International Technical Support Organization

SG24-6053-00

Application Service Provider Business Model: Implementation on the iSeries Server

April 2001

First Edition (April 2001)

This edition applies to V4R5 of OS/400, Program Number 5769-SS1.

Comments may be addressed to:
IBM Corporation, International Technical Support Organization
Dept. JLU Building 107-2
3605 Highway 52N
Rochester, Minnesota 55901-7829

Contents

Preface

This IBM Redbook shows you how to implement an exciting and new business model, called Application Service Provider (ASP), on the IBM @server iSeries server. ASP is the "how to" base for offering outsourced access to mission-critical applications on a subscription basis over the Internet, your intranet, or via a dedicated line. This redbook explains how to implement the ASP business model on your iSeries server by extending the focus of other reference materials to include ASP and by including short configuration and programming examples.

This book begins with a high level of what we believe currently represents the ASP business model and to what it will evolve. Next, it breaks up the application requirements of ASP into the functional components of network, accounting and billing, administration, user registration, security, service level management (SLM), high availability, and scalability. You will see how the iSeries server and architecture directly support the ASP business model.

Then, this redbook examines the ASP application model, which supports the argument that there is no single way to correctly implement an ASP solution on the iSeries server. You learn just how to implement ASP for Domino, WebSphere, and the more traditional enterprise-out application models on the iSeries server.

This redbook is written especially for the hardware and software distributors who want to sell or rent their products and for independent software vendors (ISV) looking for alternative means of licensing their products.

Note: This redbook reflects the IBM @server iSeries server name. Throughout this redbook, we use the shortened version "iSeries" to refer to both AS/400e and iSeries servers.

The team that wrote this redbook

This redbook was produced by a team of specialists from around the world working at the International Technical Support Organization Rochester Center.

Brian R. Smith is a Senior Consulting I/T Specialist in the IBM International Technical Support Organization (ITSO) Rochester Center. The first half of his career was spent in the Rochester Lab with the design, coding, and testing of the System/38 and AS/400 in the area of communications. He then "jumped the wall" into technical marketing support in 1990 to pursue the life of teaching and writing. Brian is the team leader of the iSeries e-business team at the ITSO Rochester Center. You can reach Brian at: brsmith@us.ibm.com

Louis Campbell is a Senior AS/400 Systems Engineer for Innovative Business Systems, an IBM Business Partner in San Antonio, Texas. He has 15 years of IT experience and 12 years of AS/400 experience. He holds the following five IBM certifications: V4R3 Technical Solutions, Professional System Administrator, Professional Network Administrator, Client Access, and e-business Infrastructure. His areas of expertise include TCP/IP and APPC communications configuration, basic network infrastructure design and implementation, AS/400 CISC-to-RISC software and hardware migration, and general AS/400 system configuration and administration.

Lam Seng Cheah (Jordan Cheah) is the Information Architecture Manager with EA Consulting, an IBM AS/400, Lotus, and SAP Business Partner based in Folsom, California. He has more than seven years of experience in Lotus Domino and Notes. His expertise includes infrastructure planning, Domino/Notes application development and enterprise integration. He holds a B.S. First Class degree in computer science from the Australian National University. You can reach Jordan at: jordancheah@email.com

Axel Lachmann is a Systems Engineer and Project Manager with FoxCom, an AS/400 Business Partner in Germany. He has nine years of experience in the OS/400 field. He is an IBM Certified Solutions Expert in AS/400 Technical Solutions and Domino R4.6 for AS/400 Technical Solutions. His areas of expertise include e-business enablement of LOB applications and Lotus Domino planning and implementation. You can reach Axel at: alachmann@foxcom.de

Steven Milstein is a Senior Solutions Architect for LOGISIL in Montreal, Canada, an IBM Premium Business Partner and provider of education, mentoring, and development/deployment resources for the AS/400 and other object-oriented technologies. He has 18 years of midrange and PC application development experience, specializing in integrated technologies solutions. He has spent the last few years working with Java and the AS/400, VisualAge for Java, WebSphere Studio, and more recently WebSphere Application Server for AS/400 Advanced Edition. He has been a major contributor to an Internet-based training (IBT) venture specializing in the IBM family of VisualAge and WebSphere products for the AS/400 system. He is primarily responsible for bring LOGISIL's AS/400 ASP division to market. Steven can be reached at: smilstein@logisil.com

Delilah Morgan was a Software Analyst at the IBM Rochester AS/400 Support Center at the time this redbook was written. She has since left IBM to pursue other opportunities.

Aleksandr V. Nartovich is a Senior I/T Specialist in the IBM International Technical Support Organization (ITSO) Rochester Center. He joined the ITSO in January 2001 after working as a developer in the IBM WebSphere Business Components (WSBC) organization. During the first part of his career, Aleksandr was a developer in AS/400 communications. Later, he shifted his focus to business components development on WebSphere. Aleksandr holds two degrees: in Computer Science from the University of Missouri-Kansas City and in Electrical Engineering from Minsk Radio Engineering Institute. You can reach Aleksandr at: alekn@us.ibm.com

Jan Roelofs is a Senior IT Specialist in the AS/400 Software Support department at IBM in the Netherlands. His areas of expertise include WebSphere, Java, Net.Data, IBM HTTP Server, and Client Access. You can reach Jan at: roelofs@nl.ibm.com

A special thank you goes to Dick Kiscaden and his entire team at the AS/400 Prime Solution Center for AS/400 in Rochester's PartnerWorld for Developers. They can be found at http://www.as400.ibm.com/developer/asp/ and are an excellent source of information, guidance, and resources for those AS/400 partners starting down the ASP road.

We also thank the following people for their invaluable contributions to this project:

Marcela Adan
Debbie Landon
Bob Maatta
International Technical Support Organization, Rochester Center

Eric Barsness
Ken Dittrich
Rui Fan
Pat Fleming
Les Fullem
Larry Hall
Mike Koranda
Fred Kulack
Dave Legler
Travis Nelson
George Weaver
IBM Rochester

Graeme N. Dixon
WebSphere Development, IBM Transarc Lab

Angela Surkau
FoxCom OHG

Alan Thomas Payne
Internet AG

Bill Scott
CIO StoreReport Inc.

Comments welcome

Your comments are important to us!

We want our Redbooks to be as helpful as possible. Please send us your comments about this or other Redbooks in one of the following ways:

- Fax the evaluation form found in "IBM Redbooks review" on page 261 to the fax number shown on the form.
- Use the online evaluation form found at http://www.redbooks.ibm.com/
- Send your comments in an Internet note to redbook@us.ibm.com

Chapter 1. Zen and the art of ASP

Believe it or not, but if you are a user of applications, you already have a relationship with an Application Service Provider (ASP). Whether your applications reside on your personal computer (PC) or organization's mainframe, midrange system, or PC network, somebody is responsible for providing your applications to you. The primary difference between these alternative providers actually lies in the amount of responsibility that you, the user, have. Such issues as hardware and software installation, upgrades, backup, security, problem determination and troubleshooting, training, and support are all shared responsibilities.

1.1 ASP pioneers

If you are a home user or small office/home office (SoHo), for example, then you most likely install your own software, maybe even your own hardware. When an issue arises, you are your first level of support. Maybe you call the help line of a particular software or hardware vendor. Maybe you "perform surgery" on your PC or experience the joys of the uninstall, install, reboot, and "let's-just-reboot-to-be-safe-again" scenario. In the end, resolution is directly related to the amount of time, energy, patience, and funds you can, or are willing to, spend.

If your business fits the Small and Medium Business (SMB) mold, maybe your needs are serviced by a small information technology (IT) shop to which you delegate your technical issues. Resolution is directly related to the amount of time, energy, patience, and funds your SMB can, or is willing to, spend.

If your needs are serviced by your large organization's information technology (IT) shop, then you most likely place a call to your internal support line and delegate the matter. Resolution is directly related to the amount of time, energy, patience, and funds your organization can, or is willing to, spend.

Think back to the days when the idea of Internet connectivity was an issue for you. If you were your own IT shop, you probably started looking into Internet service providers (ISPs). Oddly enough, chances are when your organization's IT shop desired a connection to the Internet, they too looked at various ISPs to provide it to them. Why didn't they simply connect themselves directly into the Internet? It probably had something to do with the amount of time, energy, patience, and funds they could, or were willing to, spend. If your organization ever used electronic data interchange (EDI) to communicate information back and forth to business partners, then they most likely used a provider of those services for the same reasons.

If an issue were to arise relating to your Internet connection, the problem would be delegated to the respective ISP. Notice that as we move away from the home or SoHo user towards, an SMB IT shop, an Large IT shop, and an ISP, the problem is delegated to an individual or organization that possesses greater resources to resolve the issue in a more timely fashion. Better yet, the more our IT resources evolve, the easier it is to replace a provider in the event that the quality of service (QoS) does not meet a certain expectation level or service level agreement (SLA).

Let's review what has happened. As user needs became more standard, the ability to provide a source for them became easier. Consider custom applications and off-the-shelf applications, such as office productivity suites, or specialized communication needs and packaged ones, such as ISP and EDI. The more common the need is, the more likely it will be available in a packaged form.

1.2 The skill-set shuffle

Now let's extrapolate common IT shop funtionality and promote it to a higher level service provider. Figure 1 represents a traditional generic IT shop.

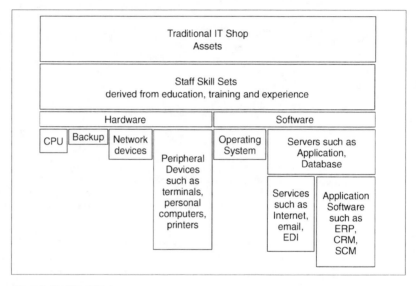

Figure 1. Traditional IT shop

Imagine promoting CPU, backup, network, operating system, and maybe application and database server responsibilities to an ASP. Continuing along the same pattern, it is conceivable to promote some backoffice applications such as General Ledger, Accounts Payable, Accounts Receivable, Order Processing, and Inventory Management. These applications may be provided by an independent software vendor (ISV) or by custom applications developed by your IT shop.

Figure 2 represents the big picture relationship between an ASP, its business partners, and their customers.

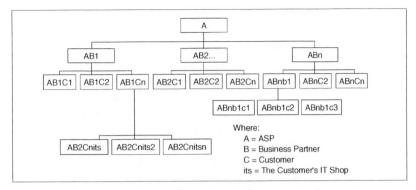

Figure 2. ASP, business partner, customer, and the customer's IT shop relationship

At one point in time, an ASP IT shop may resemble a current traditional IT shop. It is at that time where the IT shop consists of a skill set whose sole responsibility is to extend or enhance the applications being served by the ASP. In other words, it is capable of reflecting a business' competitive advantage by programming its business rules.

An OO analogy

If you are familiar with the world of object orientation (OO), consider the following scenario. The traditional IT shop represents the procedural approach. There is considerable redundancy across these IT shops with respect to their assets such as hardware, software, and skill sets. If you wanted to create a traditional IT shop, then it's simply a matter of copying another IT shop's structure and making some modifications. By encapsulating common assets and promoting them to an ASP level, you gain re-usability. Everyone may inherit these assets and extend them for their own purposes. Therefore, it can be said that the ASP model represents the potential object-oriented IT shop.

1.3 ASP in the big scheme of things

Now that we justified the theory behind the ASP business model, let's see where it fits into the big picture.

ASPs may most likely require the services of a Wholesale Service Provider (WSP), which would place their hardware within an ISP's secure environment. Two immediate benefits of the WSP are that the security provided for the installation can be shared across many systems (and hence customers) and, in general, that ISPs are closer to the Internet. Figure 3 on page 4 shows the relationship between the Internet, an ISP, customers, WSPs, ASPs, and ISVs.

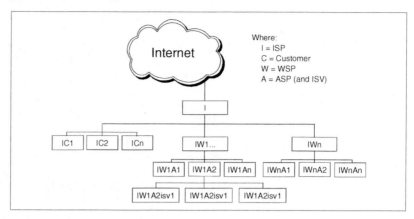

Figure 3. Relationship between the Internet, an ISP, customers, WSPs, ASPs, and ISVs

1.4 The driving forces

Gone are the days when one single person was a jack-of-all-trades. As technology has grown, so have the skill set requirements. It started with the separation of systems operations and application programming. It is said that an experienced application programmer was quite capable of delivering a complete solution — analysis, design, coding, testing implementing, support, and maintenance. It wasn't too much to expect of an individual. The same analogy can be made of the systems operator.

Wait a minute!

The same business application environment that has made the iSeries server great for over ten years is still alive and well. Existing and new applications built for the enterprise represent many millions of lines (in RPG, COBOL, and CL) of well tested business logic. Web-facing or using such tools as Host-on-Demand can quickly turn these legacy applications *enterprise-out*. That is, an ISV can already have the quality focus on the enterprise application, but now it only uses new tools to carry that information across the Internet. The core iSeries server features that make it a great ASP platform and the "how-to" behind moving from an enterprise application to enterprise-out are covered in Chapter 2, "Core OS/400 components for enterprise-out ASP" on page 9.

But things are different now. The acceptance of the Internet as a means of conducting business has spurred the face of technology. The complexity and cost of deploying new business applications have become over-whelming. The drivers of this complexity include the new multi-tier application architectures, rapidly changing technologies, the need for 24x7x365 application availability, the rapid increase in user connections typical of Internet environments, and the growing importance of the Internet as a means of communicating with suppliers, partners, and customers. Keeping up with this technology churn requires highly skilled IT personnel and more rapid turnover in the infrastructure investment.

At the same time, businesses see the rapid deployment of these new applications as critical to their competitiveness. This is as true for SMBs as it is for large enterprises.

Lou Gerstner says

2000 IBM Annual Meeting of Stockholders
L.V. Gerstner, Jr.
Cleveland, Ohio
25 April 2000

"And in this networked world, there are going to be new ways of providing these services. Companies that once had to own all the hardware and software, and all the staffs to manage them, are finding that they can buy computing, applications, and networking the same way they buy electricity. They pay for what they use and leave ownership and management of the infrastructure to someone else.

This opportunity is what's known as "Web hosting", and it's pegged at $35 billion in the U.S. alone by 2005."

1.5 What ASP actually is

Here is the working definition of ASP that we used as a basis to write this redbook:

> *Application Service Providers (ASP) deliver and manage applications and computer services from remote data centers to multiple users via the Internet or a private network.*

The three major characteristics of the ASP model are:

- One to many: Mass customized standardized services
- Subscription pricing: Per user or per month
- Bundled services: Operations (network and server) and application support

The customer categories in the ASP marketplace are:

- Personal/consumer
- Single-office, home office (SOHO)/Very Small Business (VSB)
- Small and Medium Businesses (SMB)
- Enterprises
- Industry specific verticals

These marketplaces drive the following application topologies offered by an ASP:

- Business-to-business (B2B)
- Business-to-customer (B2C)
- Customer-to-customer (C2C)
- Customer (C)
- Business (B)

To support these marketplaces and topologies, ASPs use the following models:

- **Dedicated**: An outsourcing model where the ASP provides dedicated machines to a business (traditional ERP applications). The ISV manages both application content and infrastructure support such as network connections.
- **Co-locating**: The ISV co-locates the machines running the application with a bandwidth provider (ISP). The ISV is responsible for managing machines remotely or on site.
- **Shared Hosting of Applications**: The ASP is responsible for providing bandwidth and machines for shared applications. The applications are shared among multiple enterprises with multiple users on a virtual host.

The ASP operational environment is determined by the following factors:

- Rapid change and constant flux
    - New applications, subscribing companies, additional users
    - New versions of operating systems, hardware, networking
    - *Power surges* of unexpected spikes of connected users
- Potentially *rapid* growth
    - Order of magnitude increases in scope possible
    - Scalability of infrastructure becomes a critical success factor
- Complex, multi-tier, application architectures
    - Web transaction servers, application servers, data servers
    - Routers, dispatchers, firewalls
- Multiple companies sharing individual applications
    - Secure isolation of data
    - Shared recovery groups and services
- Service level agreement/cost of ownership trade-offs
    - The SLA may be contractual with penalties for non-conformance
    - The data center is a for-profit business, not a cost center

1.6 The objectives of this book

To help you better understand the content and philosophy of this IBM Redbook, we should establish a common ground.

As the title of this IBM Redbook states, we will describe the implementation of a business model as opposed to a particular product. In fact, this redbook describes how to implement the ASP business model on several products and technologies by extending other reference materials. For example, we did not want this book to become an all-inclusive WebSphere Application Server manual. Instead, we wanted it to show you how to extend the WebSphere Application Server to support the ASP business model.

Domino, WebSphere, and traditional ILE applications are certainly not the only means of achieving the ASP business model. Other possibilities include, but are not limited to:

- Client Access
- Host On-Demand
- Screen scrapers

- Net.Data
- WebSphere Commerce Suite (was Net.Commerce)

While Client Access, Host-On Demand, and screen scrapers enable users to access existing iSeries applications and provide alternatives to the 5250 terminal, they do not enable application sharing. You must still make changes to your enterprise-out application to extend it to the ASP opportunity.

Net.Data Web-enables OS/400 data and applications. However, doing so, simply represents a technology that may or may not be used in an ASP business model.

Oddly enough, WebSphere Commerce Suite (formerly known as Net.Commerce) is for the most part excluded from this IBM Redbook because it is already an ASP implementation. WebSphere Commerce Suite not only provides a store-front application, it is also capable of implementing it within a shopping mall model. With WebSphere Commerce Suite's ability to have multiple instances running on the iSeries and the iSeries server's ability to cleanly handle virtual hosts, this is a solution if your business metaphor is shopping or the more powerful business-to-business (B2B). It should be noted, however, that the iSeries server does not support WebSphere Commerce Suite, Service Provider Edition. This Edition allows you to build a complete, scalable, extensible solution to easily set up and efficiently operate hosted e-commerce services and communities for your Small and Medium Business customers. This does not eliminate your ability to do these things in an ASP environment. For more information about WebSphere Commerce Suite, see the Web site at:

http://www-4.ibm.com/software/webservers/commerce/

Chapter 2. Core OS/400 components for enterprise-out ASP

Whether you are planning to implement Application Service Provider (ASP) on your iSeries server in one of these seven (more exist, of course, but these are the major ones) application development environments, the core components of OS/400 will provide an integrated base of functions.

- **Enterprise-out**: As defined by the traditional ILE application. This kind of application would be seen to use the native DB2 Universal Database (UDB) for AS/400. Its core business value would be written in such languages as RPG, COBOL, and CL. The client view of the application would most likely be via the 5250 protocol, although many variations of this are possible.

- **Legacy Web**: Applications using the CGI-BIN API of the HTTP server.

- **Domino**: Applications that are built on the Lotus Domino collaborative server model.

- **WebSphere Commerce Server**: For the "shopping" and B2B business metaphor.

- **WebSphere Application Server**: Used for a servlet, JavaServer Pages (JSP), and Enterprise JavaBeans (EJBs).

- **PASE**: OS/400 PASE (Portable Application Solutions Environment) is a new technology designed to expand the iSeries solutions portfolio. It is an integrated runtime that provides simplified porting of selected solution provider UNIX applications. For more information, see *Porting UNIX Applications Using AS/400 PASE*, SG24-5970.

- **Personal office applications**: The iSeries is a very good file and print server for clients. Features built into OS/400, such as NetServer (see *The AS/400 NetServer Advantage*, SG24-5196, for more information), provide a powerful and flexible environment to support remote clients. These clients can be thought of as either the ubiquitous PC or a thin client like a Network Station (see *IBM Network Station Manager V2R1*, SG24-5844, for more information). Solutions for an intranet or the Internet in this area could be a great opportunity for an ASP.

---
iSeries advertisement

More than anything, the above list yells loud and clear that the AS/400 legacy (if we can use this term in a positive future-looking frame of mind) for iSeries customers is of unparalleled application development environment choices. This is far from being a closed proprietary system.

It gives you, as the owner of an iSeries server, the ability to choose the path down which you will extend your business model to include ASP. It gives us, the writers of this redbook, the difficult task of showing you many different ways to "achieve ASP", none of which is the best.

This chapter documents many of the core functional components of OS/400 and other features available on the iSeries server that can be used by most any application. It focuses on the enterprise-out application as defined by the traditional legacy ILE application.

Figure 4 illustrates the application hosting services and which party in the offering is involved with its usage. It is a guide only. The actual implementation for your own solution may define the borders differently. All of the application hosting services are provided by the Service Provider (SP) with the following usage patterns:

- The SP uses a set of publishing and administration interfaces to define and manage applications and their execution environment.
- The Application Provider (AP) uses a set of the services related to customer, application, billing provisioning, and usage tracking.
- The customer uses a set of customer-type services for registration, support, application browsing, and usage tracking.

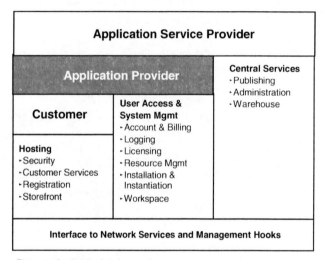

Figure 4. Application hosting services structure

This chapter examines the architecture of the application hosting services by describing the following building blocks and relating each component to the iSeries server:

- Network infrastructure
- Accounting and billing
- Administration
- Security
- User registration
- Printing
- Service level management (SLM)
- High availability
- Scalability

The application hosting services provide the ISV with a single set of interfaces that enable the application to participate in the life cycle (installation, usage, suspension, and removal) and billing aspects of the application. Existing framework-based applications can evolve to take advantage of these services, which means they can be integrated into and offered by SPs with little or no change. Over time, the application can be modified to leverage the services to automate the integration and customization tasks required for hosted applications.

Hopefully you can see that the SLM and service level agreements (SLA) play a critical role in the "glue" that holds together all the roles and responsibilities shown in Figure 4. You can find more information in 2.8, "Service level management (SLM)" on page 60.

2.1 Enterprise-out or e-business-in?

Investing in your OS/400 application is good business. There are over 700,000 iSeries servers shipped worldwide. In 1998, more servers were shipped than any previous year, and over 20 percent of these servers were for new customer use. The iSeries server has over 30,000 industry leading native applications in numerous market areas or industries such as ERP, distribution, manufacturing, finance, and more.

The core business applications for the iSeries server are written in RPG and CL and are tightly integrated with DB2 UDB for AS/400. COBOL and C/C++ account for a smaller portion of the core business applications for the iSeries. To remain a vital business franchise, the existing core business applications need to remain competitive on the iSeries server. Meanwhile, the iSeries server needs to attract and retain applications from other platforms. There are three sources of applications that will fuel this franchise into the future and grow the business:

- Upgrading existing iSeries applications
- Porting applications from UNIX and Windows NT to iSeries
- The development of new applications targeting the iSeries server

This section focuses on two sources that are covered in the following section and in 2.1.2, "Building an e-business-in solution" on page 14.

2.1.1 Building an enterprise-out solution

The first task for ASP applications is to upgrade existing iSeries server applications. It is a common strategy to upgrade or modernize existing iSeries applications. This method extends the RPG (or COBOL) green screen (5250 terminals) to a graphical user interface on a Windows client or a browser interface.

Another approach is to extend the core business application to the client/server model or the Web model with "side-car" business logic on the server that connects to the client. A more aggressive approach is to redesign the core business application to separate the user interface, from the business logic, from the back-end services such as database or communications.

In all of these cases, it is prudent to evolve the application and not to re-engineer or create a totally new core business application design. In addition, there are simple actions, such as moving today's RPG (or COBOL) application to the Integrated Language Environment (ILE), that take advantage of the application partitioning and performance benefits. Another fundamental is that the "new" application environment must coexist with the existing application environment through program call mechanisms (Java to RPG, for example) or data interchange.

2.1.1.1 Updating existing iSeries applications

This section explores updating existing iSeries applications using ILE technology. This shifts the applications and computing resources back to a centralized location (much like the mainframe model), while maintaining the power of Windows and UNIX applications. ASP increases the power of server-based computing by allowing these traditional applications to be centrally deployed and maintained:

- **OS/400 Common Gateway Interface (CGI) support**: On the iSeries server, CGI programs can be written in most OS/400-supported languages, including RPG, C, COBOL, and Java. CGI is the lowest level API available on the iSeries server to create dynamic content for Web pages that are served by IBM HTTP Server for iSeries. It is powerful, but creating large and complex applications like the ones that most ASP solutions create in CGI would be difficult.

- **Workstation Gateway**: IBM Workstation Gateway (WSG) allows the conversion of 5250-based applications into HTML files on the fly. WSG sends a request for a 5250 screen to your iSeries Web server. Then the WSG interpretation of that screen is sent to the client in HTML format. With WSG, 5250 applications that you either purchased or created can be placed on the Internet without modification.

  One of the problems with the WSG is that the data entered at the client's remote Web browser is not checked for accuracy before it is sent to the iSeries server. Also, the keyboard mapping between the client using the Web browser and the 5250 data stream is not handled well by the WSG. All-in-all, if you need a robust solution that will convert 5250 data streams into HTML and back again, we suggest you consider IBM WebSphere Host On-Demand.

  Another tool that is coming soon is the WebFacing tool that will allow you to give your green-screen user interfaces a Web look and feel. For more information about this tool, see:

  http://www-4.ibm.com/software/ad/wdt400/news.html

  You can also use http://www-4.ibm.com/software/ad/ as a portal into the ever-changing world of iSeries application development news and products.

- **IBM WebSphere Host On-Demand**: Host On-Demand (HOD) gives you secure access to your host applications and data, using a simple, Java-enabled Web browser. With secure to your host data on many platforms (including Microsoft Windows NT, IBM AIX, Linux, S/390, and iSeries), HOD requires no client installation or middle-tier server. Centralized deployment means that you always have the latest version of code, and software maintenance costs are minimized with only the Web server needing code installation.

  The ability to transfer files and perform remote print emulation are equally important to the secure access of 5250 applications that HOD provides. That is, the customer can run an application via the Internet on your iSeries and easily print a report on the printer in their office attached to their PC.

- **Net.Data**: Net.Data offers a fast way to create HTML documents that make queries into your database. IBM does not call Net.Data a Database Markup Language (DBML). However, it has DBML-like qualities that allow database calls via text-based documents residing on the iSeries. Unlike a CGI program, Net.Data requires no code compilation. The text document uses macros that the iSeries interprets before the document is served. The macros' results are returned in HTML format.

- **Telnet**: Telnet gives users remote terminal emulation sessions or any Telnet server-support platform. An OS/400 native Telnet interface maps well when it is accessing another iSeries server, but working between the iSeries and other platforms requires extensive remapping of the function keys.

- **Client Access/400**: A 32-bit Windows client that allows users to connect to the iSeries over TCP/IP, APPC over TCP/IP (AnyNet) SNA/APPC, and IPX/SPX by providing PC5250 emulation or print and graphical access. It supports V3R2 through V4R5, and improvements/modifications are planned through future releases. Depending on the version of Client Access, it can support Secure Sockets Layer (SSL) and uses OS/400 built-in support.

These are only IBM products. IBM is not alone in its quest to offer powerful solutions to connect your iSeries server to the Internet. There are several third-party developments.

For core application development/deployment, the following tools are available:

- VisualAge (RPG, C/C++, Java)
- Inprise Jbuilder for AS/400
- AS/400 ToolBox for Java
- InstallShield Java edition
- Aldon (SCM)

For specialized tools, such as screen scrapers, GUI builders, embedded databases, and object-relational schema mappers, the following tools are available:

- Jacada Family of Products
- Seagull Jwalk
- Cloudscape

An integrated application environment that provides a platform for application development, deployment, and running is available through LANSA. LANSA has a new product that it supports independent software vendors (ISV) who want to become Application Service Providers (ASP). Using a new product called *e.ssential*, ASP Portal Manager ISVs can dramatically reduce the effort required to host their applications for multiple customers over the Web. e.ssential ASP Portal Manager is a solution that delivers a broad range of features that include Web administration, security management, user profiling, personal pages, Web reporting, multiple menu structures, and graphics and content to the look and feel desired by the individual user of the hosted applications.

Now, under one umbrella, Web site management is possible for a mixture of applications that use technologies such as LANSA, Domino, JAVA, XML, Microsoft Office Products, and GUI tools. For more information visit:
http://www.lansa.com

For more information and details on partners that support iSeries application development and deployment, see the PartnerWorld for Developers, iSeries Web site at: http://www.ibm.com/as400/developer

2.1.2 Building an e-business-in solution

The value of Web and Java application servers today is that they provide an easy way to develop N-tier distributed e-business applications. The infrastructure required to support these applications (communications support, security, data access, transactional context) is provided by the application server platform. This allows programmers to abstract themselves to solve business problems quicker and spend less time on sockets level programming, for example. Most of these application servers provide support for Web-centric application models such as HTML/CGI for basic Web serving and servlets or JSPs for simple Java/Web serving. Further, these application servers provide or intend to provide EJB support for the distributed enterprise application environment.

Another key value these application servers provide is "connectors" to existing core business application systems. The connectors provide access to the existing business assets that allows a strategy of "coexistence" and gradual "transition" to the new application models and environments. This enables a much lower risk of evolution to the new technology versus a revolutionary approach of re-engineering and building the next business systems from scratch.

One way to implement such applications is by using IBM WebSphere, which is explained in the following section.

2.1.2.1 WebSphere Application Server Advanced Edition

WebSphere Application Server Advanced Edition allows you to implement and manage server-side Java components, such as servlets, enterprise beans, and JavaServer Pages (JSP) files. These Java components can add complex business logic and dynamic functions to static HTML Web pages. Use servlets to access legacy data and perform programmatic functions. Use enterprise beans to model more complex data and to process more complex logic, especially transaction-based work. Use JSP files to present dynamic data in a Web interface.

Note

WebSphere Application Server does not provide an interface to create servlets, enterprise beans, and JSP files. While you may use a variety of tools to code Java components, WebSphere Studio (which includes VisualAge for Java Professional Edition) provides a suite of tools that are customized for the WebSphere Application Server environment. For more information about WebSphere Studio, see the WebSphere Studio product Web site at:
http://www-4.ibm.com/software/webservers/studio/

In addition, VisualAge for Java Enterprise Edition provides a complete development and test environment for Enterprise JavaBeans. For more information about VisualAge for Java, see the VisualAge for Java product Web site at: http://www-4.ibm.com/software/ad

Select the product **VisualAge for Java**.

Figure 5 shows the high-level architecture of the WebSphere Application Server environment on the iSeries server.

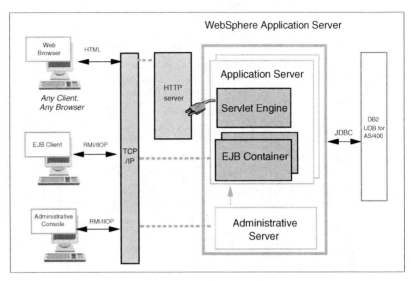

Figure 5. AS/400 WebSphere architecture

2.1.2.2 WebSphere Host Publisher V2.2 for AS/400

WebSphere Host Publisher V2.2 for AS/400 lets you implement Web applications such as Web self-service from existing 3270, 5250, Virtual Terminal, Java, and JDBC host applications without modifying the host applications. Host Publisher V2.2 consists of two major components:

- **Host Publisher Studio**: This provides a collection of easy-to-use, task-oriented, point-and-click tools that provide a development environment for creating Host Publisher applications. This component requires a Windows 32-bit platform.

- **Host Publisher Server**: This includes IBM WebSphere Application Server Standard Edition and Host Publisher runtime components for executing the applications created with the Host Publisher Studio. This component is currently available for AIX, NetWare, OS/2, OS/390, OS/400, Solaris, and Windows NT.

2.1.2.3 WebSphere Commerce Suite

WebSphere Commerce Suite (previously called Net.Commerce) is a merchant solution that provides a framework to conduct business on the Internet in a secure and scalable manner. It supports both business-to-business as well as business-to-consumer environments. WebSphere Commerce Suite works together with DB2 UDB for AS/400 and the IBM HTTP Server for iSeries to give users and companies a simple and secure environment. WebSphere Commerce Suite is architected to be scalable to meet the needs of the small to very large business. Merchants can take advantage of their existing operating environment and expand to larger systems.

2.1.2.4 MQSeries

MQSeries is the middleware that provides secure and flexible process integration between almost all major computing systems and any key network protocol. MQSeries provides *message queuing*:

- A message in this sense refers to any data in any format that applications care to exchange. It is not a message in the EDI sense of a communication between two people (although MQSeries can carry EDI messages too).

- Message queuing is different from what transaction monitors do. The benefits they share are that they both provide protection from network complexity, include client/server interoperability, and have reliability and integrity.

Transaction monitors process transactions. MQSeries simply carries messages between applications and assures their delivery. MQSeries provides time independence because it works asynchronously. It has a common application programming interface (API) so that once the code is written for one platform, it can be used on another.

With MQSeries, applications communicate by putting messages on message queues and by taking messages from message queues.

2.1.2.5 DB2 Universal Database (UDB)

IBM is the only database vendor to provide complete data management solutions for OS/400, in addition to other user platforms scaling from the laptop to the enterprise.

A universal database extends the benefits and capabilities of modern database technology to nontraditional forms of data, such as information stored in documents, spreadsheets, and multimedia objects. Traditionally information from relational databases, which has been evolved into "business data in a business context", has been done with the aid of tools such as documents and spreadsheets. Therefore, it is natural to the business user that it also be stored in this format. DB2 Universal Database provides the new and advanced functions necessary to store, manage, index, and control all forms of information, ranging from traditional database data to documents and multimedia, in a single consistent database architecture.

Third-party offerings

The direction of the iSeries for application servers is to lead with IBM WebSphere in the long term as the carrier of Java and EJB technology for future distributed applications. WebSphere Standard and Advanced Edition are available on the iSeries today. You can start taking advantage of EJB support with WebSphere Advanced Edition. The iSeries server also has a long history of partnering with third-party tool or middleware providers. Key partner application servers include:

- BEA/WebXpress and their WebLogic server: http://www.bea.com
- Bluestone's Sapphire/Web server: http://www.bluestone.com
- Novera's jBusiness: http://www.novera.com

These are complete application servers that include leading EJB support since the Fall of 1998 and have an iSeries integration focus.

2.2 Network infrastructure

The network infrastructure consists of the physical hardware and communications protocols needed to make the ASP systems accessible and secure to remote users, regardless of whether they are connecting via the Internet or private dedicated communications lines.

2.2.1 Networking in an ASP environment

The ASP network infrastructure is traditional in nature. ASP hosting systems are connected into a network medium (Ethernet, token-ring, FDDI, and so on). There may be multiple subnetworks (possibly consisting of different network mediums) interconnected by routers or bridges.

Customer access may be accomplished over the Internet or by dedicated communications lines (T1, fractional T1, T3, ISDN, and so on). One or more firewalls may be used to ensure ASP security.

Network security the SecureWay

While every effort has been made to address security issues related to the iSeries and ASP issues, we do not address the more global topic of network topology security. As stated in the white paper *Using Tivoli SecureWay to Manage e-business Security* (`http://www-4.ibm.com/software/secureway/library/whitepapers/intro_wp.html`), the difference between a controlled and an uncontrolled reaction doesn't depend on the participants as much as the environment because the right setting limits any damage. For example, fuel, oxygen, and a spark encased in a carefully engineered, controlled casing enable a rocket to travel to other planets at speeds in excess of 40,000 km per hour (25,000 miles per hour). Yet these same ingredients combined in a vulnerable shell plagued by structural weaknesses can become a potent and deadly bomb.

These laws apply to e-business as much as they do to chemistry. In a controlled environment where Internet technology serves as the catalyst reacting with business processes and users, e-business can prosper and supplement or even replace traditional operations. In a not-so-controlled setting (such as one lacking scalability, flexibility, or security), the results are unpredictable. Reactions that appear positive at first can quickly degenerate into a series of negative events that can adversely affect and in the worst case even destroy a business.

See the SecureWay home page at `http://www-4.ibm.com/software/secureway/` and remainder of the above white paper for a better appreciation of this topic.

2.2.2 iSeries networking in an ASP environment

To meet the requirements for application hosting, ASPs will want to provide reliability, availability, and security. In any business environment, these factors are extremely important. In a software-as-services model, they assume even greater significance. In a traditional, in-house deployment, the customer's own IT department typically is responsible for keeping the software up, running, and secure. Solution Providers supporting multiple customers on the same solution will have an extra burden in service and support as any glitches in reliability, availability, or security multiply across these customers. All ISVs want ASP partners that provide adequate data-center and networking capacity and redundancy, guaranteed service levels, and the support competencies to provision customers quickly and keep them happy. Your network infrastructure will play a very important role in the ASP's success in providing quality service.

Enterprises around the world have recognized the shift of networking to TCP/IP technologies and the business potential of leveraging these technologies as well as the Internet itself. It is being used in many fashions for internal company, intercompany, or public access. As the awareness and adoption rate of TCP/IP has increased, the iSeries has enhanced its TCP/IP and related technologies. As a result, the iSeries has built-in leading-edge security and enterprise-class TCP/IP. Because of its enhanced TCP/IP and related technologies, again the iSeries is a frontrunner as an ASP solution.

2.2.2.1 The protocols that carry your data
This section explores the services provided by TCP/IP that allow you to implement interconnectivity from the data center to the client site.

TCP/IP stack support
TCP/IP, as a set of communications protocols, is based on layers. Unlike SNA or OSI, which distinguish seven layers of communication, there are only four layers in the TCP/IP model. They enable heterogeneous systems to communicate by performing network-related processing such as message routing, network control, error detection, and correction. The layering model of TCP/IP is shown in Figure 6. The following sections explain each layer.

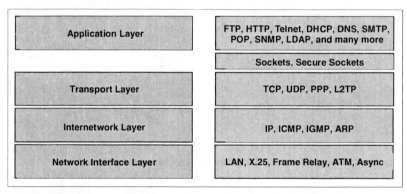

Figure 6. iSeries TCP/IP protocol stack

Application layer
The application layer is provided by the program that uses TCP/IP for communication. Examples of the applications are Telnet, FTP, HTTP, and SMTP. The interface between the application and transport layers is defined by port numbers and sockets. The applications that are part of the iSeries offering are discussed in "TCP/IP suite" on page 21.

Transport layer
The transport layer provides communication between application programs. The applications may be on the same host or on different hosts. Multiple applications

can be supported simultaneously. The transport layer is responsible for providing a reliable exchange of information. The main transport layer protocol is TCP. Another is User Datagram Protocol (UDP), which provides a connectionless service in comparison to TCP, which provides a connection-oriented service. That means that applications using UDP as the transport protocol have to provide their own end-to-end flow control. Usually, UDP is used by applications that need a fast transport mechanism.

Internetwork layer
The internetwork layer provides communication between computers. Part of communicating messages between computers is a routing function that ensures that messages will be correctly delivered to their destination. The Internet Protocol (IP) provides this routing function. Examples of internetwork layer protocols include IP, ICMP, IGMP, ARP, and RARP.

Network interface layer
The network interface layer (also referred to as the *link layer*, *data link layer*, or *network layer*) is implemented by the physical network that connects the computers. Examples are LAN (IEEE 802.x standards), Ethernet, X.25, ISDN, ATM, Frame Relay, or async. Note that the RFCs actually do not describe or standardize any network layer protocols. They only standardize ways of accessing those protocols from the internetwork layer.

Internet Protocol (IP)
The IP layer hides the underlying physical network from the upper layer protocols. It is an unreliable, "best-effort", and connectionless packet delivery protocol.

Note

Best-effort means that the packets sent by the IP may be lost, received out of order, or even duplicated. IP will not handle these situations. It is up to the higher-layer protocols to deal with these situations.

One of the reasons for developing a connectionless network protocol was to minimize the dependency on specific computing centers that used hierarchical connection-oriented networks. The US Department of Defense intended to deploy a network that would still be operational if parts were destroyed.

IP uses IP addresses to specify source and target hosts on the Internet. This can be compared to a fully qualified NETID.LUNAME in SNA. An IP address consists of 32 bits, which is usually represented in the form of four decimal numbers, one decimal number for each byte (or octet). For example, a 32-bit address would be represented as the decimal notation 9.67.38.1.

An IP address consists of two logical parts: a network address and a host address. An IP address belongs to one of four classes depending on the value of its first four bits. A fifth class, class E, is not commonly used.

Transmission Control Protocol (TCP)
Transmission Control Protocol (TCP) provides a reliable delivery of a stream of bytes in sequence. TCP takes a stream of data, breaks it into segments (a TCP header and application data), sends each one individually using IP, and then reassembles the segments back into the original steam. If any segments are lost

or damaged during the transmission, TCP detects this and resends the missing segments. From a performance perspective, the iSeries server supports TCP extensions for high-performance (RFC 1323) that provides for large TCP transmissions over high-bandwidth connections.

User Datagram Protocol (UDP)
UDP enables an application to send datagrams to other programs on other systems with a minimum of protocol overhead. Unlike TCP, UDP is datagram oriented and does not guarantee the delivery of data in sequence. Datagrams may possibly be dropped or reordered as they travel from the source to the destination. UDP can be used instead of TCP when the application does not want to incur the overhead of TCP connecting and disconnecting. It then becomes the responsibility of the application to ensure reliable data transfer and sequencing of datagrams. iSeries UDP also includes multicast support, which allows a host to send packets to a group of hosts in a single transmission.

Point-to-Point Protocol (PPP)
Dial-up TCP/IP, known as Point-to-Point Protocol, is used to dial into remote systems or to allow remote systems to dial into the iSeries over a telephone line using a modem. Null modems or non-switched connections are also supported. The Serial Line Internet Protocol (SLIP) and Point-to-Point Protocol (PPP) are supported on the iSeries server. In addition, the iSeries supports dial-on-demand PPP connections and routing over point-to-point connections.

Layer 2 Tunneling Protocol (L2TP)
Layer 2 Tunneling Protocol (L2TP) enables connections, which are also called virtual lines, that provide cost-effective access for remote users regardless of whether their IP address is dynamically assigned. Furthermore, L2TP connections secure access when they are used in conjunction with IP Security (IPSec). L2TP is actually a variation of an IP encapsulation protocol. An L2TP tunnel is created by encapsulating an L2TP frame inside a UDP packet, which in turn is encapsulated inside an IP packet. The source and destination addresses of this IP packet define the tunnel's endpoints. Because the outer encapsulating protocol is IP, you can apply IPSec protocols to the composite IP packet. This protects the data that flows within the L2TP tunnel. You can then apply Authentication Header (AH), Encapsulated Security Payload (ESP), and Internet Key Exchange (IKE) protocols in a straightforward manner. Using IPSec protocols to encrypt an L2TP tunnel provides encryption for all sessions contained in the tunnel. The iSeries can serve as either an L2TP-enabled client or an L2TP network server (LNS).

Internet Control Message Protocol (ICMP)
The Internet Control Message Protocol (ICMP) provides error and control messages between host systems and routers. Routers and host systems use ICMP to send reports of problems. ICMP also includes an echo request or reply message that is used to test whether a destination can be reached and is responding (via Packet InterNet Groper (PING)).

Internet Group Management Protocol (IGMP)
The Internet Group Management Protocol (IGMP) is used by IP hosts to report their host group memberships to neighboring multicast routers. Multicast routers send host membership query messages to discover which host groups have members on their attached networks. Hosts respond to the query by generating host membership reports reporting each host group to which they belong. The

multicast routes use this information to determine where multicast datagrams need to be forwarded.

Address Resolution Protocol (ARP)

The Address Resolution Protocol (ARP) dynamically associates Internet addresses to physical hardware addresses on a local network. ARP relies on the broadcast capabilities of the underlying media to provide this function.

Send MIME Mail API

The Send MIME Mail API allows applications to use SMTP and TCP/IP to send mail to the Internet.

Communications line interface support

The iSeries provides several types of physical interfaces for networking connectivity. The iSeries supports:

- Token-ring (4 Mbps, 16 Mbps, and 100 Mbps)
- Ethernet (10 Mbps, 100 Mbps, and 1 Gbps)
- Distributed Data Interface (DDI), including fiber
- Wireless LAN
- Frame Relay

    An interesting feature of Frame Relay support on the iSeries is that it can carry both SNA and TCP/IP traffic simultaneously. As a WAN technology, this can come in handy when you are interested in delivering your ASP solution.

- X.25 Permanent and Switched Virtual Circuits (PVC and SVC)
- X.25 over ISDN
- PPP over ISDN
- Netfinity Integrated PC server LAN
- Asynchronous
- ATM
- Twinaxial

TCP/IP suite

The TCP/IP suite is made up of several applications that provide services. The iSeries provides many of these servers as part of the optional program products library. Table 1 describes several of the more popular servers.

Table 1. TCP servers and descriptions

Server	Description
Domain Name Server	The iSeries supports the Domain Name Server. The Domain Name Server is used by applications to translate domain names of hosts to IP addresses. The Domain Name Server is the network naming service of intranets and the Internet.
File Transfer Protocol (FTP)	iSeries TCP/IP provides client and server support for transferring files. FTP allows a user to transfer data between local and remote hosts. FTP is built on the services of TCP in the transport layer. FTP transfers files using either an ASCII or EBCDIC mode. ASCII mode is used to transfer data that contains only text characters.
HyperText Transfer Protocol (HTTP)	The HTTP server provides World Wide Web browser clients access to iSeries information and supplies a rich application deployment environment. In addition, the HTTP Server for iSeries supports secure HTTP and multiple instances of the HTTP server running on one iSeries server.

Server	Description
Internet Daemon (INETD)	The INETD super server eliminates the need for many individual servers to be up and running at all times waiting for incoming connections. Instead, the INETD listens for connections on a set of configured ports, and when a connection request is received, it decides to which service the port corresponds and invokes a program to service the request. After the program is started, the INETD continues to listen on the port for additional requests. Essentially, INETD allows one running daemon to invoke several others, reducing the load on the system.
Post Office Protocol Mail server (POP)	The POP server is the iSeries implementation of the POP Version 3 mail interface. This server allows iSeries servers to act as POP servers for any clients that support the POP mail interface. One of the key benefits of the POP server is that it allows users to exchange multimedia mail.
Remote Printing: Line Printer Requester/Line Printer Daemon (LPR/LPD)	The iSeries server provides client and server support for remote printing. The client, line printer requester (LPR), allows the user to send spooled files to a remote system running a remote line printer daemon (LPD). This enables printing files remotely to any system that supports and is running an LPD. In turn, the iSeries supports remote printing to its printers by being a remote printer server using LPD.
Route Daemon (RouteD)	The route server provides support for the Routing Information Protocol (RIP) Version 1 and Version 2. Routing Information Protocol on the iSeries is an Interior Gateway Protocol (IGP) used to assist TCP/IP in the routing of IP data packets.
Remote Execution (REXEC)	The remote execution server enables a client user to submit system commands to a remote server for processing.
Simple Mail Transfer Protocol (SMTP)	The iSeries server provides support for the Simple Mail Transfer Protocol. SMTP enables the exchange of electronic mail between hosts running TCP/IP. The SMTP function on the iSeries is coupled with iSeries SNA distribution services (SNADS). SNADS is part of the OS/400 operating system, and it contains extensions to support SMTP. SNADS allows you to send mail to various types of users (not just SMTP users) with one consistent user interface. The distribution services (send, receive, and forward electronic mail) for the OfficeVision licensed program are provided by SNADS.
Simple Network Management Protocol (SNMP)	The iSeries can be an SNMP agent in an SNMP network. That is, the iSeries gathers information about the network and performs the management functions requested by some remote SNMP manager. The iSeries TCP/IP SNMP provides the means for managing a TCP/IP environment. SNMP allows network management by elements, such as routers and hosts. Network elements act as servers and contain management agents that perform the management functions requested. Network management stations act as clients; they run the management applications that monitor and control the network. SNMP provides a means of communicating between these elements and stations to send and receive information about network resources.

Server	Description
SOCKS client	The OS/400 SOCKS client support enables programs that use sockets, such as AF_INET or SOCK_STREAM, to communicate with server programs that run on systems outside a firewall. In addition, by using SOCKS client support, both iSeries FTP and iSeries Telnet client connections can be directed through a firewall. The key advantage to OS/400 SOCKS client support is that it enables client applications to access a SOCKS server transparently without changing any client code. The SOCKS client support operates with any SOCKS server that supports Version 4 SOCKS protocols.
Telnet	Telnet makes your computer act like a mainframe computer's workstation. In other words, when using Telnet, your computer (the client) pretends to be, or emulates, a terminal attached to the remote computer (the Telnet server).
	The iSeries server provides client and server Telnet support. Both client and server support 5250, 3270, VT220, and VT100 full-screen modes. In addition, the AS/400 Telnet server supports an ASCII line mode.
	The Telnet server also supports Secure Sockets Layer (SSL) client requests for encrypted data flow.
Trivial File Transfer Protocol (TFTP)	TFTP is a protocol used to provide basic file transfers with no user authentication to and from a remote server. TFTP is used to support the IBM Network Station for AS/400 solution.
5250 Work Station Gateway	5250 HTML Workstation Gateway Server is an application that automatically transforms OS/400 5250 applications to HTML. This server enables users to run iSeries applications from any client supporting a Web browser.

Dynamic Host Configuration Protocol (DHCP/DHCP relay agent)
DHCP provides a framework for passing configuration information to hosts on a TCP/IP network. DHCP is based on the bootstrap protocol, which adds the automatic allocation of reusable network addresses and additional configuration options. This could be highly effective for Application Service Providers.

Services provided by DHCP
The first service provided by DHCP offers persistent storage of network parameters for network clients. A client can query the DHCP service to retrieve its configuration parameters. The client interface to the configuration parameters repository consists of protocol messages to request configuration parameters and responses from the server carrying the configuration parameters.

The second service provided by DHCP is the allocation of temporary or permanent network (IP) addresses to hosts. The basic mechanism for the dynamic allocation of network addresses is simple: a client requests the use of an address for a period of time. The allocation mechanism (the collection of DHCP servers) guarantees not to reallocate that address within the requested time and attempts to return the same network address each time the client requests an address. The client may extend its lease with subsequent requests. The client may issue a message to release the address back to the server when the client no longer needs the address. The client may ask for a permanent assignment by asking for an infinite lease. Even when assigning permanent addresses, a server may choose to give lengthy, but not infinite, leases to allow detection of the fact that the host has been retired.

In some environments, it is necessary to reassign network addresses due to exhaustion of available addresses. In such environments, the allocation mechanism reuses addresses whose lease has expired. The server should use whatever information is available in the configuration information repository to choose an address to reuse. For example, the server may choose the least recently assigned address. As a consistency check, the allocation mechanism may probe the reused address, with an ICMP echo request, before allocating the address, and the client will probe the newly received address with ARP.

A particular network will use one or more of these mechanisms, depending on the policies of the network administrator.

Dynamic allocation is the only one of the three mechanisms that allows automatic reuse of an address that is no longer needed by the host to which it was assigned. Therefore, dynamic allocation is particularly useful for assigning an address to a host that will be connected to the network only temporarily or for sharing a limited pool of IP addresses among a group of hosts that do not need permanent IP addresses. Dynamic allocation may also be a good choice for assigning an IP address to a new host being permanently connected to a network. This is important where IP addresses are sufficiently scarce and it is important to reclaim them when old hosts are retired. Manual allocation allows DHCP to be used to eliminate the error-prone process of manually configuring hosts with IP addresses in environments where (for whatever reasons) it is desirable to manage IP address assignment outside of the DHCP mechanisms.

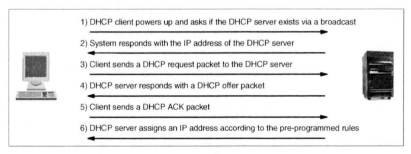

Figure 7. DHCP on the iSeries server

The iSeries server has provided a DHCP server as a part of the base operating system (BOS). It is automatically installed as option 3 of the BOS (5769-SS1 *BASE) during the operating system installation. The DHCP integrated server in the iSeries added the ability for the iSeries to act either as a DHCP transaction server or as a BOOTP/DHCP Relay Agent. Since we have only one set of attributes associated with the DHCP server, that is *SERVER or *RELAY, it is not possible for a single system to assume the roles of a SERVER and a RELAY at the same time.

2.2.2.2 Multihoming support
Given the iSeries server's strength as a server and scalable business computer, the iSeries fully supports multihoming. Multihoming is the support of multiple IP addresses by a single host, which can be thought of as logical interfaces. These logical interfaces may be associated with one or more physical interfaces, and these physical interfaces may be connected to the same or different networks.

The iSeries TCP/IP implementation supports multihoming by allowing the specification of either a single interface or multiple interfaces for a communications line. You can have your iSeries appear as any one or combination of the following scenarios:

- A single host on a network over a communications line
- Multiple hosts on the same network over the same communications lines
- Multiple hosts on the same network over multiple communications lines
- Multiple hosts on different networks over the same communications lines
- Multiple hosts on different networks over multiple communications lines

Related to multihoming is the IBM HTTP for iSeries server's ability to have multiple instances running at the same time on one iSeries. Each instance of the HTTP server can be bound to a specific host name (or IP address), thereby allowing a single iSeries to have multiple instances of an HTTP server that all accept requests on a single port (port 80 for example). This is called *virtual hosts*. You can find more information about this topic in 3.2, "Multihoming" on page 81, and in 3.9, "Virtual hosts" on page 100.

2.2.2.3 Multiprotocol support (AnyNet/400)

iSeries supports AnyNet/400, which is part of the AnyNet family of products. AnyNet products allow application programs written for one communication protocol to run over non-native protocols without changing (or recompiling) the application programs. The destination address determines if the request is sent over the native protocol or through the AnyNet code and on to a non-native protocol.

AnyNet/400 allows sockets, intersystem communications functions (ICF), CPI communications (CPI-C), and CICS/400 applications to run over APPC, TCP/IP, and Internetwork Packet eXchange (IPX). AnyNet/400 is based on the Multiprotocol Transport Network (MPTN) architecture and is designed to allow any application to run over any networking protocol. AnyNet/400 can be used to:

- Access APPC using TCP/IP if your applications were developed for the System Network Architecture (SNA), but they are using TCP/IP to connect the systems.

- Access APPC using IPX if your applications were developed for SNA, but they are using IPX to connect the systems.

- Access sockets using SNA if your sockets applications were developed for TCP/IP, but they are using SNA to connect the systems.

Access sockets using IPX if your sockets applications were developed for TCP/IP but they are using IPX to connect the systems.

2.2.2.4 Conclusion

In conclusion, as discussed above, the iSeries server and TCP/IP offer many services and solutions for your ASP networking needs. Built-in DHCP, multihoming, and IPSec are just a few of the features that we mentioned to help launch your network and give you the "e-edge".

More information, consult these resources:

- For TCP/IP information, see the *TCP/IP Configuration and Reference Guide*, SC41-5430.

- For Version 3-related information, see *Cool Title About the AS/400 and Internet*, SG24-4815.

- For Version 4 information, see *V4 TCP/IP for AS/400: More Cool Things Than Ever*, SG24-5190.

2.3 Accounting and billing

Services and rates are the basis for a billing system. Each service provided by the ASP has a rate or fee that falls into one of two categories: sign-up fees or usage fees. The *sign-up fee* is a one-time flat fee charged to set up the user account for the service. The *usage fee* is a predetermined, recurring charge that occurs during each billing cycle. The usage criteria may be based on several models ranging from a simple scheme where a flat fee is charged for the use of the service, to sophisticated schemes where the exact usage of each ASP resource (CPU, memory, disk, etc.) is metered and billed to the user. Promotions and discounts are frequently offered to encourage new users to sign up and current users to use more services.

At the end of the billing cycle, the billing software computes the total charge for each user and mails an invoice or debits a credit card account, depending on the user's payment type.

2.3.1 ASP accounting and billing

The Application Provider (AP) must have an accurate way of billing the customer for such things as application and system resource usage. Additionally, the Service Provider (SP) must have an equally accurate way of billing the AP for hardware resource usage such as CPU time used.

Application usage is easily tracked by ways as simple as using timestamp checkpoints embedded in the application programs. The customer signs on to the application, and the time is recorded and stored. When the customer signs off, the time is once again recorded and stored. When the time comes to generate the bill, the start and end times are used to calculate the charge for that particular user's session.

The challenge is in accurately billing the hardware resource usage that the SP is to charge to the AP. Such things as CPU time used, total number of operating system-level transactions, and total transaction time are not commonly available to billing report-generating programs.

2.3.2 iSeries accounting and billing in an ASP environment

A billing system has been incorporated in OS/400 for many years. This means
that no extra programs have to be written to overcome the billing issue. This is a
simplistic approach to billing that can be considered if you are hosting traditional
applications launched from 5250 screens. Even if the application is converted to
a Web format by a tool, such as Host On-Demand, you could still use OS/400
accounting and billing.

2.3.2.1 Usage accounting

The job accounting function gathers data so it can determine who is using the
system and what system resources are being used. It also assists in evaluating
the overall use of the system. The system may be requested to gather job
resource accounting, printer file accounting data, or both. Accounting codes may
be assigned to user profiles or specific jobs. A charge may be needed for:

- Specific jobs that run
- Identifying charges by user or company that is being supported
- High priority jobs
- Work done during peak hours
- Use of critical resources

Typical job accounting data details the jobs running in the system and the
resources they are using, such as the use of the processing unit, printer,
database, and communication functions. Job accounting statistics are kept by
using the journal entries made in the system accounting journal
QSYS/QACGJRN. The knowledge of how to perform journal management
operations, such as saving a journal receiver, changing journal receivers, and
deleting old journal receivers, is needed. When analyzing the job accounting
data, it must be extracted from the QACGJRN journal by use of the DSPJRN
command. With this command, the entries can be written into a database file.
From there, applications programs can be written, or one of the many database
query and reporting tools available on the iSeries can be used.

2.3.2.2 Resource accounting

Resource accounting data is summarized in the Job resource information (JB)
journal entry at the completion of a job. In addition, the system creates a JB

journal entry summarizing the resources used each time a Change Accounting Code (CHGACGCDE) command occurs. The JB journal entry includes:

- Fully qualified job name
- Accounting code for the accounting segment just ended
- Processing unit time
- Number of routing steps
- Date and time the job entered the system
- Date and time the job started
- Total transaction time includes service time, ineligible time, and active time
- Number of transactions for all interactive jobs
- Auxiliary I/O operations
- Job type
- Job completion code
- Number of printer lines, pages, and files created if spooled or printed directly
- Number of database file reads, writes, updates, and deletions
- Number of ICF file read and write operations

2.3.2.3 Printer file accounting

There are two types of journal entries for printer file accounting:

- Direct print (DP) information for non-spooled printer files
- Spooled print (SP) information for spooled printer files

These two types of journal entries share a common journal entry format, although some of the information is available only in the SP entry. The DP and SP journal entries include information such as:

- Fully qualified job name
- Accounting code
- Device file name and library
- Device name
- Device type and model
- Total number of pages and lines printed (if multiple copies occurred, this is the sum of all copies)
- Spooled file name (only in the SP entry)
- Spooled file number (only in the SP entry)
- Output priority (only in the SP entry)
- Form type (only in the SP entry)
- Total number of bytes of control information and print data sent to the printer device. If multiple copies occurred, this is the sum of all copies. This only applies to the SP entry.

The DP and SP journal entries occur when the file is printed. If a spooled file is never printed, the SP journal entry will not appear.

2.3.2.4 Using accounting codes

The initial accounting code, up to 15 characters in length, for a job parameter is determined by the value of the ACGCDE (accounting code) parameter in the job description and user profile for the job. When a job is started, a description is assigned to the job. The job description object contains a value for the ACGCDE parameter. If the default of *USRPRF is used, the accounting code in the job's user profile is used. Note that when a job is started using the Submit Job (SBMJOB) command, its accounting code is the same as that of the submitter's job. You can change the accounting code after the job has entered the system by using the Change Accounting Code (CHGACGCDE) command. The CRTUSRPRF and CHGUSRPRF commands support the ACGCDE parameter. The default is *BLANK. If all of the work for a particular user is recorded under one accounting code, only the user profiles need to be changed. The accounting codes for specific job descriptions can be changed by specifying the desired accounting code for the ACGCDE parameter on the CRTJOBD and CHGJOBD commands. The CHGACGCDE command also allows different accounting codes in a single job. The Retrieve Job Attributes (RTVJOBA) command and the APIs that retrieve jobs allow access to the current accounting code in a CL program.

2.3.2.5 Resource accounting data

A JB journal entry is written at the end of every job and any time the job accounting code is changed by the CHGACGCDE command. A JB journal entry is written even if the accounting code is changed while the job is in the queue although no resources have been used. Each resource accounting journal entry contains information about the resources used while the previous accounting code was in effect.

Figure 8 illustrates a job with two accounting segments. At the mid-point, the CHGACGCDE command was issued. The accounting code is changed, and the JB journal entry is sent to the journal. The JB journal entry contains data for the first accounting segment. When the job ends, a second JB entry is made for the job containing data for the second accounting segment.

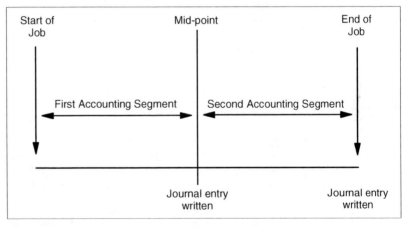

Figure 8. Accounting job

If the job accounting code was not changed during the existence of the job, the single JB entry summarizes the total resources used by the job. If the job accounting code was changed during the existence of the job, then you must add up the fields in the multiple JB entries to determine the total resources used by the job. The creation of a job log does not count toward the processing unit used for a job or its printed output in the JB accounting entries. However, if print file accounting is used, the job log printed is included in the printer file journal entries.

2.3.2.6 Processing the accounting journal

The accounting journal QSYS/QACGJRN is processed as any other journal. Files can also be recorded in this journal. However, for simplicity, we recommend that it be kept solely for accounting information. The Send Journal Entry (SNDJRNE) command can be used to send other entries to this journal. While there are additional operational considerations involved in using several journals, there are advantages to not allowing any file entries in the QACGJRN journal. It is usually easier to control the QACGJRN journal separately so that all job accounting entries for a particular accounting period are in a minimal number of journal receivers and that a new journal receiver is started at the beginning of an accounting period. System entries also appear in the journal QACGJRN. These are the entries with a journal code that relate to IPL and general operations performed on journal receivers.

Job accounting entries are placed in the journal receiver starting with the next job that enters the system after the CHGSYSVAL command takes effect. The accounting level of a job is determined when it enters the system. If the QACGLVL system value is changed after the job is started, it has no effect on the type of accounting being performed for that job. The DP and SP print entries occur if the job that created the file is operating under accounting and the system value is set for *PRINT. If spooled files are printed after the accounting level has been set to *PRINT or if the job that created the file was started before the accounting level was changed, no journaling is done for those spooled files.

While the most obvious use for the accounting data is to charge users for system resources, the data may be analyzed in other ways. Some methods of analyzing the job accounting information would be to sequence by the following fields or combinations of fields:

- Accounting code
- User
- Job type
- Time of day

The data from the journal can then be queried and used to generate billing reports for the customer. For more information on job accounting, refer to *OS/400 Work Management V4R4*, SC41-5306.

2.3.2.7 Disk space accounting

In an ASP environment, it is not uncommon for subscribing companies to have their own independent library or group of libraries. The subscribing company may be billed based on how much disk space is occupied by this library.

While the iSeries server doesn't provide a simple command to show the disk space utilization at the library level, there is a simple way to retrieve this information. The Display Object Description (DSPOBJD) command displays basic information about OS/400 objects. Object size is one of these items. The command also provides the ability to send the object attribute information to a DB2 Univeral Database (UDB) for AS/400 file.

Once this information is stored, a monthly-bill-producing high level program reads this information, and the subscribing company is billed accordingly. The procedure for obtaining this library disk utilization is explained here:

1. The DSPOBJD command (an example is shown in Figure 9) is run for the library (or libraries) for the subscribing company in question. The parameters for the command are shown in Figure 9. In this figure, LIBRARY01 is the subscribing company's production library, and a bill will be processed based

on the amount of disk space in this library. The command will place in the DISKUTIL DB2 UDB for AS/400 file, in the QGPL library, a list of all the objects in LIBRARY01. There will be one record per object in the library. The individual object size will be part of the individual file records in the form of a physical file field (named ODOBSZ).

2. Once this information is collected, a high-level program (RPG IV or COBOL/400) or query (Query/400 or SQL) will be run that reads each record for the subscribing company and keeps a running total of the object sizes. After the last record is read and processed, the total disk utilization of this subscribing company's library is available for processing.

```
                    Display Object Description (DSPOBJD)

Type choices, press Enter.

Object . . . . . . . . . . . . > *ALL           Name, generic*, *ALLUSR...
  Library  . . . . . . . . . . >   LIBRARY01    Name, *LIBL, *USRLIBL...
Object type  . . . . . . . . . > *ALL           *ALL, *ALRTBL, *AUTL...
          + for more values
Detail . . . . . . . . . . .       *BASIC       *BASIC, *FULL, *SERVICE
Output . . . . . . . . . . . . > *OUTFILE       *, *PRINT, *OUTFILE
File to receive output . . . . > DISKUTIL       Name
  Library  . . . . . . . . . . >   QGPL         Name, *LIBL, *CURLIB
Output member options:
  Member to receive output . . > *FIRST         Name, *FIRST
  Replace or add records . . . > *REPLACE       *REPLACE, *ADD
```

Figure 9. *Display Object Description command example*

2.3.2.8 Work management API
The QUSRJOBI API, when called from a high-level programming language such as RPG/400 or COBOL/400, returns the following information, which is useful for billing purposes:

- Job name
- User name
- Job number
- CPU time used
- Number of interactive transactions
- Response time total

To make billing more accurate, this API also returns the following values to the calling program:

- Time spent on database lock waits
- Time spent on non-database lock waits
- Time spent on internal machine lock waits

Once this information has been read into the application program, the billing calculations may be done and the results saved into a master Billing database file.

2.3.2.9 Application-level accounting and billing
Depending on the application, this service may also be done strictly at the application level.

2.4 Administration

Administration in a typical IT environment consists of user profile maintenance. This helps to make sure that users have the correct level of access to the applications, that the disk utilization is kept as low as possible, and that the production systems are as well-tuned as possible for optimal performance.

2.4.1 ASP administration

ASP administration takes place at two levels: the AP and the SP level (see Figure 4 on page 10). At the AP level, administration consists of adding and deleting users (customers) and controlling what applications each user is allowed to access.

The usual and constant housekeeping tasks, such as keeping disk utilization low and the ASP serving systems optimally tuned, are done at the SP level. Additionally, maintenance of the higher-level AP administrator's user profiles is done at this level.

2.4.2 iSeries ASP administration

The iSeries server provides robust administration facilities in the following areas:

- User profile support
- Automated cleanup
- Performance monitor
- Work management commands
- Disk management commands

2.4.2.1 User profile support

OS/400 user profile and work management support provides each ASP subscribing company with its own unique and independent operating environment. This environment consists of:

- **Initial program**: This is the user's entry point to the system of application programs.

- **Group profile**: This is a way of managing, such as assigning authorities, to a group of users.

- **Supplemental groups**: This feature allows a user to belong to more than one group.

- **Current library**: This is the user's default library. All object searches begin here.

- **Maximum storage allowed**: This sets a storage limit on each user to prevent the individual from taking up too much disk storage.

- **Initial library list**: This, along with the current library, defines the user's object search path. Objects outside of this list (for example, other subscribing company's applications and data) are not accessible.

2.4.2.2 Automated cleanup

The iSeries provides the ability to perform automatic cleanup of message and output queues. This cleanup procedure may be scheduled for off hours.

2.4.2.3 Performance monitor

iSeries server performance may be monitored on a regular basis by using the Start Performance Monitor (STRPFRMON) CL command. This starts the OS/400 performance monitor (shipped free of charge as part of the base operating system). The performance monitor may be automatically scheduled by using the Work with Performance Collection (WRKPFRCOL) and Start Performance Collection (STRPFRCOL) commands. The performance data collected may be taken at regular intervals and archived for comparison.

Once the performance data is gathered, the Performance Tools/400 (5769-PT1) licensed program provides the ability to generate various types of performance-related reports from the data collected by the performance monitor.

Additionally, the iSeries has a facility to perform capacity planning tasks. The BEST/1 capacity planner (part of Performance Tools/400) is used to build iSeries server models based on the performance data gathered by the performance monitor. Once this model is built, the workload may be increased by a certain percentage (or a series of percent increases) to determine if a possible hardware upgrade is needed. If it's determined that an upgrade is needed, BEST/1 will even make recommendations as to which iSeries model can handle the additional workload.

2.4.2.4 Work management commands

Performance may be more loosely monitored on an on-demand basis by using the Work with Active Jobs (WRKACTJOB) and Work with System Status (WRKSYSSTS) CL commands. Using these commands, it's possible to monitor:

- Total system CPU utilization
- CPU percent per job
- CPU time used per job
- Disk utilization in system auxiliary storage pool
- Database and non-database paging and faulting in main memory
- Number of jobs in system

Additionally, the WRKSYSSTS command allows an SP administrator to move memory from under-used subsystems to ones that are busier.

2.4.2.5 Disk management commands

The iSeries server provides the following disk management tools:

- **Work with Disk Status (WRKDSKSTS) CL command**: The WRKDSKSTS command shows how each individual disk unit, regardless of the storage pool to which it belongs, is used. It also shows how busy the disk arm is. This is an important statistic because, generally, disk performance is only as fast as the busiest disk.

- **Disktasks menu**: There are two options in the Disktasks menu that allow an SP administrator to acquire information on how the disks are used on a per library basis. This is useful for determining when a disk "cleanup" may be needed.

- **System Service Tools (SST)**: SST gives an SP administrator the ability to add and remove disk units to the system. This may be done while the system is in production.

2.5 Security

Security is an important aspect of every IT environment. Any discussion about IT security should begin with the protection of mission-critical data and applications, regardless of whether user access is local or over the Internet.

2.5.1 ASP security

To provide an ASP offering, the vendor must provide a secure product. Network security needs are tied directly to the growing number of network enabled applications. As more and more user-to-business and business-to-business applications are deployed, the challenge of determining security needs and providing security for internal networks becomes increasingly difficult. Businesses must determine the information they need to protect. They also need to understand how to grant and restrict access and how to manage the access controls. Also, the growing trend of using semi-private and public networks, in place of private networks, adds additional security issues. Therefore, due to the increasing sophistication of "hackers", layered security architectures are often needed.

To study security, you must take a holistic approach. A firewall, for example, does not provide security. It simply enforces some of your security rules at one layer (or a few layers) of your overall security plan.

2.5.1.1 Basic security concepts

The five main elements of network security are: authentication, authorization, integrity, confidentiality, and monitoring.

Authentication

Authentication is the assurance that the people (or systems) at the other end of the connection are really who they say they are. Two primary mechanisms are used by the iSeries to provide authentication on the Web: *user ID and password authentication* and *digital certificate authentication*.

An often used example of user ID and password authentication is the HTTP basic authentication used by many Web servers today. HTTP basic authentication requires clients (usually browser users) to pass user IDs and passwords to identify themselves to a protected server. The iSeries supports two types of users that can be validated in this way. The first type is standard system users, with valid OS/400 user profiles. These users are allowed to use their granted authorities to access objects within the system. The second type is network users, which are defined by either OS/400 validation lists or as LDAP users defined in a directory. These users can obtain access only to resources that are authorized to the Web server or applications running on behalf of the Web server. This allows you to control access by the Web site users without having the chance for a Web user to access objects outside the scope of the Web server.

Another authentication method that is emerging is called *digital IDs* or *digital certificates*. Digital ID support relies on a third-party certification authority (such as VeriSign) to vouch for the identity of the client by providing them with a signed certificate and associated private key. When users connect, they pass their certificate to the server, which then checks the certificate, verifies that each certificate was issued by a trusted authority, and verifies that the user has the private key associated with the certificate. A digital certificate can be used to establish people's identities online and define their relationships or privileges within a certain business, group, or community, much like a driver's license or passport can be used for identification in face-to-face transactions.

Digital certificates also allow users to encrypt and send information over open or private networks with the confidence that unauthorized persons won't open the data and that any compromise to the data enroute can be detected. These concerns become magnified when transacting business electronically over unsecured public networks such as the Internet, because it is more difficult to detect or prevent fraudulent transactions. *Public Key Infrastructure* (PKI) technology is fast emerging as the preferred trust mechanism for addressing these concerns. PKI consists of a certificate authority (CA) that provides digital credentials to participants and a public-key cryptographic system that uses these digital credentials to ensure overall message integrity, data privacy, signature verification, and user authentication. Together these technologies provide the trusted infrastructure required for secure electronic transactions.

User IDs and password authentication is considered weak authentication because passwords sometimes flow in the clear or when encrypted, are usually encrypted via basic hashing algorithms that can be easily compromised. Digital IDs are considered strong authentication, because the certificates are digitally signed by the authority and are protected with digital signatures.

Authorization or access control
Authorization is the process of granting a user either complete or restricted access to an object, resources, or function. Web-based authorization is traditionally tied very closely with authentication and is done by the HTTP server, an application server like WebSphere, or by the application itself. The server establishes protection domains or realms of protection (typically directories) that the administrator wants to protect. These realms are defined in the HTTP server configuration file or WebSphere user directory. When a protected realm is accessed, authentication is done by using either user ID and password authentication or digital ID authentication. Authorization is done by looking up the user in a user or group file (which contains passwords) to ensure that the user is registered for that realm before access is allowed.

The iSeries uses protection domains as well as the authorization mechanisms built into the operating system. Unauthenticated users and authenticated "Internet users" run under an identity specified by the server. Real iSeries users are authenticated (via basic or digital ID authentication) and run under their own user ID. The authentication information passed by the client (user ID and password or digital ID serial number) is mapped to a valid OS/400 user profile. The iSeries provides very granular authorization down to the object level.

An interesting CL program and table driven approach to provide three tiers of access for a given OS/400 user profile can be found in Appendix A, "Security study: ScotSystems' StoreReport" on page 217.

Integrity
Integrity is the assurance that the information that arrives at a destination is the same as the information that was sent, and that any changes are detected. This is typically accomplished by running a hash function over the data to create a message digest, which is then encrypted using a one-way encryption algorithm. The encrypted message digest is sent along with the original data. The receiver

can execute the same hash and encryption functions on the data received and verify that it matches the encrypted message's digest received.

Digital certificates use public key cryptography and message digest techniques to ensure the integrity of the certificate contents. In public key cryptography, a pair of asymmetric keys are used. The first key is the *private key*, which is kept secret by the owner. The second key is the *public key*. The owner of the public key published this key to everyone to which they want to communicate. Data, encrypted with the private key, can be unencrypted with the public key and vice versa. The iSeries also has the ability to extend this concept and sign applets sent to the user's browser. This protects the users and provides authentication of the applet.

Another important aspect of integrity is *content control*, which is looking at what's in a data stream to ensure it's free of viruses, junk mail, and confidentiality breaches. This is especially important when dealing with e-mail, but it can also be applied to other data types. Because of the need to encrypt data that flows over the Internet, it becomes necessary to do content scanning at the end nodes as opposed to the gateways (like firewalls), where it may be done more efficiently. There are several commercially available software products for content scanning. Some examples are IBM Antivirus and MIMEsweeper from Content Technologies, which works with a Domino mail server. You can find additional information at: http://www.us.mimesweeper.com/

Virus scanners for content already on the server are also available from companies like Symantec and Norton.

In the future, the iSeries plans to add additional ability to prevent unwanted software from running on the system. This would be done by digitally signing objects to help protect the server and provide for the secure distribution of program objects.

Confidentiality and encryption
Confidentiality means that anyone who might be able to intercept the data is unable to interpret its meaning. Encryption techniques are used to scramble the data that is transferred between two machines so that eavesdroppers won't understand the information. Only the intended receiver has an appropriate key that can be used to decrypt the data that was sent. A variety of encryption algorithms are available on iSeries both in hardware and software and are used by different techniques to ensure confidentiality.

Encrypting the data to be transported can be done at several levels: at the application itself, at the application API, or in the network layer.

Application encryption
On the iSeries server, certain encryption services are available to an application. One example is the Common Cryptographic Application Services (CCA). These services are used by the application to perform application controlled encryption. Most financial and banking applications need to control the encryption and, therefore, use these interfaces.

Application programming interface (API) encryption
Some applications do not want to control the encryption, but want to ensure that the data they send and receive is always encrypted. On the iSeries, the key servers (such as HTTP, Telnet, Operations Navigator, Management Central,

LDAP, Java servers, Client Access, DDM, and DRDA) support Secure Sockets Layer (SSL). The application interface uses SSL to take over the responsibility of providing encryption for the application's data. SSL uses a two-step key negotiation to provide the encryption for a session. First, *asynchronous handshakes* are used to determine the key pair to be used on the session. Then, new keys are used to provide the encryption of the data using synchronous encryption. SSL APIs are available for C, C++, and Java programs natively on the iSeries server. RPG IV is also supported with maps to the native C interface.

Another way to look at giving clients secured access to iSeries applications is via SecureWay Host On-Demand (HOD) to dynamically convert the 5250 data stream to a Java-based host access. More information about HOD can be found at: http://www.ibm.com/software/network/hostondemand/

Network-based encryption
Because of the global reach provided by the Internet, companies are using the network (considered to be for local use only) for access to key business applications and data that reside in traditional I/T systems. Companies can now securely and cost effectively extend the reach of their applications and data across the world through the implementation of secure virtual private network (VPN) solutions.

The iSeries supports native VPN solutions. For more information, see "Virtual private networks (VPN)" on page 44.

Monitoring
The last element of network security is the ability to monitor for certain types of attacks and to audit or log what has occurred. For an e-business site, the inability to process requests is often more costly than the loss or corruption of a piece of data. Therefore, e-business sites must protect themselves from what is known as *denial of service attacks*.

Collection of the logs is only part of the solution. Auditing tools are also key to overall security. By studying logs, you can find both individual attempts at security breaks, but also patterns of attempts that you can use to determine if additional security measures are required.

2.5.1.2 Technologies of network security
Several technologies are used, in many combinations, to provide the level of security that meets the specific requirements for a given security policy. There are two general levels of network security technologies: application and network.

Application level
The possible application level security you can implement includes proxy server, socks server, Secure Sockets Layer, and Domain Name Server.

Proxy server
A proxy server is a TCP or UDP application. Its purpose is to receive requests from a client and resend them to a server. It also resends responses from the server back to the client. To do this, the proxy must keep state information so that it can send the responses back to the appropriate client. Proxy servers are unique to the particular protocol that they handle. This is why you will hear references to Telnet proxies and HTTP proxies. One area of confusion is that people sometimes call the hardware on which the proxy runs a "proxy server".

Because this is ambiguous, we always use the term *proxy server* only to mean a TCP/IP application. You may be wondering why you would want to do this since it obviously introduces additional overhead. Most importantly, proxies break the TCP/IP connection. Clients no longer talk directly to servers. If a proxy is being used, what source IP address does the server see? It only sees the IP address of the proxy server, because it is unaware that the request actually originated at a client. This is useful for keeping internal network information private. Because a proxy is an application and understands the protocol, it also can perform a number of tasks such as:

- Authenticating users
- Logging access
- Caching information

Proxies are commonly used to relay requests from internal users to servers on the Internet. They can be used for incoming connections as well, but there is a major problem with authenticating users from the Internet. Because passwords sent in the clear can't be trusted, you need some form of encryption or one-time password support to do it. That is why most installations will not allow inbound proxying. The client needs to be smart enough to know to send the request to the proxy instead of the server with which it wants to ultimately communicate. That means the client application needs to be proxy-aware or the user must be told to perform some special procedure (browser configuration). The servers, on the other hand, are standard. They have no knowledge that a proxy is being used. One of the bad things about proxies is that they are unique to a particular application. If you obtain a new TCP/IP application, you may have a difficult time finding a proxy server to support it. Let's look at a couple of popular proxies.

Probably the most common example of a proxy is the *HTTP proxy*. An HTTP proxy relays requests from a Web browser to a Web server. The browser is configured to send requests for URLs to the proxy instead of directly to the server. The HTTP proxy can perform caching. When it receives a request, it first checks to see if the requested HTML file or GIF file is in its cache. If so, it simply sends it back to the browser. If not, it forwards the request to the Web server. When it receives the response, it stores it in its cache and sends it back to the browser.

A proxy can significantly improve average response times since the Web browser only needs to talk to the proxy if the page was cached (LAN speed versus Internet speed). Our experience in IBM Rochester is that a 40% cache hit rate is possible. This will vary based on the access patterns by your users. There is some overhead introduced by the proxy when the page is not cached. The HTTP proxy can also log all URL requests by IP addresses of the Web browser from which they came. This can be used to ensure that users are using company resources appropriately. Not all proxies are quite so easy to use.

Telnet proxies, for example, require the user to connect to the proxy and log in, and then Telnet again to the system with which they ultimately want to communicate. Another common proxy is one that relays mail between internal mail servers and other mail servers on the Internet. Because the proxy simply relays mail, sometimes it is called a *mail relay*. Users on the Internet send mail for your users to the mail proxy. The proxy relays all incoming mail to an internal mail server where it can be accessed by internal users.

All outgoing mail is also routed through the mail proxy. Mail proxies use Simple Mail Transport Protocol (SMTP), which is the mail protocol of the Internet. Post Office Protocol (POP), another popular mail protocol, can be used internally when communicating with the internal mail servers. The mail proxy has a relatively simple mail configuration. Complex mail routing should be handled on internal mail servers after they receive mail from the relay. The idea is to avoid placing too much policy or configuration information on the proxy. As mail passes through it, the mail proxy may rewrite the mail addresses to hide the original address and make it appear as if the mail originated on the proxy. A major benefit of using a mail proxy is that your internal mail servers will never communicate directly with the Internet. Many attacks in the past have been mounted against internal mail servers.

Table 2. Proxy server

Platform	Technology
Native OS/400	Contains an HTTP proxy server and a mail relay, but no others.
Firewall	Most firewalls support proxies on an individual basis. See your specific firewall manufacturer.
Appliance	Typically, appliances do not support proxies, but it is possible.
Router	Typically, router software does not support proxies.

Socks server

There is another TCP/IP application that resends requests and responses between clients and servers. It is called a *sockets server*, but everyone calls it a "socks server" for short. The socks server is like a multi-talented proxy. Instead of handling one type of application protocol, it handles them all: HTTP, Telnet, FTP, and so on. The purpose of the socks server is the same as a proxy. It breaks the TCP/IP connection and hides internal network information. However, to use a socks server, the client must be written to support the socks protocol. Some applications, such as popular Web browsers, support socks.

There are also some systems (such as OS/2) that support socks in their TCP/IP protocol stack (versatile clients) so that all client applications can use a socks server. The client configuration gives the name of the socks server to use and rules for when it should be used. The Internet servers are standard, the same as with proxies. Socks servers have no knowledge of the application protocol that they are using. They don't distinguish Telnet from HTTP. As a result, they can be written in a more efficient manner than a proxy. The down side is that they can't perform such tasks as caching or log URLs that are accessed.

Socks servers support a rule set, somewhat similar to the packet filtering rule set, which describes which subnetworks can use the socks server and which protocols they can use. A socks server can log general information about which Internet sites are accessed, what protocol is used, and how much data was transmitted. More and more people are moving to a socks server as a way to avoid having individual proxies for HTTP, Telnet, and FTP. A socks server can be used by your own proprietary TCP/IP applications.

Table 3. Socks server

Platform	Technology
Native OS/400	OS/400 contains SOCKS client support, but does not currently provide a socks server. A socks server is in our plans.
Firewall	Socks servers are typically found in firewall software, but not all products support a socks server.
Appliance	Typically, appliances do not support socks servers, but it is possible.
Router	Typically, router software does not support socks servers.

Secure Sockets Layer

The Secure Sockets Layer (SSL) protocol consists of two separate protocols: the *record protocol* and the *handshake protocol*. The handshake protocol is encapsulated within the record protocol. The SSL handshake is used to establish an SSL session on the TCP/IP connection between a client and a server application. The SSL handshake usually occurs immediately after the TCP connection is established. During the handshake, the client and server agree on the encryption algorithms and the encryption keys that they will use for that session. In all SSL handshakes, the client authenticates and verifies the identity of the server. The server can optionally authenticate and verify the identity of the client. After the SSL handshake has successfully completed, information exchanged between the client and server is encrypted using the negotiated keys.

An important advantage of SSL is its ability to negotiate unique encryption keys for each SSL session between a client and a server even if they have not previously communicated with each other. During the SSL handshake, the client and server exchange digital certificates. Digital certificates provide identifying information that enable the client and server to identify each other. Digital certificates are issued by trusted third-parties called *certificate authorities*. An SSL client must trust the certificate authority that issued the server's certificate in order for the SSL handshake to complete successfully.

The SSL protocol engine provides a set of published application programming interfaces (APIs) that are used by socket applications. It uses the services of a cryptographic service provider to perform all cryptographic services.

SSL gateways also exist. In this implementation, the IP segment between the server running the application and the security device is not encrypted. The security device establishes a secure session to the remote end. This offloads the encryption processing from the main server to a specialized device.

Table 4. Secure Sockets Layer (SSL)

Platform	Technology
Native OS/400	Supports SSL Version 2 and 3 implementations, with plans for TLS support.
Firewall	Some firewalls support the SSL gateway function.
Appliance	Is available today as a gateway function.
Router	No known product is available.

Domain Name Server

Domain Name Servers (DNS) are another technology that is often employed when building a secure network. Most of the time, people use host names, such as www.mycompany.com, when talking about hosts on the Internet. However, to send packets on the Internet, you need to know the IP address of the destination host. You may recognize the Domain Name Server as the application that enables a client to determine the IP address given a host name. For example, a host name, such as www.mycompany.com, might be translated into IP address 10.5.7.9. When constructing a firewall, we use DNS in a very particular way so that internal users can locate the IP addresses of all systems (internal and public), while users on the Internet can only locate the IP addresses of our public systems. This is part of the effort to hide internal network information from the Internet.

This is done by using two Domain Name Servers: one for internal names and one for external or public names. You may already have an internal DNS. It has a table of all of your internal systems that maps host names to IP addresses. It does this for a particular domain for which it is responsible.

For example, 192.168.67.3 is the IP address of the host with host name client1.private.mycompany.com. This internal Domain Name Server lets all of your internal systems locate each other. An external Domain Name Server is also needed. This DNS keeps the names of hosts that you want visible to users on the Internet. It will have the name of your mail proxy and your public Web server. You configure your *internal* Domain Name Server to forward name resolution requests to the external Domain Name Server if it doesn't know the host name. You configure the *external* Domain Name Server to forward requests to domain name servers on the Internet if it doesn't know the host name. This allows internal users to access hosts on the Internet. Users on the Internet will send requests to the external Domain Name Server to locate your public systems.

Table 5. Domain Name Server (DNS)

Platform	Technology
Native OS/400	Contains a DNS
Firewall	Typically support DNS. See your specific firewall.
Appliance	Typically, appliances do not support DNS, but it is possible.
Router	Typically, router software does not support DNS.

2.5.1.3 Network level security

The options for network level security are IP packet filtering, stateful packet filtering, network address translation, virtual private network (VPN), and monitoring audit logging.

IP packet filtering

IP packet filtering is a technology that is inserted at a low level in the IP protocol stack. IP, or Internet Protocol, runs on every host and is responsible for routing packets to their destination. As packets are ready to be received or ready to be sent, the packet filter decides if the operation should be performed or if the packet should be discarded. It does this by comparing the packet with a set of rules that say which packets are permitted.

Packet filters are a good way to selectively allow some traffic into a subnetwork. They are also a good way to protect the higher communications layers and applications from unwanted traffic. Because good traffic goes through unchanged, the protection is completely transparent to users and applications. Packet filters look at the first few bytes of each packet, called the *packet header*. The packet header describes the connection protocol and application protocol that are being used. Using this information, the packet filter determines whether it should allow the packet through or discard it.

Although there are some differences between products, most packet filters allow you to filter on:

- Source and destination IP addresses.
- Protocols TCP, UDP, or ICMP. TCP is the connection-oriented protocol used for most services, such as FTP and Telnet. UDP is connectionless and is used by SNMP and RealAudio. ICMP is the low-level management protocol for the Internet.
- Source and destination ports. Ports identify the application for TCP/UDP such as FTP, Telnet, SNMP, or RealAudio. For ICMP, you can use the equivalent service identifier.
- Whether the packet is the first of a new TCP/IP connection or a subsequent packet.
- Whether the packet is destined for, or originated from, a local application or if it is being routed through.
- Whether the packet is inbound or outbound. This is useful for filtering packets to local applications.

Your initial thought may be that this is going to be real easy. You let the good traffic go out and don't let in anything from the Internet. This would be fine if you never want to access again the Web page from that Web server on the Internet. You need to distinguish between inbound or outbound packets and inbound or outbound connections. Inbound packets resulting from an outbound connection are okay. They are the responses, and we need to let them pass through the filter. That means packet filters need to pay attention to the flags in the TCP header (SYN and ACK), which indicate if this is a new connection or response in an existing connection.

Some other problems with packet filters are:

- Trust is based on IP addresses. If a host lies about its IP address (that is, spoofing), then the rule can't work properly.
- Because packets that are not discarded flow unmodified, everyone sees the real IP addresses that are used. In other words, packet filters don't help with privacy at all.
- There are some attacks based on IP fragments that can bypass filter rules. A subsequent fragment changes the TCP/IP header after the original header has already been validated with the packet filter.

Table 6. IP packet filtering

Platform	Technology
Native OS/400	Contains a packet filter with wizard and graphical configuration support.
Firewall	Typically support packet filters. See your specific firewall.
Appliance	Packet filter appliances exist.

Platform	Technology
Router	Most routers provide optional packet filter support.

Stateful packet filtering

To address some of the shortcomings of simple packet filtering, some companies are introducing an enhanced packet filtering capability known as *stateful packet filtering*. Where simple packet filtering works by examining and filtering on the source and destination IP address and ports, stateful packet filtering devices look at some of the payload of the packet. This technique allows for higher performance, because patterns are quicker to check than to test against all of the filter rules. If the pattern is recognized as part of an already approved connection, the filtering rules are not checked. If the pattern is not recognized, the packet will be checked based on the filtering rules.

Network address translation

Network address translation (NAT) allows you to hide internal network information, such as Internet Protocol (IP) addresses from the network. For example, you can use NAT to hide the IP address of a public server on the secure side of the firewall. You can use NAT to dynamically translate secure client IP addresses to a reserved pool of registered IP addresses for communicating with the untrusted network. This is sometimes referred to as *masquerading*. NAT also allows you to use private IP addresses on your internal network rather than publicly registered ones. With NAT, internal addresses are translated to a reserved, publicly registered IP address. Outsiders only see the public address. If you use NAT port mapping, you can use the non-secure NAT device IP address as the publicly registered address for your public server.

NAT is more efficient than socks or proxy servers. Because NAT uses fewer computing resources, your firewall may have better performance. NAT also supports a much wider range of services than the proxy server. Your internal clients do not have to provide support for proxy or socks. Because some types of clients do not provide this support, using NAT allows you to support Internet access for a wider range of clients.

NAT also has some disadvantages. When you use NAT and support transactions initiated from the Internet, you must have a pool of public addresses to use for translation purposes. However, when you use socks and proxy servers, you need only one public address for the firewall nonsecure port. NAT is also not as adept as either the socks or proxy servers in detecting attacks. NAT does not provide logging services. The firewall only logs traffic that matches those filter rules that have a log field value of "yes".

Additionally, NAT requires you to permit IP forwarding to open a hole in your firewall. Using IP forwarding can increase your internal network's security risk.

And, finally, be careful about NAT issues in conjunction with VPNs. If you are using private IP addresses and need to access public resources on the Internet, you may have a need for NAT. If you are going to deploy an IPSec-based VPN, there are scenarios where using NAT would be detrimental to what you are trying to achieve.

Using NAT is ideal when you want to locate public servers behind the firewall. With NAT, the server can keep the secure (unpublished) IP address to communicate with the internal network, while being accessed from the Internet using a mapped registered IP address. Without NAT, the public server behind the firewall needs to be assigned a registered IP address that makes the communication with other systems in the internal network more difficult besides having to use a publicly known IP address in the internal network.

Table 7. Network address translation (NAT)

Platform	Technology
Native OS/400	Contains NAT support.
Firewall	Typically support NAT. See your specific firewall.
Appliance	NAT appliances exist.
Router	Most routers provide optional NAT support.

Virtual private networks (VPN)

Virtual private networks (VPN) are a by-product of network security. Today, network security is primarily handled by firewalls, products that create a software barrier between corporate network resources and the Internet at large. Many of today's firewall products do their job by filtering packets that go onto and off of the intranet. VPNs move beyond basic filtering and leverage encryption technology. In this first encryption phase, the payload (data contents) of each IP packet sent out over the Internet is encrypted, but the source and destination address information in the packet header is left intact. The next stage of network security focuses on delivering VPN services. The element that distinguishes the VPN from the current network security offering is the ability to encapsulate (or tunnel) entire IP packets including address information from the source station to the destination host. This is shown in Figure 10.

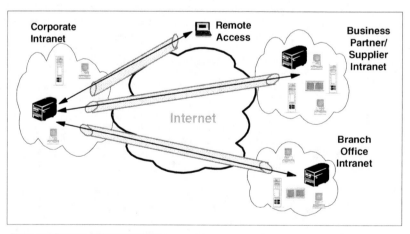

Figure 10. Example VPN configuration

A VPN is an extension of an enterprise's private intranet across a public network, such as the Internet, which creates a secure private connection essentially through a private tunnel. VPNs securely convey information across the Internet that connects remote users, branch offices, and business partners into an extended corporate network. Internet service providers (ISPs) offer cost-effective access to the Internet (via direct lines or local telephone numbers). They enable companies to eliminate their current, expensive leased lines, long-distance calls, and toll-free telephone numbers.

VPN implementations come in two forms: endpoint (host) and gateway. An *endpoint solution* is when the VPN implementation exists at the applications initial entry into the TCP/IP domain. In this case, the data never travels on an IP segment without encryption. In a *gateway implementation*, some IP segments are not secured, and another node provides encryption for other segments in the path.

Native VPN solutions provide better security than firewall or gateway encryption solutions. This is because they provide encryption support between the network endpoints, and therefore, thwart both external and internal hackers.

Within the layered communications protocol stack model, the network layer (IP in the case of the TCP/IP stack) is the lowest layer that can provide end-to-end security. Network-layer security protocols provide blanket protection for all upper-layer application data carried in the payload of an IP datagram, without requiring a user to modify the applications.

VPN offerings can be categorized by the protocol layer on which the VPN is realized. In this context, the following different approaches to VPN implementation exist:

- **IP Security Architecture (IPSec)**: This network layer-based protocol defines the protocols that are used to provide authentication and encryption in the IP layer.
- **L2TP**: This data link layer-based, enhanced link protocol provides a multi-hop virtual circuit link through the network.
- **Internet Key Exchange (IKE) protocol**: This protocol is key to making up VPN solutions and is used to negotiate and exchange the encryption keys and security policies that define the link security.

IP Security Architecture (IPSec) is an open framework, defined by the IPSec Working Group of the Internet Engineering Task Force (IETF). IPSec is called a framework because it provides a stable, long lasting base for providing network layer security. It can accommodate today's cryptographic algorithms and can also accommodate newer, more powerful algorithms as they become available. Future IPv6 implementations are required to support IPSec, and current IPv4 implementations are strongly recommended. In addition to providing the base security functions for the Internet, IPSec furnishes flexible building blocks from which robust, secure virtual private networks can be constructed.

The IPSec Working Group concentrates on defining protocols to address several major areas:

- Data origin authentication verifies that each datagram was originated by the claimed sender.
- Data integrity verifies that the contents of the datagram were not changed in transit, either deliberately or due to random errors.
- Data confidentiality conceals the clear text of a message, typically by using encryption.

- Replay protection assures that an attacker cannot intercept a datagram and play it back at some later time without being detected.

- Automated management of cryptographic keys and security associations assures that a company's VPN policy can be conveniently and accurately implemented throughout the extended network with little or no manual configuration. These functions make it possible for the VPN size to be scaled to the size that a business requires, as well as increases its security since the cryptographic keys are refreshed on an interval specified in the security associations.

The principal IPSec protocols are:

- **IP Authentication Header (AH)**: Provides data origin authentication, data integrity, and replay protection. The IP Authentication Header provides connectionless (that is, per-packet) integrity and data origin authentication for IP datagrams and also offers protection against replay.

  There are two modes that can be used: tunnel mode and transport mode. In *tunnel mode*, the entire IP packet is used to create the AH header, and a new IP header is added to ensure proper routing of the packet. In *transport mode*, only the packet payload is used to generate the AH, and the original IP is used for routing. Tunnel mode is used whenever one end of the security association is a gateway. Because tunnel mode places a new IP header on the packet, it hides the IP address of the final endpoint. This technique is similar in nature and is the same, in effect, as network address translation (NAT).

- **IP Encapsulating Security Payload**: Provides data confidentiality (encryption), connectionless (that is per-packet) integrity, data-origin authentication, and protection against replay. ESP always provides data confidentiality and can also optionally provide data origin authentication, data integrity checking, and replay protection. In comparing ESP to AH, only ESP provides encryption, while either can provide authentication, integrity checking, and replay protection.

  ESP also works in tunnel mode and transport mode. In *tunnel mode*, the entire IP packet is used to create the ESP header, trailer, and authentication package. A new IP header is added to ensure proper routing of the packet. In *transport mode*, only the packet payload is used to generate the ESP information, and the original IP is used for routing. Tunnel mode is used whenever one end of the security association is a gateway. Because tunnel mode places a new IP header on the packet, it hides the IP address of the final endpoint. This technique is similar in nature, and the same in effect, as NAT.

Either ESP or AH may be applied alone, in combination with the other, or even nested within another instance of itself. With these combinations, authentication and encryption can be provided between a pair of communicating hosts, between a pair of communicating firewalls, or between a host and a firewall.

L2TP is an IETF draft and combines the efforts of several companies to bring together PPTP and L2F. The iSeries server can:

- Be an L2TP network server
- Provide PPP dial-up to an ISP
- Act as an L2TP enabled client for voluntary tunnels when establishing a secure tunnel with a server

Before using a VPN solution, you need to ensure compatibility between the endpoints of the secure network. Industry sponsored compatibility "bake-offs" continue to try and ensure this. Also, the International Computer Security Association (ICSA) provides certification for VPN solutions in the same manner that they have been certifying firewalls. You should check the ICSA Web site (http://www.icsalabs.com/index.shtml) for more information on certification.

For a good source of information on iSeries VPN, see the IBM Redbook *AS/400 Internet Security: Implementing AS/400 Virtual Private Networks*, SG24-5404.

2.5.1.4 Application level security
Sometime there are no built-in features to secure access to the production data. Therefore, there is no other option, but to implement security at the application level.

Lightweight Directory Access Protocol (LDAP)
LDAP is based on the client/server model of distributed computing and has evolved as a lightweight protocol for accessing information in X.500 directory services. It has since become more independent of X.500 and is now more commonly supported than the X.500 Directory Access Protocol (DAP).

LDAP has the following advantages over the X.500 DAP:

- LDAP runs over TCP/IP rather than the Open Systems Interconnect (OSI) protocol stack. TCP/IP is less resource-intensive and is much more widely available, especially on desktop systems.

- The functional model of LDAP is simpler. It omits duplicate, rarely-used, and esoteric features. This makes LDAP easier to understand and to implement.

- LDAP uses strings to represent data rather than complicated structured syntaxes such as ASN.1 (Abstract Syntax Notation One).

LDAP defines the content of messages exchanged between an LDAP client and and an LDAP server. The messages specify the operations requested by the client (search, modify, delete, and so on), the responses from the server, and the format of the data carried in the messages. LDAP messages are carried over TCP/IP, a connection-oriented protocol. Therefore, there are also operations to establish and disconnect a session between the client and server.

However, for the designer of an LDAP directory, it is not really the structure of the messages being sent and received over the wire that is of interest. What is important is the logical model that is defined by these messages and data types, how the directory is organized, what operations are possible, how information is protected, and so forth.

Without going into much detail, we mention a few important points about LDAP. For more information about LDAP, refer to *Understanding LDAP*, SG24-4986.

The philosophy of the LDAP API is to keep things simple. The directory stores and organizes data structures known as *entries*. Each entry has a name called a *distinguished name* (DN) that uniquely identifies it. The DN consists of a sequence of parts called *relative distinguished names* (RDNs). This tree of directory entries is called a *directory information tree* (DIT). Each entry contains one or more attributes that describe the entry. Each attribute has a type and a value. A directory entry describes an object. The object classes that a directory server can store and the attributes they contain are described by a *schema*. A schema defines what object classes are allowed where in the directory, what attributes they must contain, what attributes are optional, and the syntax of each attribute. In other words, a schema defines the type of objects that can be stored in the directory. The basic directory structure is shown in Figure 11.

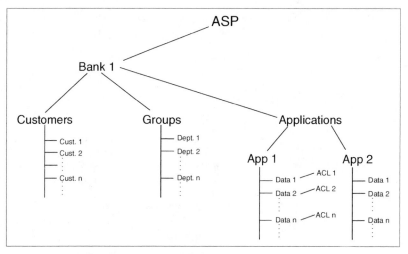

Figure 11. LDAP directory information tree (DIT)

LDAP defines operations to access and modify directory entries such as:

- Searching for entries meeting user-specified criteria
- Adding an entry
- Deleting and entry
- Modifying an entry
- Modifying the DN or RDN of an entry (move)
- Comparing an entry

LDAP access control

Access control lists (ACLs) provide a means to protect information stored in an LDAP directory. Using ACLs, administrators can restrict access to different portions of the directory or specific directory entries. Each entry within the directory has an associated ACL.

ACL information is broken into two distinct subgroups: the entry owner and the entry ACL. Each directory entry must have both an entry owner and an entry ACL:

- **Entry owner**: The entry owner has complete permission to perform any operation on the object regardless of the ACL entry. Additionally, the entry owner is the only one, besides the directory administrator, who has permission to administer the ACL for that object. The entry owner is defined to be an ACL subject.

- **ACL subject**: The ACL specifically grants a subject permission to perform a given operation. Subjects are considered the combination of a privilege attribute and a DN.

For more information about ACLs, refer to the IBM Redbook *LDAP Implementation Cookbook*, SG24-5110.

The purpose of introducing LDAP at this point is because, in the absence of built-in methods of user authentication in an ASP environment, LDAP serves this purpose.

An LDAP ASP schema

The scenario shown in Figure 11 shows an ASP at the top of the DIT. Each ASP subscriber (which, in this example, is a bank) is at the second level. From there, the tree branches out in the following directions:

- **Customers**: These are the bank's customers (the ASP subscriber's customers).

- **Employees/groups**: These are the bank's individual departments that consist of the bank's employees.

- **Applications**: These are the different applications.

- **Access control lists**: The ACLs control who has access to what. Whenever a customer wants to view their data (account balances, loan payoff amounts, and so on), the ACL ensures that only that customer can view this information.

This is only one example. LDAP is flexible enough so that simpler or more complex directory structures can be designed. However, we recommend that you implement as shallow of a hierarchy as possible. As the nesting in an LDAP DIT grows, so can the complexity of both finding the right information and keeping it up-to-date.

2.5.2 iSeries ASP security

All the previous technologies and security layers (as detailed in 2.5.1, "ASP security" on page 34) can be implemented in OS/400. We mention a few points in this section that are OS/400 specific.

2.5.2.1 OS/400 system security levels

Use the Work with System Value (WRKSYSVAL) command to display or change your current system security level. On an OS/400 command line, you would enter:

```
WRKSYSVAL SYSVAL(QSECURITY)
```

A valid user profile and password is required for each of the security levels:

- **Level 20**: The user has access to all system resources. Obviously, this is not an appropriate security level for an ASP environment.

- **Level 30**: The user must have explicit authority to access objects and system resources.

- **Level 40**: The user must have explicit authority to access objects and system resources. Programs fail if they try to access objects through interfaces that are not supported.

  For ASP on the iSeries server, we recommend you implement a security strategy based on Level 40 because this is the first level that enforces operating system integrity. With an ASP, you will most likely host users of different companies with direct access to the Internet and, therefore, require this additional level of security.

- **Level 50**: The user must have explicit authority to access objects and system resources. Programs fail if they try to pass unsupported parameter values through supported interfaces or if they try to access objects through interfaces that are not supported.

In addition, the iSeries provides security methods that may be imposed on Internet user connections using:

- Digital certificates
- Secure Sockets Layer (SSL) encryption
- Virtual private networks (VPN)

2.5.2.2 Monitoring: Auditing and logging

Sometimes the ability to prove that security is working can be as important as what the security does. Most security products provide some form of logging or auditing of security events. Because each product is different, we only describe the methods that OS/400 provides. OS/400 provides a wide array of auditing support to help you in this task. As with the security functions, auditing is integrated throughout the entire operating system to provide completeness, and to make it extremely difficult to bypass when your system is running at the proper security level (40 or 50). OS/400 journaling functions provide integrity in your audit journal by preventing a user from deleting individual entries from a journal receiver. Someone with the right authority could delete an entire journal, but an audit entry is then sent to a new journal receiver to record the deletion.

OS/400 auditing capabilities are quite comprehensive. You can audit system-wide security actions, the security actions of a particular user, system-wide access of an object, or a specific user's access of an object. For example, you can audit the creation of user profiles, the deletion of all objects on the system, or all sign-on attempts that are not valid. You can perform these audit functions for everyone on the system or for one particular user. For vendors and security officers, you may want to use the Change User Auditing (CHGUSRAUD) command to log the command strings entered by that user. If you want to monitor who reads or updates your payroll file, you can use the Change Object Auditing (CHGOBJAUD) command.

OS/400 auditing is also a handy debugging tool. For example, applications sometimes fail because a user isn't authorized to an object, but the error message gives no indication of the object's name. You can turn on system wide or user-based auditing, monitor for authorization failures, run the failing application, and view the journal entry created. The object name is in the audit entry. For complete instructions on configuring OS/400 auditing and a list of auditing settings, see Chapter 9 in *AS/400e Security - Reference*, SC41-5302.

In addition to the auditing tools, OS/400 provides tools to help you manage your users and groups and the authorities they have to the objects on your system. For example, by using one simple command, you can see which users have passwords that are the same as their user profile name and force them to change their password the next time they sign on. You can also schedule to delete or disable profiles on a date you specify. Authority reports let you keep track of the private authorities on your most sensitive files and directories. Or, you can examine the security-relevant characteristics of your job descriptions, job queues, output queues, subsystem descriptions, device descriptions, or trigger programs to see if they follow your security policy's requirements. If you aren't familiar with these tools, you can learn about them by typing either of the following commands on any OS/400 command line:

```
GO SECTOOLS
GO SECBATCH
```

2.6 User registration

User registration is a common practice in every IT environment. User profiles are constantly added, deleted, and modified.

2.6.1 ASP user registration

In the three-tier ASP model (see Figure 4 on page 10), there are three levels of users. From the topmost level down, they are:

- ASP hosting system administrators
- Administrators for the subscribing APs
- Individual users of each subscribing AP

User profile administration at the two topmost layers is relatively straightforward, especially in a traditional enterprise-out environment and even when the newer Domino and Web-based applications are used by the APs.

In an enterprise-out application environment, AP customer user profile maintenance is straightforward. You can find an interesting CL program and table driven approach to provide three tiers of access for a given OS/400 user profile in Appendix A, "Security study: ScotSystems' StoreReport" on page 217.

However, when the ASP applications are Domino or Web-based, matters of user registration become complicated. Traditional methods no longer apply.

In a WebSphere or Domino application environment, users may be authenticated in one of the following ways:

- Lightweight Directory Access Protocol (LDAP)
- HTTP Access Control Lists (ACL)
- HTTP validation lists

2.6.2 iSeries ASP user registration

Refer to 2.4.2.1, "User profile support" on page 32, for a description of iSeries user profile support.

Appendix A, "Security study: ScotSystems' StoreReport" on page 217, offers an interesting CL program and table-driven approach to provide three tiers of access for a given OS/400 user profile.

2.7 Printing

This section looks at printing in an ASP environment and then digs deeper into the printing solutions available from the iSeries server.

2.7.1 ASP printing considerations

Often overlooked in this day and age of "e-everything" is the fact that your ASP customers may want to actually print the data they have stored in your application. The reasons might include printed reports (daily, weekly, monthly, and yearly), invoices to be faxed to customers, information for tax purposes, and sometimes merely to provide a physical backup in case of a system or network crash.

As you decide how to provide your customers with the ability to generate and print *their* information extracted from your ASP application, step back and ask one question: Who will manage the printing of the documents? That is, who (or what) will be the *print server*?

The role of a print server is to:

- Queue print jobs and send them to the printer.
- Ensure the appropriate data stream is being created for specific printer, and perform a transform if necessary.
- Send documents to the printer.
- Instruct the operator to load specific forms (if used).
- Load printer resources (fonts, overlays, images, and so forth).
- Perform error recovery procedures. Send print-related messages to operators or other destinations.
- Set up printer and jobs per job attributes.

How the operator sees and interacts with any error recovery procedures may be key to your decision.

Look at Figure 12, which shows that, in terms of the network configuration, there is not much difference between the print server function residing on the ASP server or the client's network attached printer. However, as you will see, once you make the decision about where the print server will reside, you can start making choices about print data streams and protocols.

Note: The left-hand side of Figure 12 shows an example of a network where the iSeries is the print server – controlling the network attached printer (or, as depicted by the dashed line, the printer could also be directly connected to a PC). The right side of Figure 12 shows that the print server function is now the responsibility of your ASP customer. In this case, the print server function most likely will reside on a system that is directly attached (or attached via a network attachment as shown by the dashed line) to the printer.

Either way, you must decide if the print server function resides on your ASP server (the iSeries) or in the customer's location.

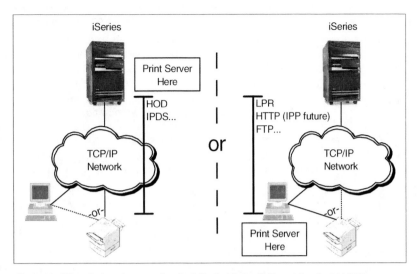

Figure 12. Where is the print server function? On the iSeries (left) or at the client (right)?

2.7.2 iSeries printing in an ASP environment

The iSeries server provides a robust printing solution that works well in both of the environments shown in Figure 12. When you make the choice as to where the print server resides (either on the iSeries or at the customer's location), you are limited to the following solutions for printing.

2.7.2.1 Print server resides on the iSeries server

Handling the print server function on the iSeries server can give you greater control over the printing process and, therefore, the quality of the final printout. This kind of solution fits well in the following ASP environments:

- The enterprise-out solution where your ASP application is largely based on a traditional ILE language solution. In this case, you most likely already have solutions for generating printed reports and now simply must be concerned about how to transport the printer data stream across either an intranet or the Internet.

- The enterprise-out solution, but using solutions such as Host-on-Demand as a tool to convert the SNA character string (SCS) or Advanced Function Printer (AFP) data stream generated by your ASP application into an ASCII data stream. The ASCII data stream is then formatted and sent to an ASCII printer through a Host On-Demand 5250 printer session. The conversion is done on the iSeries via the Host Print Transform (HPT) function.

- Pre-printed forms can cause an additional level of complexity because the output generated must match the form in the printer. By handling the print server function from the iSeries, you will have greater control over the actual position of the text on the paper.

- Keeping the printer data stream or document on the iSeries provides increased protection to the loss of data. If the print documents are moved to the client's environment to be stored, they are at risk to being destroyed or lost, all depending on the quality of each and every client's backup and recovery plan (that is, if they have one, of course).

- An enterprise-out solution that is now front-ended (faced) with a WebSphere Application Server (WAS) servlet or some other Web-based application development environment. In this case, the "print" servlet makes calls to your existing enterprise-out print program to create the output.

- A Java servlet can use native iSeries server calls to generate printer data streams on the iSeries that will now have to be sent from a print server running on the iSeries to the remote client location. The list of tools available in Java to manage this situation are increasing all the time.

  The easiest way to accomplish this is to use the print classes as part of the Java Toolbox to put data into iSeries spooled files.

  Another way is to use the 2D Graphics APIs with the remote Abstract Window Toolkit (AWT). To learn more about how to do this, search for AWT on the iSeries 400 Information Center at:
  http://publib.boulder.ibm.com/pubs/html/as400/infocenter.htm

Let's take a quick look at the types of printer data streams that can be created on the iSeries and how you can transport these data streams to remote clients.

Note: Much of the following information comes from the IBM Redbook *IBM AS/400 Printing V*, SG24-2160. Further study of printing solutions on the iSeries should be directed to this IBM Redbook.

Data streams supported on the iSeries server
Printed output is the result of the interaction between your ASP application and the printer file (see Figure 13). The output of this interaction can be controlled by the printer device type selected in the printer file as shown in Figure 14.

Back to Figure 13, this printer data stream or document is created as a spooled file in an output queue. Later, this printer data stream or document may need some kind of transformation into the actual data stream of the printer, via a print writer.

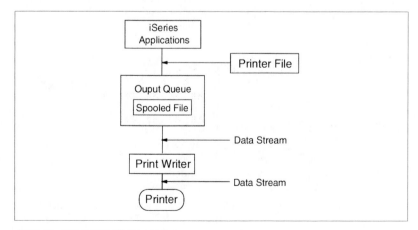

Figure 13. Data stream: iSeries server

The iSeries server supports different data streams and can automatically create the majority of them. The Printer device type parameter (Figure 14) in the printer file determines the type of data stream or document to be created.

```
                            Create Printer File (CRTPRTF)
  Type choices, press Enter.

  File . . . . . . . . . . . . . . > MYPRTF        Name
    Library . . . . . . . . . . . >   MYLIB        Name, *CURLIB
  Source file . . . . . . . . . .   *NONE          Name, *NONE
    Library . . . . . . . . . . .                  Name, *LIBL, *CURLIB
  Source member . . . . . . . . .   *FILE          Name, *FILE
  Generation severity level  . . .  20             0-30
  Flagging severity level  . . . .  0              0-30
  Device:
    Printer . . . . . . . . . . .   *JOB           Name, *JOB, *SYSVAL
  Printer device type  . . . . . .  *SCS           *SCS, *IPDS, *LINE...
  Text 'description' . . . . . . .  *SRCMBRTXT

                                                                      Bottom
  F3=Exit    F4=Prompt    F5=Refresh    F10=Additional parameters    F12=Cancel
  F13=How to use this display          F24=More keys
```

Figure 14. Create Printer File: Printer device type parameter

The Printer device type parameter can be set to one of the following values:

- ***SCS** (SNA Character String):

  Used to control line mode printers and has a relatively simple structure. The Data Description Specifications (DDS) FONT keyword is not supported. The font specified in the printer file or the printer default font is used.

  An extension of SCS, Final-Form Text Document Architecture (FFT-DCA) is used within the iSeries Office environment.

- ***IPDS** (Intelligent Printer Data Stream):

  A host-to-printer data stream used for AFP subsystems. It provides an attachment-independent interface for controlling and managing all-point-addressable (APA) printers. It supports an interactive, two-way dialog between the print driver and the printer (printer information, cooperative recovery, and resources management).

  Note: The iSeries-generated IPDS is a subset of the full IPDS.

- ***AFPDS** (Advanced Function Printing Data Stream):

  A data stream for advanced function printers (independent of operating systems, independent of page printers, and portable across environments). AFPDS is a structured data stream divided into components called *objects*. AFPDS includes text, images, graphics, and barcodes and references AFP resources (for example, overlays, page segments, and fonts).

- ***LINE** (Line data stream):

  A LINE data stream referencing a page definition and a form definition with the spooled file. The Printer device type parameter was enhanced in V3R2 and V3R7 (and later) with a new value *LINE.

- ***AFPDSLINE**: AFPDS line (also called Mixed) data stream:

  AFPDSLINE data stream is a mixture of AFP structured fields and LINE data. Only certain AFP structured fields can be mixed with the line data. Programmers must specify AFP structured fields in applications. The Printer device type parameter was enhanced in V3R2 and V3R7 (and later) with the new value *AFPDSLINE.

- ***USERASCII**: ASCII data stream:

  There is no formal structure that controls the use of the American National Standard Code for Information Interchange (ASCII) data stream to control printers attached to systems providing ASCII support. There is no architectural data stream standard to which ASCII printers can conform in the interest of uniformity.

  To create a spooled file in *USERASCII on the iSeries server, programmers must specify ASCII escape sequences in applications that use the transparency mode. We do not recommend this approach because the escape sequences required in the application depend on the type of printer.

  A *USERASCII spooled file can contain any form of ASCII printer data stream (for example, PCL5, PPDS, or PostScript).

Spooled files can also be received from other systems:

- From another iSeries server, you can receive spooled files in SCS, IPDS, LINE, AFPDSLINE, AFPDS, or USERASCII data streams.

- If the spooled file is from a System/390, LINE, AFPDSLINE, and AFPDS are supported. By using object distribution (SNADS), the spooled file is placed directly in an iSeries output queue.

- From a PC running Client Access for AS/400 network printing, you can receive spooled files in SCS, AFPDS, or USERASCII.

- From a RISC system (pSeries), you may receive spooled files in AFPDS or USERASCII.

- From an Other Equipment Manufacturer (OEM) system, spooled files are normally received in USERASCII.

A spooled file stored in an iSeries output queue can be in different data streams. On the other end, many printers support only one data stream (for example SCS, IPDS, or ASCII PCL5). Some others (for example, the IBM Infoprint 20, 21, 32, and 40) support IPDS, PCL, and Postscript. Figure 15 shows data streams and printer devices.

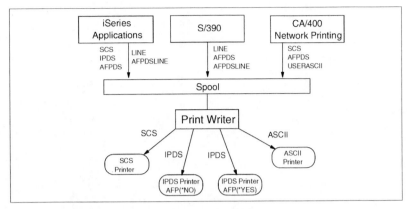

Figure 15. Data streams and printer devices

On the iSeries server, the print writer can convert some of the data streams to others. The following section explains the possible conversions.

The job of the printer writer

The printer writer program is a system-supplied program. This program takes the spooled file from an output queue and sends it to a printer. The printer writer handles spooled files by using one of the following options:

- Print Writer
- Print Services Facility/400 (PSF/400)
- Host Print Transform

Each of these writer options supports different data streams and printer types. They can also perform certain data stream conversions.

Figure 16 on page 58 shows the three options with the supported input data streams, the resulting data streams, and the required printer types.

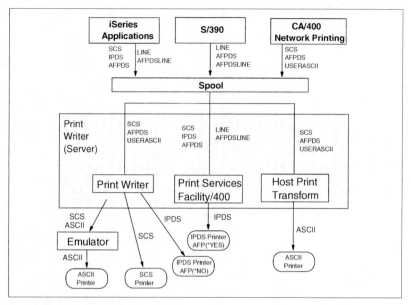

Figure 16. Printer writer and data streams

The IPDS data stream generated by the iSeries server (when the printer file device type parameter is set to *IPDS) is not the full IPDS data stream. Many functions are not included in this subset, including the use of external resources such as fonts or page segments.

The IPDS data stream generated by Print Services Facility/400 (PSF/400) includes the full IPDS set of commands and supports a two-way dialog between PSF/400 and the printer (Figure 17).

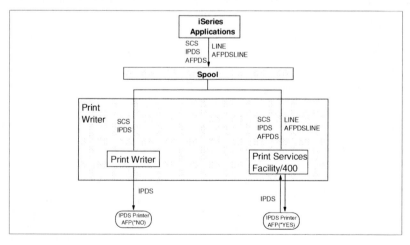

Figure 17. iSeries-generated IPDS: Full IPDS

The iSeries-generated IPDS is supported by the print writer or transformed to full IPDS by PSF/400. iSeries-generated IPDS cannot be transformed to an ASCII data stream and can only be sent to another iSeries server. Because of these restrictions, we recommend you use device type *AFPDS in place of *IPDS in the printer file to allow portability, more conversion possibilities, and full IPDS support.

For more details of the functions and features of the three different Printer Writers (Print Writer, PSF/400 and Host Print Transform) on the iSeries server, see the IBM Redbook *IBM AS/400 Printing V*, SG24-2160. Also, *Printer Device Programming Version 4*, SC41-5713, can be useful as a guide to programming.

2.7.2.2 Print server resides at customer location

Handling the print server function at the client location may be one of the easiest ways to handle printing in an ASP environment. The reason is that you have offloaded many of the responsibilities of the print server to the customer. If you consider an example of this, performing error recovery procedures, you can see how difficult this might be. However, removing your ASP application from the direct contact with the printer also reduces your ability to provide a quality printed document.

Having the print server residing at the customer location fits well with the following ASP scenarios:

- A Domino server runs on the iSeries to a Web or Notes client. The client in this case is responsible for printing locally.

- You can give the customer the choice as to when and where to print. Also, now that the print document is local, they can print it a number of times and not cause the information to be resent over the network.

- The customer now implicitly has a copy of the document. This can allow them to share this information within their own organization more efficiently. For example, information could be copied out of a PDF that was originally generated on the iSeries and then pasted into another document (report, Web page, presentation, and so on).

- An HTTP server (with or without the associated WebSphere Application Server) generates reports online and displays them via HTML. The client would print locally.

    Note: The quality of this solution is not high because your control over the "white space" (or the placement of text and graphics) in HTML is poor.

- Reports and other print documents are generated on the iSeries server (as PDFs, for example) and then made available for download to the client environment. The client would then have the responsibility to manage the print server.

    Two examples of third-party vendors that have solutions in this area are:

    – **Datalogics**: Look through their Adobe PDF Library, which is a collection of toolkits associated with Adobe's Acrobat products that allow for PDF creation available on the iSeries server. Their Web site is located at:
    http://www.datalogics.com

    – **Help/Systems**: Look at their Robot/REPORTs, which converts reports to PDF or HTML output. You can find them on the Web at:
    http://www.helpsystems.com/

Remote system printing

Remote system printing (Figure 18) is particularly useful for customers who have networked systems for automatically routing spooled files to printers connected to other systems. Output queue parameters define the target system. Depending on the target system or printer, Host Print Transform can be called to convert the spooled file into an ASCII printer data stream before it is sent to a remote system.

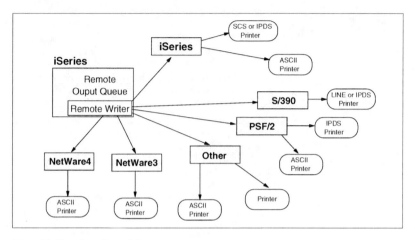

Figure 18. Remote system printing

Note these considerations:

- If the spooled file is *AFPDS, *LINE, or *AFPDSLINE, PSF/400 is only needed on the target system.

- Host print transform is only supported if the connection type parameter is set to *IP, *IPX, or *USRDFN.

- If Host Print Transform is used, SCS, AFPDS, and USERASCII data streams are supported.

- USERASCII must be in the ASCII printer data stream of the target printer (for example, PCL5 or PPDS). TIFF, BMP, GIF, and PostScript level 1 are supported if you are using the image print transform function.

For more information on remote system printing, see the IBM Redbook *IBM AS/400 Printing V*, SG24-2160.

2.8 Service level management (SLM)

Service level management (SLM) and monitoring supports the administration of the execution environment, management of storage and network connections, and monitoring service levels. This includes quantitative measures, such as application availability and response time, and qualitative factors such as responsiveness of the data center technical support staff.

2.8.1 ASP service level management

System management tools are primarily required for centralized management of the ASP. These tools enable monitoring the operation of the hardware and software components of the ASP, provide early warnings of impending failures, help diagnose faults, and assist with inventorying the hardware and software of the components of the ASP nodes. The total cost and effort required to manage an ASP environment largely depend on the system management solution selected. Centralized system management and problem detection significantly reduce the total cost of ownership.

Since system management forms an integral part of the ASP operation, it needs to be planned and incorporated into the solution from the very beginning. Careful consideration must be given to the scalability of the system management solution to ensure that it scales with the growth of the ASP.

For small ASPs, the return on investment (ROI) on the system management solution may not be as significant, but as the ASP adds more users, applications, and hardware, the ROI grows exponentially. While system management tools are primarily responsible for administering the ASP, the benefits of a well-managed environment are far reaching, from higher quality of service to greater customer satisfaction.

The system management tools for an ASP environment should provide the following functionality:

- Deployment of software
- Inventory control
- Job scheduling
- System monitoring and diagnosis
- Capacity planning

2.8.2 iSeries service level management

Some of the tools that can be used for system management are covered in the following sections.

A document on the ASP Prime Solution Center's Web site offers a sample service level agreement that is written specifically with the iSeries in mind. Although the sample is not complete, it offers an excellent place for you to start because it asks many of the right questions. You can find the ASP Prime Solution Center on the Web at: `http://as400.rochester.ibm.com/developer/asp/index.html`

Click **Papers & Pointers**, and then click **Sample Service Level Agreement** in the right panel.

2.8.2.1 Tivoli Cross-Site

Tivoli's Cross-Site product suite is targeted at e-business management. The product provides a set of core services that are used by specific application modules. The core services include an event service, resource management, security (authorization and authentication) report generation, administration, and a repository.

A module that could be useful is Cross-Site for Security. The Security Agent monitors traffic at the Data Link layer of the network stack (using the Open Systems Interconnect (OSI) terminology). It uses a "signature" technology to detect certain known attacks as well as the following list of intrusions:

- Floods and other network-based attacks
- Windows network attacks

- Remote procedure attacks (SUN/ONC RPC)
- Service exploitations
- Unauthorized network traffic
- Suspicious activity

In addition, the Security Agent provides a heartbeat monitored at the server to indicate basic system state. Intrusion alerts are sent to the Cross-Site server.

Cross-Site for Availability

This module measures end-to-end service time and runs on the end-user (browser) system. In a sample scenario, the ASP administration would deploy this agent on a sample user PC that could be used for routine measurement of performance. The operation of the PC could, in fact, be automated.

It would also be possible to deploy the agents on a customer PC, given proper agreements. This would allow the individual ASP providers a performance window into their specific application. The Availability tool also includes a Web scanner that should be used to routinely scan the ASP Web servers for broken links and so on. The scanner runs as a separate process from the Cross-Site server and is not linked to the Availability Agent.

However, take into consideration that Tivoli Cross-Site is a very expensive product and is used to manage several hundred computers and servers.

Tivoli Management Framework

This is the full-featured enterprise-class framework. The Tivoli Management Framework (TMF) is implemented as a three-tier system. The TMF server is a CORBA-based platform that provides the full set of CORBA services. The server communicates with a CORBA-based client, the Managed Node. The Managed Node acts as a gateway for a third client tier, the Light Client Framework (LCF). Like Tivoli Cross-Site, TMF is a very expensive product. Modules that can be used with TMF include:

- **Tivoli Distributed Monitoring**. Tivoli Distributed Monitor provides a long list of monitors including those that are process-specific and resource-specific. Monitors can be greatly customized. Automated monitor responses can include starting and restarting a process on monitored hosts or any other controlled platform.

- **Tivoli User Administration**. Tivoli User Administration provides a single GUI interface for creating and administering users across multiple platforms. This will be used for internal user control only.

- **Tivoli Software Distribution**. Tivoli Software Distribution focuses on continually deploying and synchronizing applications on an enterprise scale. Tivoli Software Distribution is a key solution for customers who need to rapidly and efficiently deploy complex mission-critical or desktop productivity applications to multiple locations from a central point.

BMC Patrol

BMC Patrol is a lower-cost alternative to TMF. Patrol is a two-tier application with an extensive list of application monitoring functions, including a full set of Oracle monitors.

LCCM

LCCM or LANClient Control Manager is used for software distribution.

Tivoli IT-Director

IT-Director is a lower-cost systems management tool available on the Microsoft Windows platform and on the iSeries.

Microsoft System Management Server (SMS)

SMS is another tool that can be used at smaller ASPs.

2.8.2.2 Systems management tools summary

The systems management tool should be chosen depending on the size of the ASP's data center. Some of the tools described above are very comprehensive and expensive, for example Tivoli Management Framework, and should only be used for large data centers with hundreds of servers. Small ASPs will be better off with, for example, Tivoli IT-Director or Microsoft SMS.

2.8.2.3 Deployment of software

Installing software on multiple nodes is often a time-consuming and laborious task. Therefore, deployment of software and software distribution is a must.

The software deployment tool should be able to install and uninstall applications, and perform upgrades on remote ASP nodes. These tasks should be scheduled for a particular date and time, or when other predefined criteria are met. Reporting facilities should be available to track the progress of the distribution.

Scheduling of tasks to manage configurations is particularly difficult for systems running multiple applications that have multiple dependencies. For example, multiple applications may run on a single platform servicing multiple companies. Each application depends on other components, such as operating system level and patch level. As applications change, dependencies change too. It is conceivable that one application upgrade could render another application unsupportable. At the same time, many applications are required to be available 24 hours-a-day, 7 days-a-week (24x7). Configuration management software is needed to track dependencies and alert the ASP staff of pending upgrades. Such upgrades must be coordinated to maintain service levels.

As we show later, clustering and load balancing may also be used to facilitate the deployment of upgrades. System management plays a role in optimizing upgrade management so that maximum benefit can be achieved without adversely affecting other activities of the ASP.

2.8.2.4 Inventory control

In a large heterogeneous ASP environment, it is cumbersome, if not impossible, to manually keep track of all the system resources of the nodes. Inventory control tools are required to automate the process of tracking these system resources. The hardware inventory tool should be able to track such resources as:

- Number of physical disk drives
- Processor types and version numbers
- Amount of main memory
- Operating system type
- Display monitor settings
- Computer names and IP addresses
- Configured peripheral devices
- Network interface card types
- System BIOS information

Similarly, the software inventory control tools should be able to manage multiple application versions and provide details such as the application name, manufacturer, version number, and installation date.

2.8.2.5 Job scheduling

In an ASP environment, several tasks need to be performed at regular intervals, including running certain batch jobs such as generating invoices at the end of each day, or taking inventory of the hardware and software resources of the systems every week. The system management tools should provide an easy means of automating such tasks and also provide feedback to the central controller of any resulting errors or warnings from the tasks.

2.8.2.6 System monitoring and diagnosis

System monitoring tools are required to monitor the general health of the ASP and performance of the hardware and software resources. An insufficient hardware or software resource usually manifests itself with unstable performance ahead of actual failure. Monitoring these resources often results in early detection and diagnosis of impending failures.

The system management tool should easily monitor the performance and usage of the different resources of the system such as processor, memory, disk, network, and application software packages. It should allow for associating thresholds with these resources, so that appropriate action may be taken for faulty resources, or a resource that is nearing its performance limits.

2.8.2.7 Capacity planning

Capacity planning is the process of ensuring that just the right amount of resources are available for use in the ASP. Insufficient resources cause bottlenecks and poor quality of service especially during peak load periods, while excess resources unnecessarily increase the investment cost. The goal is to have just enough resources. Capacity planning involves continuous monitoring of system resources and identifying any increasing usage trends to plan for additional resource requirements in the future.

The system management tools must be able to capture the relevant system resource (for example processor, memory, disk, and network) data required for capacity planning utilization. Then, it must be able to present it in an easily comprehensible and usable format. It should also be able to make recommendations on possible bottlenecks and ways to resolve them.

With all the different possible information and warning messages generated by the system management tools, their usefulness quickly fades away if there is no way to filter and summarize the messages into an easily comprehensible report format. A message summarizing and filtering tool helps filter out the messages of interest and generates real-time status information in a predetermined report format.

Similar to the ASP itself, the system management tools should be scalable from the smallest to the largest environment. To achieve this, the system management solution should have a scalable architecture without any bottlenecks and be able to control the network bandwidth used for maintenance tasks. Furthermore, it should also be configurable and easy to use in all environments from the smallest to the largest.

When the ASP environment grows, it may be necessary to use several different system management tools to cater to different needs. Therefore, the chosen solution should be able to interoperate with other industry-standard management tools.

Specifically for the iSeries, in the area of capacity planning, is PM/400e. PM/400e is a dynamic tool shipped with OS/400 that automates many of the functions associated with capacity planning and performance analysis. Personalized Web-based reports help identify potential resource constraints and help you plan future growth. For customers under hardware warranty or maintenance, basic PM/400e is available for no additional charge; more detailed PM/400e is available for all customers for a nominal fee. For more information on PM/400e, go to `http://www.as400service.ibm.com/` and then click **Services**.

The iSeries is very flexible and robust when it comes to allocating system resources where they're most needed. CPUs, disk units, and memory may be assigned to logical partitions, auxiliary storage pools, and subsystems as the workload demands. If additional resources are needed, the iSeries is highly upgradable.

2.9 High availability

The significance of high availability in the ASP environment cannot be overstated. System down time in an ASP environment directly translates into lost revenue, increased support calls, and decreased customer satisfaction. To eliminate these, the level of availability has to be factored into the design of the ASP infrastructure.

2.9.1 ASP high availability

High availability is achieved through adherence to design for availability (DFA) principles at all levels, training of operations staff, and the implementation of data center policies and procedures. DFA takes into consideration the full range of system attributes, from low-level chip design to system components, such as disk RAID technology, to the system as a whole, including network access. Any part of the system that could result in loss of data is subject to analysis. In short, a highly available system permits access to critical data and applications that keep the business running. At the implementation level, high availability is achieved by combining reliable components in a redundant way (for example, mirrored disks) or by providing redundant methods in case of catastrophic failure of non-redundant components (for example, CPU and memory within a SMP environment).

2.9.2 iSeries high availability

The reliability and high availability of the iSeries platform makes it an ideal platform for ASP. Compared to Intel-based servers running Microsoft Windows NT or UNIX, the iSeries has a much lower unplanned outage per server per year than Windows NT and UNIX-based servers (Figure 19 on page 66). The iSeries server offers system availability at 99.94% without implementation of clustering.

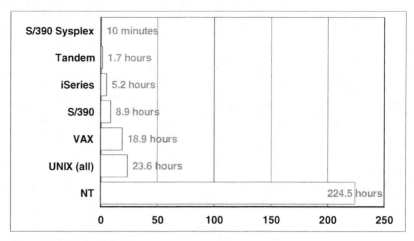

S/390 Sysplex	10 minutes				
Tandem	1.7 hours				
iSeries	5.2 hours				
S/390	8.9 hours				
VAX	18.9 hours				
UNIX (all)	23.6 hours				
NT				224.5 hours	

0   50   100   150   200   250

Figure 19. iSeries reliability: Unplanned outages per server per year

You should refer to *OS/400 Backup and Recovery V4R5*, SC41-5304, for details about iSeries high availability.

2.9.2.1 Logical partitioning (LPAR)

Logical partitions allow for the simultaneous running of multiple independent servers, each with its own processors, memory, and disks, all within a single symmetric multiprocessing iSeries server. Multiple system requirements can now be addressed in a single machine to achieve server consolidation of network servers, tiered application servers, and database servers, as well as provide configuration flexibility for multiple customers on a single server. Resources can be optimized for each customer's needs, even handling issues of multiple time zones and language support on a single system. LPARs provide the ability to better deploy modular application suites that are divided between a database server and multiple application servers. The high performance application-to-database partition communication that is needed in these environments is enabled with OptiConnect/400. Together, logical partitions and OptiConnect make it possible to try out a new application in a test partition without affecting production partitions.

Each partition's system values can be set independently. For example, each partition can have a different system name, may use a different primary or secondary national language, or may be operated using different time zones. Each partition can define its own set of security attributes, subsystems, communication attributes, job descriptions, applications, database file systems, and work management characteristics. When providing application services to customers, this can meet the requirements of customers who may be in different time zones. Setting up a server with multiple time zones also allows for the sharing of tape resources. For example, a set of IBM 3590 tape drives can perform different backup activities at different time frames by using the capability of switching I/O resources dynamically between partitions.

Opportunities to deploy logical partitions

There are numerous benefits to using LPAR for application hosting. Some of the most compelling reasons to deploy logical partitions on the iSeries server are:

- **Customized partition performance**: The ability to run multiple independent servers or partitions, each with its own processors, memory, and disks, within a single n-way symmetric multiprocessing iSeries server. This flexibility and independence permits customers to have customized partition performance, allowing a single system to be fully optimized for both interactive and e-business or advanced workloads, such as Business Intelligence, Lotus Domino, and Web applications.

- **Multi-tiered applications**: Logical partitioning provides a robust and cost-effective solution for multi-tiered application solutions offered by ERP partners. In essence, logical partitioning allows iSeries users to create multiple partitions defined as application servers, and one partition defined as a database server. A partition can also be used for the network server with VPN, NAT, mail, and HTTP proxy services. The typical "demilitarized zone" Web application servers can be in a partition, consolidating the multiple servers that would be needed for a complete e-business environment.

- **Consolidation to lower costs**: Consolidation of multiple servers to fewer, yet independently functioning, iSeries servers using LPAR. The driving factor towards these types of consolidation activities are to reduce the overall data center operational costs pertaining to maintenance and support of both hardware and software.

- **Perform high-speed data replication**: With the internal high-speed bus-to-bus communications capability, LPAR provides a method to quickly replicate data from one partition to another. Although this option does not offer any higher level of availability with planned and unplanned outages, it offers a solution to reduce the batch window required to perform save operations. The second copy of the data can also be used to perform read-only transactions such as queries, or transforming operational data, into a data warehouse for Business Intelligence.

Partition management

Each logical partition should be viewed as an independent system and will require the same systems management disciplines need for managing multiple iSeries servers. Additional functions and features have been added to OS/400 V4R4 Management Central to further automate complex systems management tasks:

- **Data Packaging and Distribution**: Allows for the packaging of a set of OS/400 objects or files that can be distributed to other partitions or iSeries servers.

- **Fix Management**: Provides the ability to compare PTF levels, distribute PTFs, and install PTFs across multiple partitions or iSeries servers.

- **Hardware, Software, and Fix Inventory**: Supports the collection of inventory hardware and software resources about multiple partitions or iSeries servers, which may be viewed, searched, or exported to a spreadsheet.

- **Remote Command**: Provides the ability to define and run commands on multiple partitions or iSeries servers. It also allows access to their results through a graphical interface. For example, the results of the Work with Active Jobs (WRKACTJOB) command on a secondary partition can be viewed from the source partition.

- **Performance Collection Control**: Provides the ability to control the performance data collection on the network of partitions or iSeries servers.

These collection objects can be converted to database files and can be exported to the iSeries performance tools for further analysis.

2.9.2.2 OS/400 availability technology

Multiple levels and capabilities exist on the iSeries for enhancing availability. These capabilities can be used in combination to create a highly reliable server for hosted applications. The total availability will use resources from IBM, High Availability Business Partners (HABPs), and solution developers.

Application Service Providers should plan on using all three of these resources as required to deliver the needed quality of service required by the customer.

2.9.2.3 Clustering

Clustering, available with V4R4, is the latest OS/400 technology for iSeries availability, building on existing iSeries technologies such as OptiConnect, mirroring, journaling (including remote journaling), and commitment control. Clustering is covered at length in the following section.

2.9.2.4 OptiConnect for AS/400

OptiConnect allows high-speed, bus-level, fiber-optic connections between iSeries servers and is a natural solution for clustering communications. However, clustering does not require OptiConnect. The systems in a cluster can be connected via any TCP/IP network (for example, a LAN or across telephone lines). And, as of V4R4, TCP/IP is available across OptiConnect.

To complement V4R4 clustering solutions, IBM reduced the price of OptiConnect by nearly 80 percent. There is also a low-cost PRPQ, called OptiMover, which delivers most OptiConnect functions. For longer distances, iSeries supports Asynchronous Transfer Mode (ATM) LAN and WAN connections, which supply transfer rates of up to 155 Mbps (about 100 times the rate offered by a T1 connection). These ATM speeds are sufficient to keep remote journals synchronized without impacting application performance.

2.9.2.5 Device parity protection

Device parity protection is a hardware function that protects data from being lost because of a disk unit failure or because of damage to a disk. Calculating and saving a parity value for each bit of data protects data. Conceptually, the parity value is computed from the data at the same location on each of the other disk units in the device parity set. When a disk failure occurs, the data on the failing unit can be reconstructed by using the saved parity value and the values of the bits in the same locations on the other disk.

Device parity protection is a high-availability function. It allows the iSeries server to continue to operate when a single disk failure has occurred. The system continues to run in an exposed mode until the repair operation is complete and the data is rebuilt. If a failure occurs, you should correct the problem quickly. In the unlikely event that another disk fails, you can lose data.

2.9.2.6 RAID-5

A minimum of four disk units of the same capacity are required for a valid RAID-5 configuration. Parity information can be spread across four or eight of the disk units in an array. It is automatically maintained as part of the RAID-5 protection feature. Internal disk units of different technology (that is, different feature numbers), but of the same capacity, can be either mirrored or RAID-5 protected.

Parity spread across eight disk units gives better performance in the event of a disk unit failure, since the data required to dynamically rebuild the data on the failed disk is accessed from an eighth of the disk units as opposed to a quarter. If one disk unit fails, it cannot be used to read or write data. The disk unit controller then reads the parity and data from the same data areas as the other disk units to dynamically rebuild the original data from the failed disk unit to satisfy ongoing read requests. When data needs to be written, the controller generates the parity information for the failed disk unit as if it were still operating. As far as the iSeries is concerned, the disk units continue to respond to I/O even though a single disk unit has failed.

A RAID controller is necessary when concurrent maintenance support is required.

2.9.2.7 Mirroring
Mirroring is the ability to duplicate disk drives and associated components, such as IOPs, at the system level. When mirroring is active, OS/400 maintains two synchronized copies of information and provides transparent protection against a disk drive failure. Mirroring provides an extremely high level of availability for critical information, but it is not selective; it simply keeps everything on a drive synchronized. This makes mirroring comparatively expensive in terms of performance and DASD, resulting in a relatively small percentage of iSeries shops use mirroring.

2.9.2.8 Journaling
Journaling is the cornerstone of existing iSeries high-availability solutions because it provides a way to record incremental changes to data. Journaling is implemented at the physical file level. Once journaling is initiated for a particular file, all changes to the file are recorded in the designated journal receiver. Journaling is the primary tool HABPs use to synchronize data between systems.

With remote journaling, which is available on iSeries servers running V4R2 or higher, the journal entries are transferred to a journal receiver on another system within the cluster using high-speed system services. Remote journaling minimizes the overhead of replicating journal receivers and, therefore, removes some of the burden of data resiliency from the HABPs by providing OS/400 tools to handle underlying services.

Developers can use commitment control, which is based on information stored in journal receivers, to implement application checkpoints and return a program and the associated data to a known transaction boundary. Commitment control code must be written for each application, but it is not complex. Essentially, commitment control designates the beginning and ending of each logical transaction as a commitment control boundary. For example, in an order entry application, one logical transaction might include creating the order header record, updating the customer open order balance, creating the associated order detail records, and updating the inventory quantities for the items ordered. An application developer can use commitment control to roll back any transaction that is incomplete, returning all the files to their state at the commitment control boundary (that is, the last complete transaction). All iSeries development languages support commitment control.

2.9.2.9 Save and restore availability

The iSeries provides dynamic save and restore availability options for your fundamental backup and recovery plan. This can be highly effective in a 24x7 concurrent maintenance environment.

SAVxxx and RSTxxx and flexibility

System management and operations are improved for V4R2 and later systems to allow more flexibility. You can customize backup plans further by saving objects in different combinations to avoid saving those objects that do not require frequent backups. Up to 300 specific- or generic-named objects can be omitted from a save. Since less information is saved, time to save decreases, which improves availability but does not sacrifice ease-of-use.

Save while active and object locks

The Save while active (SWA) function helps improve availability by allowing save operations without ending jobs or subsystems. Objects are saved even while they are in use. SWA reduces the amount of time applications are unavailable to users due to backup requirements. The SWA function offers these benefits:

- Objects with logical dependencies in the same library reach the same checkpoint.
- Objects in the same library that are journaled to the same journal reach the same checkpoint.
- Objects in the same library being processed under commitment control reach the checkpoint at a commitment boundary.

These benefits make recovery easier to manage due to the number of checkpoints involved.

Omitting objects on a SAVSYS operation

On V4R1 and later, an OMIT parameter is available on the SAVSYS command. This parameter allows the user to omit:

- ***CFG**: Configuration objects
- ***SECDTA**: All security objects (user profiles and security information)

By omitting the configuration and security data from the SAVSYS operation, you reduce the amount of time that the system must be in a restricted state during the SAVSYS operation. In large environments, saving configuration objects and security information can take a long time.

Concurrent save operations

On V4R1 and later, users can issue multiple SAVOBJ and SAVCHGOBJ commands, as well as the QSRSAVO API, against a single library at the same time. This allows users to issue multiple save operations and use multiple tape drives to save objects from a single large library.

Use optimum blocking for save and restore

Typically, tape drive performance relates to the speed of the device and to the block transfer size. Block transfer size is affected by the Use optimum block (USEOPTBLK) parameter on the save commands. Most of the throughput enhancements made in V3R1 (when the block size increased to 24 KB) and V3R6 are realized with the 3590 and 3570 tape drive and the high-end processors. The time to transfer data to the drive is also improved significantly with the PowerPC AS processor hardware.

Beginning with V4R1, the USEOPTBLK parameter has been added to the SAVCFG, SAVSYS, SAVDLO, SAVSAVFDTA, and SAVSECDTA commands. This parameter was already enabled with V3R7 for the SAV, SAVOBJ, SAVCHGOBJ, and SAVLIB commands.

The default setting for USEOPTBLK was changed to *YES beginning with V4R2. With optimum block size set to *YES, blocking is enabled for the supported value (based on the device type) and is used on the save commands. If the block size that is used is larger than a block size that is supported by all device types, performance may improve under certain conditions.

2.9.2.10 Uninterruptible power supply (UPS)
Uninterruptible power supply (UPS) provides auxiliary power to the processing unit, disk units, system console, and other devices that you choose to protect from loss of power. When you use a UPS with the iSeries server, you can:

- Continue operations during brief power interruptions (brown outs).
- Protect the system from voltage peaks (white outs).
- Provide a normal end of operations. A normal end reduces recovery time when the system is restarted. If the system abnormally ends before completing a normal end of operations, recovery time is significant.

Normally, a UPS does not provide power to all local workstations. Nor does the UPS usually provide power to modems, bridges, or routers that support remote workstations. Consider supplying alternate power to both workgroups since the inability of worker access to information disrupts productivity. You can avoid such disruption with proper availability and recovery implementation.

2.9.2.11 Battery backup and continuously powered main storage
Most (but not all) iSeries models are equipped with a battery backup. Based on the system storage size, relying on a battery backup for enough time for an orderly shutdown is not sufficient. The battery capacity typically varies between 10 and 60 minutes. The useful capacity depends on the application requirements, main storage size, and system configuration. Consider the reduction of capacity caused by the natural aging of the battery and environmental extremes of the site when selecting the battery. The battery must have the capacity to maintain the system load requirements at the end of its useful life.

For more information, refer to *OS/400 Backup and Recovery V4R5*, SC41-5304, for power down times for the Advanced Series systems. Refer to the *AS/400 Physical Planning Reference*, SA41-5109, for power down times for the AS/400 Bnn-Fnn models.

2.9.2.12 Hierarchical storage management (HSM)
Hierarchical storage management (HSM) automatically and transparently manages customer data across a storage hierarchy. The storage hierarchy can consist of high performance disk, compressed disk, and tape libraries.

When and how often data is accessed on an iSeries server depends on the type of data. A set of data that is currently being used may be accessed many times a day (hot data), or it may have become historical data that is accessed less frequently (cold data).

Through the BRMS user-defined policies, HSM can migrate or archive and dynamically retrieve infrequently used data or historical data up or down a hierarchy of storage devices.

Each level costs less per megabyte of storage.

The IBM Redbook *Complementing AS/400 Storage Management Using Hierarchical Storage Management APIs*, SG24-4450, describes how to enhance the functionality of ADSM, BRMS, and OnDemand with customized HSM strategies.

2.10 Scalability

Scalability is the ability to run an application unchanged on a variety of platforms that have different characteristics. It refers to how easily a system can grow with a customer's business by expanding to support new users, data, memory, processors, and other customer requirements.

2.10.1 ASP scalability

Most large ASPs face the same challenges, the most significant of which are unpredictable growth and the ability to have solutions ready for unknown problems. Typical Web sites most likely started with displaying company information and has evolved to processing simple, if not complex, transactions. You know now that the skills required to display information are different from those required to process transactions. Failure to optimize graphics, frequent table scans, and joins of multiple tables result in I/O bottlenecks that combine to degrade performance. Site availability is stressed by unpredictable traffic and inadequate systems management. These problems may be compounded by poor application design and systems that are poorly configured, underpowered, or both.

Shared services and infrastructure maximize the potential for realizing economies-of-scale as the size of the ASP increases. To achieve the necessary economies-of-scale, the ASP's infrastructure must be designed to explicitly address the operational cost forces introduced by the Internet environment, which include:

- **Rapid change and constant flux**: New applications, subscribing companies, and additional users need to be constantly added, as well as new versions of operating systems, applications, hardware, and networking technology.

- **Exponential growth**: The vast reach of the Internet means that ASPs or ISVs that catch fire will experience exponential growth of their subscription base.

- **Support for small to medium businesses**: Dedicating servers to a limited number of customers does not scale to Internet usage. Management personnel requirements for the dedicated server model are also significantly more than the shared model.

- **Offer and deliver service level agreements (SLA)**: ASPs need to optimize operational costs while still delivering SLA-specified levels of service. SLAs may be contractual, with substantial penalties being incurred for non-performance. This places a premium on reliability, availability, and scalability, creating the need for a robust infrastructure.

- **Support for multi-tier application architectures**: The applications that are best designed for an ASP environment are based on newer component-based architectures such as Enterprise JavaBeans. While the resulting architectures are highly flexible and well suited to Internet deployment, they also result in a more complex n-tier architecture: Web servers, application servers, and back-end database servers. An ASP must be able to cost effectively manage and monitor this environment.

In this challenging environment, the ASP must strike a balance between their costs of operation and the levels of service they provide to customers. Meeting such challenges requires flexibility and capacity for change in all areas, especially your IT operation. The success of future ASPs may be tied to the selection of site components that can be individually or collectively adjusted to meet variable demands. This flexibility is called *scalability* and is a feature your team needs to understand and measure for each site component.

Scalability allows the distribution of the same applications to workgroups of different or changing sizes. In an ASP environment, now more than ever, scalability is crucial to companies as they experience the growth, centralization, decentralization, distribution, and downsizing of today's business environment.

2.10.2 iSeries scalability

A particular strength of the iSeries solution is the extreme degree of scalability, from a small office server for one or two users to a distributed multiprocessing environment that supports thousands of users. Since the iSeries is designed to allow the same operating system (OS/400) to be used by the smallest to the largest processor models, application software designed for any iSeries server will work on all iSeries model ranges.

This allows ASPs to:

- Protect their investment in hardware, software, and user training
- Eliminate obsolescence
- Accommodate business growth
- Provide client or server functionality

Enhancements include:

- **New DB2 Multisystem**: This feature enhances the data-warehousing capability of the system. In essence, it allows businesses to create and work with large DB2 database files that are spread across multiple systems. Many operations gain improved performance by dividing tasks among several systems.
- **OptiConnect**: OptiConnect links up to 32 iSeries servers over high-speed, fiber-optic cable and lets multiple systems function as a single, large, seamless, distributed system. This offers a path for growth and increased capacity, while improving system availability and redundancy.
- **Capacity Advantage**: Newly announced for the iSeries (at the time this redbook was written, this feature was available with iSeries Model 840) is an idea born out of ASP. What if your business does too well, that is, you have more customers jumping on your solution than you can handle with the sub-second response time you agreed to? Would it be helpful to have a hot-spare processor already in the machine that you could simply "turn on"? Vertical Capacity Upgrade defines such a solution. Vertical Capacity Upgrade

on Demand ensures fast, non-disruptive growth by including extra processors held in reserve in your server. Customers also have the opportunity to try the standby capacity for a number of days without charge. The vertical approach is ideal when changing workload requirements dictate an increase in capacity on the server. Consider such examples as database serving applications, business transaction processing, and e-commerce store fronts. For more information about this feature, see:

http://www-1.ibm.com/servers/eserver/introducing/capacity.html

The scalability of the existing iSeries product range is remarkable. The plans to extend this through greater use of parallel processing should remove any concerns about limited expansion capabilities.

The iSeries allows users that are moving into or growing their ASP to:

- Connect to the global community without having to build that capability from scratch.
- Scale to accommodate the expanding customer base that can result from the increased interest generated in their products or services via e-business.

The iSeries server is also a logical choice for customers that are considering ASP. As the amount of data and access to that data grows, ASPs need a system that can accommodate the growing need for:

- Large amounts of memory
- Increased disk space
- Additional processor power

The iSeries server's scalability advantages extend far beyond the number of processors. Other factors critical to scalability include the server's ability to support multiple applications and dynamic tuning as well as the reliability of the server. The iSeries server supports running multiple applications on the same system, dynamic tuning, and an average of 99.9+% availability. With the Windows NT server, a separate server is typically used for each application, a reboot is required to put many tuning changes into effect, and reliability is an issue. As a result of these factors, the maximum capacities that the Windows NT Server supports is often times irrelevant.

ASP is an important and growing environment that has a unique set of requirements. To satisfy these requirements, existing framework services must be extended and new services defined. These services enable the service provider to minimize operational costs and achieve the appropriate economies-of-scale that are proven by using the iSeries. As the number of users increases, the iSeries platform is considerably more cost-efficient.

2.11 Summary of iSeries integrated solutions

In this chapter, you learned about several reasons why the iSeries is your ASP solution. ASP is a natural extension of what the iSeries has been successfully doing since its existence – serving applications. The iSeries offers ways to integrate existing applications or create e-business solutions for your ASP, secure and robust network and security alternatives, high availability and scalability, and lots of operating system features and licensed programs to help you implement ASP. See Table 8 to recap the iSeries integrated solutions.

Table 8. iSeries integrated solutions

Functional components	Solutions
Network	iSeries TCP/IP includes, multihoming, DHCP, IPSec, NAT, SSL, and other related technology.
Accounting and Billing	AS/400 Usage Accounting, incorporated in AS/400. IBM WebSphere Payment Manager, electronic billing. Several third-party software providers offer electronic billing software for AS/400 such as ROI, Jigsaw, Signio, CISoft, and I/NET.
Security	Virtual private network (VPN), IP Packet Filtering, IPSec, NAT, DNS, SSL, OS/400 auditing, and object level security.
Service Level Management (SLM)	Tivoli Cross-Site, Tivoli Management Framework, BMC Patrol, LCCM, Tivoli IT-Director, Microsoft System Management Server, and built-in OS/400 properties such as job scheduling, performance collection tools, dynamic performance adjustments, message logging, and security auditing.
High Availability	LPAR, clustering, OptiConnect, device parity protection, RAID-5, mirroring, journaling, save and restore availability, UPS, battery backup, CPM, hierarchical storage management (HSM)
Scalability	The iSeries supports a wide range of systems and servers. It also supports multiple applications on the same system, DB2, OptiConnect, clustering, and SMP.

The following list identifies Wholesale Service Providers (WSP) who support the iSeries and who can offer additional information:

- ACS: http://www.acs-inc.com
- AmQUEST, Inc.: http://www.amquest.com
- Berbee Information Networks: http://www.berbee.com
- Digica: http://www.digica.com
- DPS, Inc.: http://www.dpslink.com
- Eviciti: http://www.eviciti.com
- J.J.Croney & Associates: http://www.j2ca.com
- Prominic.NET: http://www.prominic.net
- SunGard Computer Services: http://www.sungard.com
- Triangle Hosting Services: http://www.bcafreedom.com

Chapter 3. WebSphere Application Server (WAS) for AS/400

To extend your application to the Web or to develop a new Web-based application, you should move to the new e-business model. This chapter looks at this model and what you can gain from this model as an ASP.

WAS Version 3.5 versus 3.02

At the time most of the examples in this chapter were written, WebSphere Application Server (WAS) 3.02 was the primary version available for us to use. See 3.17, "WebSphere differences between Version 3.02 and 3.5" on page 150, which lists the differences between WAS Advanced Edition 3.02 and 3.5.

A three-tier e-business model is shown in Figure 20. A client uses a Web browser to send a request to an application. The application server performs the required step to fulfill the request and sends back a response. To do that, it communicates with a back-end system which may be a database or another application. In this model, an application is located on a server.

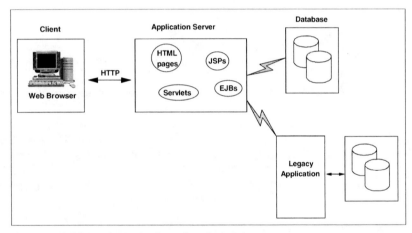

Figure 20. WebSphere Application Server three-tier model

Using a server-based application has several advantages:

- The number of Web users (and, therefore, the clients who can access your application) is huge. Most of them (if not all) use Java-compatible Web browsers.
- There is no maintenance cost for software running on a client's system.
- An application has to be updated on the server only.
- It is easier to scale your application.
- Your application is available 24 hours-a-day, 7 days-a-week.
- It offers seamless upgrades to a new version of an application.

There are two main scenarios for deploying a three-tier model:

- Extending your existing application to the Web
- Developing new Web-based application

In the case of extending your existing application to the Web, the middle tier, an application server, will mediate between the Web and business application. You need to provide a set of software components (sometimes called *connectors*) to link the Web and "legacy" application together (in this scenario, the "legacy" application provides business logic and database support).

In the case of developing a new Web application using the three-tier e-business model, you encapsulate most of your business logic into the middle tier. Therefore, your middle tier does most of the work in your application.

Depending on the application, there are different technologies to use:

- **Servlets**: Server-side Java components that provide services using request-response model. Servlets can encapsulate business logic, database connection support, and so on.
- **JavaServer Pages (JSPs)**: Used to create dynamic content for the Web pages. In fact, they are compiled into servlets and run on the server.
- **Enterprise JavaBeans (EJB)**: Used to do a more sophisticated level of business logic.

With this brief introduction to the role of the application server, let's see what IBM offers to its customers to participate in the three-tier e-business model.

WebSphere

WebSphere is a brand name for a set of IBM products. They enable the building, deploying, and management of Java applications. WebSphere has the following four main components:

- **WebSphere Application Server (WAS)**: Provides the application runtime environment.
- **WebSphere Edge Server**: Provides Web-facilities management software that supports the rapid growth of high-volume Web sites. It brings together, in a single package, caching, load balancing, and Web site replication support. It presently does not run on the iSeries.
- **WebSphere Site Analysis**: The set of tools that provide site administration and analysis. These tools can be used to administer and monitor usage of a Web site.
- **WebSphere Studio**: This is a PC-based tool to build Web applications. WebSphere Studio allows the integration of various technologies, for example, HTML, EJB, JSP, and servlets. VisualAge for Java is one of the IBM products included in the studio.

WebSphere Application Server is the main interest of this chapter.

3.1 Overview of IBM WebSphere Application Server Advanced Edition 3.x

WebSphere Application Server 3.x for AS/400 is the first server of the WebSphere Application Server family to bring a true Java-based IBM Enterprise Application environment to the iSeries server. There are three editions of WAS:

- **Standard Edition**: The Standard Edition is intended for use by Web application developers who focus on the issues of presentation logic, data access, and the business logic that resides in the middle tier.

- **Advanced Edition**: The Advanced Edition adds support for EJBs. EJB support includes bean-managed persistence (BMP) and container-managed persistence (CMP), full support for sessions beans, relational database connectivity using JDBC, and support for EJB to MQSeries and CICS.

- **Enterprise Edition**: The Enterprise Edition is designed to integrate applications across the entire enterprise. It uses the robust architecture and services provided as a part of CORBA support. The iSeries doesn't support this edition of WAS.

We focus our attention in this chapter on the WebSphere Application Server Advanced Edition. The Advanced Edition of WAS goes beyond the capabilities of the WebSphere Standard Edition product, servlets, and JavaServer Pages (JSP) support, to provide support for Enterprise JavaBeans (EJBs). EJBs allow you to develop sophisticated server-side components (or objects) to implement your business logic. This model may include developing:

- Business applications

- Internet- or intranet-based applications that require integration into existing iSeries applications

- New business applications that require complex database integration with a heterogeneous, multi-database vendor environment

To support complex business applications, WebSphere Application Server Advanced Edition 3.02 provides the following features, most of which are described in the remainder of this chapter:

- Servlet API 2.1 support

- JSP 1.0 Core support

- JSP 1.0 XML (LotusXSL) support

- Application isolation through the support of multiple instances of Java Virtual Machine (JVM)

- True virtual hosting for servlets

- EJB support

- Multi-server per node, multiple nodes, and domain configurations

- Improved security, integrated security for WebSphere resources, single signon, Lightweight Third Party Authentication (LTPA)

See 3.17, "WebSphere differences between Version 3.02 and 3.5" on page 150, for details on the level of support provided by WAS Version 3.5.

When used with development products, such as VisualAge for Java Enterprise Edition, WebSphere Application Server Advanced Edition provides a modern development environment for building Java applications. This environment brings the facilities that provide similar levels of integration, security, and transactional support that was previously only available to the traditional AS/400 developers using ILE languages. The Enterprise JavaBeans technology is *the* standard within the Java community for building components.

WebSphere Application Server Advanced Edition implements the EJB Version 1.0 specification, with some 1.1 specification enhancements, particularly in the area of the finder helper methods.

For further information on EJBs, refer to the Sun Microsystems Enterprise JavaBeans Technology page at: http://java.sun.com/products/ejb/index.html

3.1.1 iSeries-specific considerations

There are several differences between the iSeries version of WebSphere Application Server Advanced Edition 3.0 and the product shipped for other platforms. The most important differences are discussed in this section.

3.1.1.1 International and North American editions

There are two versions of WebSphere Application Server Advanced Edition 3.0 available for the iSeries server. WebSphere Application Server Advanced Edition 3.0 can use Secure Sockets Layer (SSL) support for communications between itself and the security environment.

Note: The security mentioned here is between the HTTP server and the application server, *not* the client. Due to the United States export restrictions on encryption technologies, the iSeries server is shipped with the following versions:

- 56-bit encryption support (5733-WA2) for international usage
- 128-bit encryption support (5733-WA3) for North American usage and restricted usage outside of North America

Since the US government recently relaxed these restrictions, WebSphere Application Server Advanced Edition 3.5 is shipped with 128-bit encryption support (5733-WA3) only (with some exceptions).

3.1.1.2 Installation options

Unlike WebSphere Application Server Advanced Edition 3.0 for Windows NT and AIX, which have several installation options depending on the facilities and features you require, the iSeries product has only two options. They are *BASE (client application development software only) and Option 1 (*BASE plus WAS environment).

3.1.1.3 Database support

The iSeries version of WebSphere Application Server Advanced Edition can only use DB2 Universal Database (UDB) for AS/400 for the repository database, when it is installed as the primary server.

3.1.1.4 Running the administration client

The WebSphere Application Server Advanced Edition administrative client provides a Java graphical user interface (GUI). Since the iSeries server does not support native GUI devices, the administrative client cannot run directly on the iSeries server. You must use a Windows or AIX workstation to run the administrative client locally. We recommend that you *do not* use iSeries remote AWT support to run the administrative client.

3.1.1.5 Multiple instance support

The iSeries version of WebSphere Application Server Advanced Edition supports multiple instances of the WebSphere Application Server. The motivation to create multiple instances is to have the ability to run concurrently, but completely independent instances of the server on a single iSeries. Each server instance can read from its own set of properties files, create its own set of log and trace files, and work within its own security model without affecting other server instances that might be running on the iSeries server at the same time.

You can find more details on this in 3.5, "Multiple HTTP server instances" on page 86, and in 3.8, "Multiple instances of the WebSphere Administration Server" on page 97.

3.1.1.6 HTTP server support

The WebSphere Application Server Advanced Edition is designed to integrate into existing HTTP servers by using the HTTP server extension capabilities, such as Internet Services Application Programming Interface (ISAPI) for the Microsoft Server, Netscape Connection API (NSAPI) for the Netscape Server, and Internet Connection API (ICAPI) support for the IBM HTTP Server for iSeries. Currently the IBM HTTP Server for iSeries (5769-DG1) supports ICAPI only.

Recently a new HTTP server was brought to the iSeries server – IBM HTTP Server (Powered by Apache). It too supports a WAS plug-in. For more information, see: http://www.iseries.ibm.com/products/websphere/docs/ apacheWebServerSupport35.html

3.1.1.7 WebSphere Application Server editions and versions

Table 9 show the versions of WAS for corresponding version of OS/400.

Table 9. Versions of WAS

OS/400 version	WAS editions	WAS versions
V4R3	Standard	1.1
V4R4 and V4R5	Standard	2.03, 3.02.2, and 3.5
	Advanced	3.02.2 and 3.5

Please make note of the editions for the following product numbers:

- 5733-AS1, 5733-AS2, and 5733-AS3 are the WebSphere Application Server Standard editions.
- 5733-WA2 and 5733-WA3 are the WebSphere Application Server Advanced editions.

To find out more about WebSphere Application Server, visit the IBM Web site at: http://www.iSeries.ibm.com/products/websphere/

3.2 Multihoming

The iSeries TCP/IP implementation supports multihoming. This allows you to specify either a single or multiple TCP/IP interfaces per line description. You can have your iSeries appear as any one or combination of:

- A single host on a network over a communication line
- Multiple hosts on the same network over the same communication line
- Multiple hosts on different networks over the same communication line
- Multiple hosts on the same network over multiple communication lines
- Multiple hosts on different networks over multiple communication lines

At V4R4 of OS/400, any number of TCP/IP interfaces can be defined. However, up to eight interfaces can be started with the Start TCP/IP Interface

(STRTCPIFC) command at any given time. This is true for all line types (for example: Token-ring, Ethernet, Frame Relay, and so on).

At V4R5 of OS/400, up to 512 interfaces can be defined and started with the Start TCP/IP Interface (STRTCPIFC) command at any given time. This is true for all line types (for example: Token-ring, Ethernet, Frame Relay, and so forth). At the same time, OS/400 supports up to 16K active interfaces on the entire system.

3.3 Multiple IP addresses

You can configure your iSeries TCP/IP to have multiple IP addresses active on one physical interface. With some special configuration in the HTTP server directives, it allows you to serve different files based on the IP address (or the host and domain name that is mapped to the IP address) of the request. This is especially valuable to ASPs, because you want to use one HTTP server instance to provide Web sites for multiple customers. For example, you may want to change one of the following HTTP server configuration directives based on the IP address:

- Use the Welcome page directive to determine how the server responds to requests that do not contain a file name. You can find this form under the Directories and Welcome Page listing under the Configurations section of the Configuration and Administration interface of the HTTP server.

- Use the Request routing directive to set map requests to physical files and to determine whether the server processes a request. You can find this form under Request Processing in the Configurations section of the interface.

- Use the Protection directives in the Configurations section to activate different protection rules for requests depending on which address the request comes to or which host name is specified in a URL. These forms have a help window to assist you with the configuration tasks.

- Use the HTTP server directive BindSpecific On to have a completely separate instance of the HTTP server and WebSphere Application Server active on each IP address. The details for this are explained in 3.5, "Multiple HTTP server instances" on page 86, and in 3.8, "Multiple instances of the WebSphere Administration Server" on page 97.

Implementing
You can add TCP/IP interfaces by using Operations Navigator or a 5250 terminal session by entering the Add TCP/IP Interface (ADDTCPIFC) command.

To configure multiple IP addresses, follow these steps:

1. Start Operations Navigator.

2. In the left pane expand **Network**, and click **Protocols**.

3. Right-click **TCP/IP** in the right pane. Then, select **New Interface->Local Area Network** as shown in Figure 21.

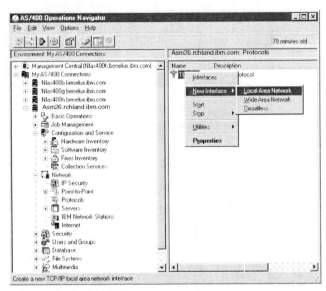

Figure 21. Configuring TCP/IP

4. Follow the steps in the wizard, and complete the form as shown in Figure 22.

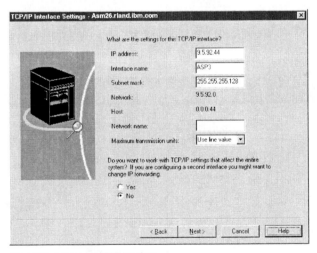

Figure 22. Adding a TCP/IP interface

3.4 Virtual IP addresses

Virtual IP address support was added in V4R3 of the OS/400 operating system. A *virtual IP address*, or circuitless IP address, is an TCP/IP interface that is defined on the system without being associated with a physical hardware adapter. A virtual IP address can always be active on the system and can be used as the system IP address.

Virtual IP addresses are always reached indirectly through a physical TCP/IP interface because the iSeries server does not respond to Address Resolution Protocol (ARP) requests to a virtual IP address. They cannot be a part of any real segment in your network. For other systems to reach the virtual IP address, they must have a route defined to reach the address.

The iSeries server accepts IP packets on any interface and processes the packets if the IP address is defined on any interface on the system. This provides a way to assign one or more addresses to the system without needing to bind the address to a physical interface. This can be used when you want to run multiple occurrences of a Domino Web server bound to different addresses, or other services, such as HTTP servers, that need to bind to the default ports of 80. A virtual IP address may be thought of as system-wide IP address. It means that your iSeries server is known by a single IP address, even when it is attached to many different networks. Also, it is possible to use a single IP address for multiple systems. In this case, you achieve a two-fold advantage: high availability and fault tolerance. Load balancing between multiple systems with the same virtual IP address helps to achieve high availability. If any system goes down, you still have other systems up and running.

Creating a virtual IP address can be done with Operations Navigator or from a 5250 terminal session.

To create a virtual IP address, follow these steps:

1. Start Operations Navigator.

2. In the left pane expand **Network**, and click **Protocols**.

3. Right-click **TCP/IP** in the right pane, and click **New Interface**->**Virtual IP** as shown in Figure 23.

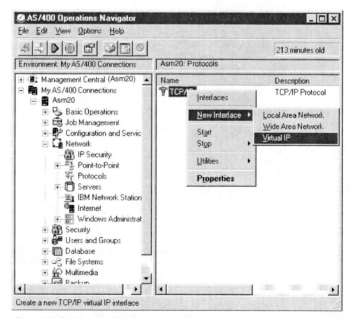

Figure 23. Creating a virtual IP address

4. Follow the steps in the wizard, and complete the form as shown in Figure 24.

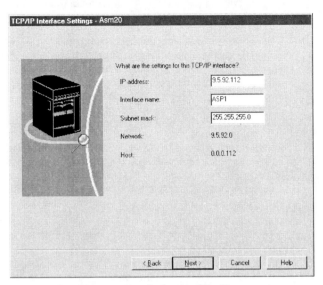

Figure 24. Specifying parameters for the virtual IP address

Make sure you specify a valid IP address. Ask you Internet service provider (ISP) or network administrator for a valid IP address.

To perform the same task using a 5250 session, run the Add TCP/IP Interface (ADDTCPIFC) command. Instead of specifying the line description, we use *VIRTUALIP for the LIND parameter. You must also specify an MTU size because there is no physical line description associated with this interface

Note: In V4R5, you may let the MTU value default to *LIND.

The MTU size does not impact performance because the interface is virtual. The route and physical interface taken out of the system determines the real MTU size.

After you create the virtual interfaces, you need to go to each system that needs to access the virtual IP addresses and add the correct routing entry. For most systems, this consists of a host route with a next hop that points to the real iSeries interface. In some cases, a more specific route entry may be needed. This information is added to a windows workstation by specifying a gateway entry in the TCP/IP properties of the network configuration.

You need to make the appropriate route entries in any routers that need to point to the system with virtual IP addresses. However, if you want anybody on the Internet to access the system with a virtual IP address, you have to use Routing Information Protocol (RIP) Version 2. You should add a route entry to the router on your local area network and start the router daemon on that system by using the command:

STRTCPSVR SERVER(*ROUTED)

With the router daemon running, your iSeries exchanges routing information with other routers on the Internet. Therefore, the route to the system with a virtual IP address is spread across Internet.

Virtual IP address versus real IP address

Virtual IP addresses work well in situations where you need unique TCP/IP addresses to bind to applications. One example of this is when you set up multiple Domino servers on the same system. We recommend that you define a new address for each new server. While you can add multiple IP addresses to a physical interface, this can lead to problems at times when a request comes in with one address but is responded to with another address.

Another problem can result if the physical interface is varied off. The IP addresses associated with this physical interface are not available. With a virtual IP address, the interface can be active as long as the system is active. This may result in higher availability if the network is dynamic enough to route around the failing physical interface. This can be accomplished with RIP Version 2.

3.5 Multiple HTTP server instances

The IBM HTTP Server for iSeries can run multiple instances of a Web server, each with a different configuration file or with shared configuration files on the same system. These multiple server instances enable you to provide multiple Web sites for customers on a single system. When you create multiple server instances, you must choose between these two options:

- A unique IP address per server
- The same IP address with a unique port per server

With this ability to run multiple HTTP server instances, you can have concurrent, but completely independent, versions of WebSphere Application Server running in parallel. These are the advantages of using this approach:

- Each server instance can read from its own set of properties files.
- Each server instance creates its own set of log and trace files.
- Each server instance works within its own security model.
- Each server instance can invoke its own Administration Manager interface without affecting any other HTTP server instances that might be running on the iSeries server at the same time.

The ability to have multiple instances allows you to keep your customer applications or application developers independent of each other. For example, you could use one instance for development, one for testing, and one for serving the Web site. Each of these instances will be independent.

Your Web server uses configuration files and server instances, and you can use as many of either as you choose. The server uses the configuration files as a basis for the server instances, but not necessarily on a one-to-one basis. You can have several server instances associated with a single configuration file. The HTTP server comes with one configuration file called CONFIG. It also comes with two server instances based on the above configuration file: the ADMIN (*ADMIN) server instance and the DEFAULT server instance.

For example, you could configure four server instances on your iSeries: DEV, PROD, INFO, and INSIDE. Perhaps two of these instances would serve a large number of customers. The PROD server instance might serve the applications you are serving as an ASP, and the INFO server instance might serve general company information and job posting. If you use a unique IP address for both of these server instances, they have the benefit of using the default port number 80. You can then access either one of these instances with a host name that you can remember easily such as *www.info.mycorp.com* or *www.as400asp.com*. However, the DEV server instance might serve a small number of employees on your company's internal intranet, so requiring a unique port number with the host name in the URL should be acceptable. Using unique port numbers in this manner allows you to reserve your IP addresses for instances that you want to identify with simple host names, such as *www.info.mycorp.com*.

If you use a unique port number, you can support any number of HTTP server instances with one communication adapter using only one IP address. If you use multiple IP addresses, you can support multiple HTTP server instances with one communication adapter.

The HTTP server directives that need to be added to the configuration file are the BindSpecific On and HostName directives with the IP address of the interface as a parameter.

Use the server instances forms in the Configuration and Administration interface to setup multiple server instances. Each form has a help window to assist you with the configuration tasks.

3.5.1 Implementing

To begin, you must change the DEFAULT server instance and any other server instances that can be active, so that they do not reply to all requests on all interfaces.

Then, you need to run a different server instance on each IP address. To do this, specify the hostname on the HostName Directive and add the BindSpecific On directive. If you specify BindSpecific On, the server binds only to the IP address specified in the HostName directive instead of binding to all local IP addresses. The default setting is BindSpecific Off. It causes the same HTML pages to be served to all IP addresses and hostnames. Now, follow these steps:

1. Start the administration server by running the command:

   ```
   STRTCPSVR SERVER(*HTTP) HTTPSVR(*ADMIN)
   ```

2. Point your browser to the configuration port 2001 on your system. Sign on and select **IBM HTTP Server for AS/400->Configuration and Administration-> Configurations**.

3. Because the DEFAULT HTTP server uses the configuration file named **CONFIG**, select this configuration from the pull-down menu, and click **Basic** (see Figure 25 on page 88).

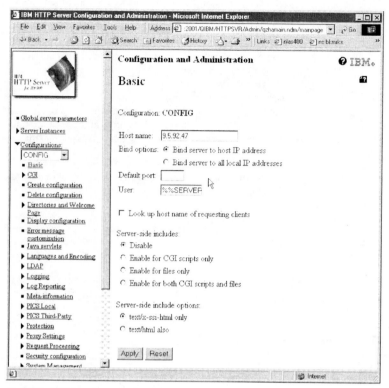

Figure 25. HTTP configuration: Basic

4. Add the IP address of the interface. For Bind options, select the **Bind server to host IP address**. Click **Apply**.

5. If you change this directive, you must stop the HTTP server that uses this configuration and then start it again. The server will not pick up the change if you only restart it. To do this, select **Server Instances->Work with server instances**. Then stop and start the DEFAULT instance.

Notice, in our example, that we use the IP address, not the name, on the HostName directive because this is what is actually used by the system. If you specify a name on the HostName directive, the system will look up the address for this name and the server will bind to this address.

If your goal is to redirect to different pages based on the hostname sent by the browser, you have to use virtual hosting as described in 3.9, "Virtual hosts" on page 100. Another way to do the same thing is to open the configuration file by running this command from 5250 session:

```
WRKHTTPCFG CONFIG
```

Then, add the following lines.

```
HostName 9.5.92.47
BindSpecific On
```

You can stop and start the server by:

```
ENDTCPSVR SERVER(*HTTP) HTTPSVR(DEFAULT)
STRTCPSVR SERVER(*HTTP) HTTPSVR(DEFAULT)
```

3.5.2 Creating an HTTP server instance

Now that you have made sure the default HTTP server will only bind to one interface, you can create the new instance. When setting up a new server, it is easiest to create a configuration file first and then create the server instance. Otherwise, you need to create the instance using a different configuration first and then change to the new configuration file later. To reduce any confusion, you may want to have the same name for the instance and the configuration.

To create a configuration, click **Configurations** in the browser window, and choose **Create Configuration** from the left frame. The form that appears (Figure 26) allows you to create an empty configuration AspHttp1. Click the **Apply** button.

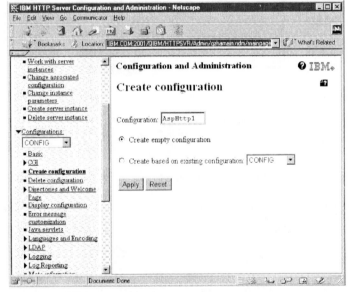

Figure 26. HTTP Create configuration

Now that you have created the configuration, you can create a server instance:

1. Create the instance by selecting **Server Instances** and **Create server instance** in the left pane.

2. Enter `AspHttp1` as the instance name, and select the **AspHttp1** configuration.

3. In a 5250 session, run the following command:

   ```
   WRKHTTPCFG AspHttp1
   ```

4. Edit the configuration file by adding the directives as shown in Figure 27 on page 90.

```
                        Work with HTTP Configuration
                                                          System:    AS20
    Configuration name . . . . . . . :      ASPHTTP1

 Type options, press Enter.
   1=Add    2=Change    3=Copy    4=Remove    5=Display    13=Insert

        Sequence
 Opt    Number    Entry

        00010     # HTTP CONFIGURATION FILE
        00020     HostName 9.5.92.112
        00030     BindSpecific On
        00040     Welcome index.html
        00050     Pass /* /asphttp1/html/*
        00060     AlwaysWelcome On
```

Figure 27. Example directives for a new HTTP server configuration

Make sure the address on the HostName directive is not specified in any other
active configuration that is using default port 80.

Create the home directory for this instance. Run the following statements in your
5250 session:

```
md '/asphttp1'
wrkaut '/asphttp1'
```

Make sure user QTMHHTTP has *RX access to the directory. Now you can create
the html directory, which should inherit authorization from its parent:

```
md '/asphttp1/html'
```

You can create a home page for your AspHttp1 instance by using the command:

```
EDTF '/asphttp1/html/index.html'
```

However, you may want to map a drive to the system and copy the home page to
the iSeries file system. Note that if you use the EDTF command to create the file,
it will be created using codepage 37 in EBCDIC.

3.6 WebSphere installation

The WebSphere Application Server Advanced Edition 3.0.2 software can be
installed from a 5250 display session or from a personal computer that is LAN
connected to the iSeries server.

This book explains how to install the WebSphere Application Server from a 5250
display session. For the other installation methods, or for more details, refer to
the online documentation at:

```
http://www.as400.ibm.com/products/websphere/docs/doc.htm
```

When you install the WebSphere Application Server Advanced Edition 3.0.2
software, the OS/400 user profile you use must have *SECOFR privileges.

To start the installation, load the CD in the iSeries, and type (on one line):

```
RUNJVA CLASS(SETUP) CLASSPATH('/QOPT/WebSphere/OS400:/QOPT/WebSphere/
OS400/INSTALL.JAR:/QOPT/WebSphere')
```

Messages appear to describe what the installation process is currently doing. It might take from 30 minutes to an hour to install WebSphere Application Server. At the end of the installation process, you should see the following message on your screen:

```
INSTALLATION COMPLETED SUCCESSFULLY.
```

After you install WebSphere, make sure you install the PTFs listed on the WebSphere Web site at:

```
http://www.as400.ibm.com/products/websphere/services/service.htm
```

Now, you can start the WebSphere Application Server by starting the QEJBSBS subsystem with the command:

```
STRSBS QEJB/QEJBSBS
```

To verify that the WebSphere Application Server has started, enter:

```
WRKSBSJOB SBS(QEJBSBS)
```

You should see two jobs started as shown in Figure 28.

```
                        Work with Subsystem Jobs                    AS20
                                                    11/29/00  09:26:16
 Subsystem . . . . . . . . . :    QEJBSBS

 Type options, press Enter.
   2=Change   3=Hold   4=End   5=Work with   6=Release   7=Display message
   8=Work with spooled files   13=Disconnect


 Opt   Job        User      Type     -----Status-----   Function
       QEJBADMIN  QEJB      BATCHI   ACTIVE
       QEJBMNTR   QEJB      AUTO     ACTIVE             PGM-QEJBMNTR



                                                                   Bottom
 Parameters or command
 ===>
 F3=Exit      F4=Prompt    F5=Refresh   F9=Retrieve   F11=Display schedule data
 F12=Cancel   F17=Top      F18=Bottom
```

Figure 28. You should see two active jobs

Check the job log of the QEJBADMIN job to verify that the message WebSphere administration server QEJBADMIN ready is displayed. If the message is shown, your first WebSphere instance is running. If this is not the case, check your job log, and look for job logs of user QEJB by executing the command:

```
WRKSPLF QEJB
```

Installing the WebSphere Administrative Console

The WebSphere Administrative Console is used to manage the application servers. You must install the Administrative Console before you use the WebSphere Application Server.

If you use the online documentation to install the WebSphere Administrative Console, pay attention to these important points:

- IBM Java Development Kit 1.1.7B for Windows NT (the supported level is included in the product package) has to be installed before installing the WebSphere Administrative Console.

- The host name of the iSeries should be the same as the name and domain name shown in CFGTCP option 12 because it is case sensitive. If the names are not the same, you will receive the error shown in Figure 32.

Note

To install the Administrative Console on your workstation, you need to use the WebSphere Application Server edition for your workstation operating system. *Do not use* the WebSphere Application Server Advanced Edition for AS/400 CD-ROM (which also came in your WebSphere Application Server Advanced Edition for AS/400 package) for this set of steps.

Insert the WebSphere Application Server 3 Advanced Edition for Windows NT, WebSphere Application Server 3 Advanced Edition for AIX, or WebSphere Application Server 3 Advanced Edition for Solaris CD in the CD-ROM drive of the Windows NT, AIX, or Solaris workstation on which you plan to run the console. If autorun is not enabled, run the either of the following commands and follow the wizard:

```
SETUP.EXE
./install.sh
```

On the Install Options page (Figure 29), select only the **Administrator's Console** option.

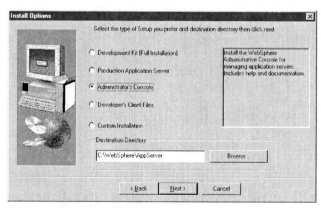

Figure 29. Installing the WebSphere Administrator's Console

At the prompt for the hostname (Figure 30), make sure that you use the correct hostname and that you can ping the system. The hostname must *exactly* match the name shown in CFGTCP option 12. Even if it is in the wrong case, you will see the error message shown in Figure 32. If you have problems starting Administrative Console, see the *Troubleshooting: Starting the WebSphere Administrative Console* section in *WebSphere Application Server 3 Advanced*

Edition for AS/400, found at:

`http://www.as400.ibm.com/products/websphere/docs/doc.htm`

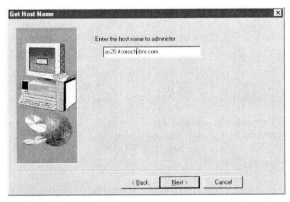

Figure 30. Host name prompt

After the installation is completed (you will need to restart your Windows NT workstation), start the Administrative Console. The amount of time that it takes for the WebSphere Administrative Console to start depends on the number of objects that you have configured. It is not uncommon for this to take several minutes when WAS configured with a large number of objects. When WebSphere Administrative Console is ready, you should see the Administrative Console window as shown in Figure 31.

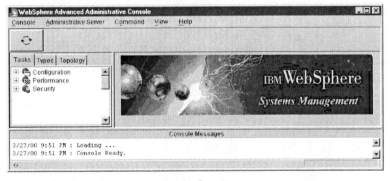

Figure 31. WebSphere Advanced Administrative Console

If, however, you specify a wrong host name during the Administrative Console installation, you should see an error window as shown in Figure 32. Simultaneously, you can see a stack dump in the command prompt window.

Figure 32. Install WebSphere Administrative Console: Could not get attributes

If you run into this problem, you do not have to reinstall. You can simply correct this error by changing the parameter on the shortcut to the WebSphere Administrative Console.

3.7 Configuring the HTTP server to enable WebSphere

To use WebSphere, you need to update the HTTP configuration file with the directives: NameTrans, Authorization, Service, ServerInit, ServerTerm, and Pass. These directives allow a Web browser to access the servlet engine and the Web applications that run on the WebSphere Application Server.

There are two ways to add the necessary directives to the configuration file. Either use the Web browser interface as described in *WebSphere Application Server 3 Advanced Edition for AS/400*, or edit the configuration file in a 5250 Terminal session.

The easiest way is via the Web browser interface. This interface allows you to configure the HTTP directives to support WebSphere Version 1 and 2, or WebSphere Version 3, or to disable servlets and JavaServer Pages (JSP) support from your Web server. To enable WebSphere Version 3 support, follow these steps:

1. Point your Web browser to your iSeries server, and specify port 2001, for example:

   `http://as20.rchland.ibm.com:2001`

2. Select **IBM HTTP Server for AS/400->Configuration and Administration**.

3. Click **Configurations** in the left pane.

4. Select from the **Configurations** pull-down menu the configuration name that matches your Web server instance.

5. Click **Java servlets** in the left pane (see Figure 33).

6. Select **WebSphere version 3**.

7. Click the **Apply** button.

Figure 33. Adding HTTP directives to allow WebSphere Version 3 to be served from the Web server

You can also manually edit the HTTP configuration file. However, this is a tedious task and we recommend that you use the previous method. If you need to edit the configuration file manually, read the *Manually adding WebSphere directives to your IBM HTTP Server* section in *WebSphere Application Server 3 Advanced Edition for AS/400*.

Now stop and start your HTTP server, and then start the WebSphere Administrative Console on your workstation.

You must now update the Host Aliases table under the virtual host, which is default_host, to reflect the correct host name and port number. Follow these steps:

1. From the WebSphere Administrative Console, click the **Topology** tab to view the Topology tree.

2. Use the tree to locate the virtual host **default_host**.

3. Click **default_host**. The settings for default_host appear in the right side of the console.

4. Click the **Advanced** tab to go to the Advanced settings page.

5. In the **Host Aliases** list, update the specified host aliases with the new hostname and correct port number. The server will only respond to the hostname and port combinations specified in the **Host Aliases** list. You can add more than one alias.

6. Click the **Apply** button.

We add hostname as20.itsoroch.ibm.com and its IP address (see Figure 34).

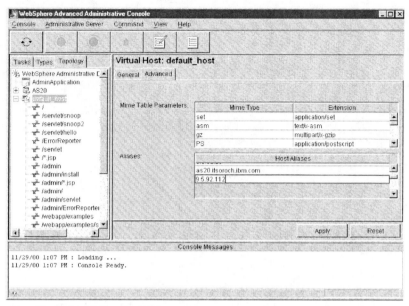

Figure 34. Configuring the virtual host

In the Topology view of the WebSphere Administrative Console, find the node that has the same name as the host name of the iSeries server, which is AS20 in our case. Expand that node, and click the application server instance named **Default Server**. Start it by clicking the green button on the tool bar, or by right-clicking and choosing **Start**.

Open a browser, and go to the following site (the address is case sensitive):

```
http://<your hostname>/WebSphereSamples/EJBs/HelloEJB/HelloEJB.jsp
```

Note: In our example, we used *as20.itsoroch.ibm.com* as the hostname.

You should see the sample page as shown in Figure 35.

Figure 35. HelloWorld EJB

You have now set up WebSphere using the default instance. To provide a higher degree of separation, you should create a separate WebSphere instance.

3.8 Multiple instances of the WebSphere Administration Server

The iSeries version of WebSphere Application Server Advanced Edition 3.0 supports multiple instances of the WebSphere Application Server.

A single administration server allows you to run many application servers. Each application server runs in its own process, so in most cases, a single administration server handles your scalability and isolation needs. Additionally, a single administration server allows you to use a single Administrative Console to manage all of the server resources.

However, since all application servers in an administrative domain share the same Persistent Name Server name space, you may want to create multiple administrative servers on a single iSeries server. Another motivation to create multiple instances is the ability to have concurrent, but completely independent, versions of the instances. In other words, each server will be able to read from its own set of property files, create its own set of log and trace files, work within its own realm security model, and have its own WebSphere Administrative Console GUI without effecting any other HTTP or WebSphere Server instances that might be running on the iSeries at the same time.

This means that you may want to create multiple administrative servers on a single iSeries for any of the following reasons:

- To apply different security rules for each customer.
- To give a customer control to their own domain, so they can use their own Administrative Console. This gives them the ability to do their own deployment.
- To handle authentication from different starting points in the LDAP tree.
- To create separate development environments for different developers. This allows them to have different versions of the same objects in their own name space.
- To create separate development and test environments. Changes made to one environment will not affect other environments.
- To run a workshop. Each person can have their own instance running on the same iSeries server. They will be able to make configuration changes, and start and stop the WebSphere Application server without impacting others.

Each administration server instance will need its own HTTP server instance.

Each HTTP server instance needs either a separate port or a different IP address (which can be on the same adapter). For development purposes within an organization, it should be acceptable to have a server using a port other than the default port number. The following section explains how to create one to use a unique IP address.

Implementing

This section shows you how to create a separate instance of the administration server:

1. Start the Qshell Interpreter. Run the script that creates all new server directories and sets up the correct authorities. Run the following two commands on your iSeries server:

```
STRQSH
/QIBM/ProdData/WebASAdv/bin/crtnewinst /asp
```

The administration server configuration is created with the server root directory /asp in the root directory of the IFS. If you decide to use a different name for the server root directory, replace */asp* with the name you choose.

2. To use a different instance of the administration server, you need to update three properties files. The first files is the bootstrap.properties file. You can do this from a mapped drive or by using the command:

```
EDTF '/asp/properties/bootstrap.properties'
```

Replace the default values of the properties with the corresponding new values listed here:

```
server.root=/asp
ose.tmp.dir=/asp/temp
ose.logs.dir=/asp/logs
```

Note that if you edit from a mapped drive, Windows Notepad does not always display the file correctly. Wordpad should work fine.

The second file to edit is the admin.properties file in the /asp/properties directory:

```
EDTF '/asp/properties/admin.properties'
```

Modify these properties:

- `mntr.admin.name=ASPADMIN`
- `install.initial.config=true`
- `admin.dbSchema=ASP`
- `admin.bootstrapPort=1910`
- `admin.lsdPort=19010`
- `admin.classpath=+/asp/properties`
- `admin.instance.root=/asp`
- `java.properties=com.ibm.CORBA.ConfigURL=file:///asp/properties/sas.server.props`

These properties are explained in the following list:

- **mntr.admin.name**: Used as the job name for the administration server job, which is listed in the Work with Active Jobs (WRKACTJOB) display. It should be unique.

- **install.initial.config**: This setting controls whether a default application server is created when the administration server is started the next time. Use "true" if you want the default server to be created. Use "false" if you do not want the default server created. This value is changed to "false" automatically when the administration server is next started.

- **admin.dbSchema**: The iSeries library name (equivalent to an SQL database collection) used for the administration database files. It is created if it does not already exist.

- **admin.bootstrapPort**: The Administrative Console uses this port number when connecting to your instance of the application server. The default value 900 (which is used by the default administration server) should not be used.

- **admin.lsdPort**: An unused port number. The default value 9000 should not be used.

- **admin.classpath**: The path to the directory that contains the properties files. Only change the last occurrence of the classpath variable in this file.

- **admin.instance.root**: The server root directory.

- **java.properties=com.ibm.CORBA.ConfigURL**: The sas server property file.

The last file you need to edit is sas.server.props:

```
EDTF '/asp/properties/sas.server.props'
```

Replace the default values of the properties with the corresponding new values listed here:

```
com.ibm.CORBA.keytabFileName=/asp/etc/keytab5
com.ibm.CORBA.bootstrapRepositoryLocation=/asp/etc/secbootstrap
```

3. Start the new instance of the administration server. The default administration server is started when the QEJBSBS subsystem is started. You must, however, manually start additional administration servers.

   To start the new administration server, run the following command (all on one line) on the iSeries:

```
SBMJOB CMD(CALL PGM(QEJB/QEJBMNTR) PARM('-p'
'/asp/properties/admin.properties')) JOB(ASPMNTR) JOBD(QEJB/QEJBJOBD)
JOBQ(QEJB/QEJBJOBQ) USER(QEJB)
```

4. Create a new copy of the HTTP server configuration based on the existing instance (AspHttp1 in our example). Name the new instance ASPHTTP. We will modify this one to use the new WebSphere instance.

5. Enter the following command:

```
WRKHTTPCFG ASPHTTP
```

   Change the line with the ServerInit directive to use the server /asp/properties/bootstrap.properties file. Change the HostName and the Pass directives with the new directory name (which is */asp* in our example).

   In our example, we use the HostName and BindSpecific On directives in the HTTP configuration file so our server binds only to one IP address.

   If you want to use the HTTP server to serve HTML files and images, create the html directory /asp/html and add *RX authority for user QTMHHTTP.

   Make sure the IP interface for this name is started and start the HTTP server.

6. Copy the shortcut to the Administrator's Console. Change only the port number to the one specified in the admin.properties file (admin.bootstrapPort parameter):

```
C:\WebSphere\AppServer\bin\adminclient.bat as20.itsoroch.ibm.com 1910
```

   > **Note**
   >
   > Do *not* change the hostname. It still has to match the hostname and domain found by running the CFGTCP command and selecting option 12.

7. Start the Administrative Console using this shortcut:

   a. From the WebSphere Administrative Console, click the **Topology** tab to view the Topology tree. Use the tree to locate the virtual host named "default_host". Click **default_host**. The settings for default_host appear in the right side of the console. Click the **Advanced** tab.

b. In the **Host Aliases** menu, add the aliases with the IP address of the iSeries server running new instance of the HTTP server. Then add the domain name www.asp.com (like the example in Figure 36), and click **Apply**.

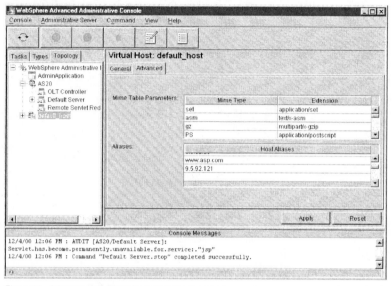

Figure 36. Administrative Console: Separating the server

c. In the Topology view of the WebSphere Administrative Console, find the node that has the same name as the host name of the iSeries server, which is AS20 in our case. Expand that node, and click the application server instance **Default Server**.

You may want to rename this default server to ASPSVR to identify the iSeries job associated with this server in the system.

8. Start the server and check the following URL to test the setup:

   http://www.asp.com/WebSphereSamples/EJBs/HelloEJB/HelloEJB.jsp

The result should appear the same as the example shown in Figure 35 on page 96.

3.9 Virtual hosts

You might use virtual hosting when you need to support multiple Web sites on your system, but have insufficient IP addresses to assign a unique address to each site. For example, you may encounter this in an intranet environment where you are hosting separate Web sites for departments within an organization. Or, an Internet service provider (ISP) might use virtual hosting to project the appearance of supporting unique sites for several customers.

3.9.1 What are virtual hosts?

A virtual host is a configuration that enables a single host machine to resemble multiple host machines. Resources associated with one virtual host cannot share data with resources that are associated with another virtual host, even if the virtual hosts share the same physical machine.

Each virtual host has a logical name and a list of one or more domain name service (DNS) aliases by which it is known. A DNS alias is the TCP/IP hostname and port number used to request the servlet, for example: *yourHostName:80*. When no port number is specified, 80 is assumed.

When a servlet request is made, the server name and port number entered into the browser are compared to a list of all known aliases in an effort to locate the correct virtual host and serve the servlet. If no match is found, an error is returned to the browser.

WebSphere Application Server provides a default virtual host with some common aliases, such as the machine's IP address, short host name, and fully qualified host name. The alias comprises the first part of the path for accessing a resource such as a servlet. For example, *localhost:80* is the alias in the request http://localhost:80/myServlet.

A virtual host is not associated with a particular node (machine) in the administrative domain. It is a configuration, rather than a "live object", explaining why it can be created, but is not started or stopped.

Virtual hosting is accomplished with the use of a Domain Name Server where multiple, fully qualified host names are recorded, all sharing a common IP address. This technique allows the Web administrator to control any number of Web sites using:

- A single instance of the HTTP server
- A single instance of WebSphere Administration Server
- A single TCP/IP address
- A single TCP/IP port, all running over
- A single physical communications interface (hardware adapter) on the iSeries

The single HTTP configuration member contains a set of directives associated with each unique host name. This set of directives per host name may contain only the Welcome, Mapping Rule, and Access Control directives to segregate the virtual sites.

Clients must support HTTP 1.1 or HTTP 1.0 with 1.1 extensions.

3.9.2 Why and when to use virtual hosting

Suppose you have two customers whose applications you want to host on the same machine. The ASP wants to keep the two sites isolated from one another, despite their sharing a machine.

The ASP can associate the resources of the first company with VirtualHost1 and the resources of the second company with VirtualHost2. Now suppose both companies' sites offer the same servlet. Each site has its own instances of the servlet, which are unaware of the other site's instance.

If the company whose site is organized on VirtualHost2 is past due in paying its account with the ASP, the ASP can refuse all servlet requests that are routed to VirtualHost2. Even though the same servlet is available on VirtualHost1, the requests directed at VirtualHost2 will not be routed there.

The servlets on one virtual host do not share their context with the servlets on the other virtual host. Requests for the servlet on VirtualHost1 can continue as usual, even though VirtualHost2 refuses to fill requests for the same servlet.

3.9.3 Mapping requests to virtual host aliases

When a user requests a resource, WebSphere Application Server tries to map the request to an alias of a defined virtual host. The mapping is case insensitive, but the match must be alphabetically exact. Also, different port numbers are treated as different aliases. For example, the request http://www.myhost.com/myservlet maps successfully to http://WWW.MYHOST.COM/MYSERVLET and to http://Www.Myhost.Com/Myservlet. But it does not map successfully to http://myhost/myservlet or to http://myhost:9876/myservlet.

If a user requests a resource using an alias that cannot be mapped to an alias of a defined virtual host, the user receives a 404 error in the browser. A message states that the virtual host could not be found.

3.9.4 How Web paths associate resources with virtual hosts

The IBM HTTP server separates the requests if the hostname is added to the Pass or Welcome directive as follows:

```
Pass /* /mycorp/* www.mycorp.com
Pass /* /asp/* www.asp.com
```

All requests for HTML pages on www.mycorp.com will now be served from the /mycorp directory. Requests for www.asp.com will go to the /asp directory.

For WAS, you can use the WebSphere Administrative Console to associate the Web paths of resources, such as servlets, Web pages, and JSP files, with virtual hosts. It is common to say that the resources are "on" the virtual host, even though the virtual host is a configuration, not a physical machine that can hold files.

The Web path of a resource, such as a servlet, is a path by which users can request the resource. For example, an administrator might specify two Web paths for a servlet class named accounts. This allows users to specify either http://www.mycorp.com/accounts or http://www.mycorp.com/accountsToo to request the servlet. An example of this is shown in Figure 37.

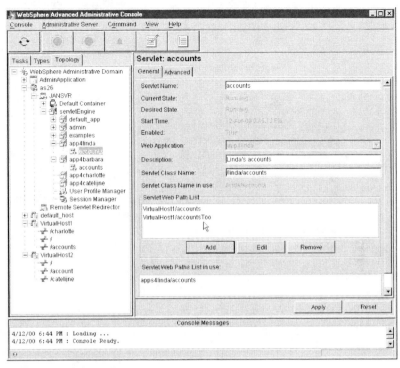

Figure 37. Web path list

Because you associate the Web path of a resource with a virtual host, and not the resource itself, you can associate one Web path of a servlet with one virtual host, and another Web path of the servlet with a different virtual host. WebSphere Application Server provides the flexibility to set up virtual hosting in the way that best suits your needs. You cannot serve the same Web path using different servlets from the same instance of the Administrative Console.

Both WebSphere and IBM HTTP server can serve different pages to different hosts, but both use different mechanisms to do this. To simplify things, you may want to consider using only WAS for all pages served, including HTML and images.

3.10 Putting everything together

This section takes you through an example that implements all the steps that were explained in the previous sections. You can find this same sample in the WebSphere Samples Gallery: Account and Transfer. This particular sample compiles and deploys two EJBs and two servlets. One bean is an entity bean with container-managed persistence and the other bean is a session bean. With these two EJBs and two servlets, you can create accounts (savings or checking) and transfer money between them. The information about accounts is saved in the database.

The purpose of this exercise is to help you see what the real deployment of the application looks like in a WAS environment. There are a lot of small, but very important, details that you don't see when deploying a sample with the default server.

Note: In this sample, note that we used the Administrative Console running on Windows NT.

Follow these steps:

1. Create a new instance of the HTTP server as explained in 3.5, "Multiple HTTP server instances" on page 86, and configure it for WebSphere (see 3.7, "Configuring the HTTP server to enable WebSphere" on page 94). We create a new instance of ASPHTTP.

2. Create a new instance of WebSphere in the /asp directory, and modify three properties files as explained in 3.8, "Multiple instances of the WebSphere Administration Server" on page 97 (using the correct directory names).

3. Start the QEJBSBS subsystem.

4. Start your instance of WAS:

```
SBMJOB CMD(CALL PGM(QEJB/QEJBMNTR)
PARM('-p' '/asp/properties/admin.properties'))
JOB(ASPMNTR) JOBD(QEJB/QEJBJOBD) JOBQ(QEJB/QEJBJOBQ) USER(QEJB)
```

5. Start the Administrative Console using the correct port number.

6. Start the HTTP server (this is ASPHTTP in our example).

7. Verify that your configuration is correct by pointing your Web browser to:

```
http://<your system DN>/WebSphereSamples/EJBs/HelloEJB/HelloEJB.jsp
```

You should see the output as shown in Figure 35 on page 96.

8. Go to your Administrative Console, and create a virtual host `BankOneVrtHost`. Add two aliases: `BankOne` (make sure this entry is added to the Domain Name Server or to the c:\Winnt\System32\drivers\etc\Hosts file) and the IP address to which your HTTP server is bound.

9. Create the following directories on the iSeries:

```
/asp/hosts/BankOneVrtHost
/asp/hosts/BankOneVrtHost/BankOneWebApp
/asp/hosts/BankOneVrtHost/BankOneWebApp/web
/asp/hosts/BankOneVrtHost/BankOneWebApp/servlets
```

10. Create the application server:

   a. In the Administrative Console, select the **Tasks** tab.

   b. Click **Configure an application server**.

   c. Click the **Start Task** button (with the green circle).

   d. Click the **Next** button (you need both types of resources for this application server: EJB and Web application).

   e. On the next panel, enter the server name, which is `BankOne` in our example. Change the location of stdout.txt and strerr.txt files to `/asp/hosts/BankOneVrtHost/` as shown in Figure 38.

   f. Click **Next**.

   g. Accept the defaults on this panel, and click **Next**.

h. In the next panel, expand the tree and select the node name under which the new application server will be placed (AS20 in our example).

i. Click **Next**.

j. Click **Next** on Enterprise Bean List panel (we add EJBs later).

k. Accept the default settings on the EJB container panel. The name of the container is **BankOneContainer**.

l. Click **Next**.

m. In this panel, expand a tree, and select **BankOneVrtHost**.

n. Click **Next**.

o. Accept the defaults, and click **Next**.

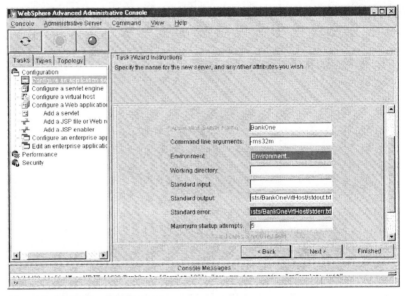

Figure 38. Application server Tasks tab

p. On the Web application panel, leave Web Application Name as **BankOneWebApp**. Select from **BankOneVrtHost** from the Virtual Host menu. Change Web Application Web Path to /banking (see Figure 39 on page 106).

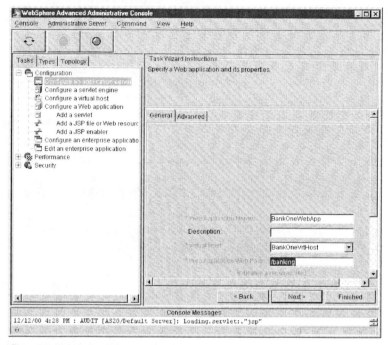

Figure 39. Web application parameters

q. Click **Next**.

r. Accept the default for the JSP version that is supported and the way the servlets are enabled.

s. Click **Finished**. Now you should see the BankOne application server in the WAS topology.

11. Create a data source:

a. Click the **Types** tab in the Administrative Console.

b. Right-click **JDBC Drivers**.

c. From the pop-up menu, select **Create...**.

d. In the new window, provide the following parameters (as shown in Figure 40):

   i. Enter NativeDB2Driver for Name.

   ii. Select **com.ibm.db2.jdbc.app.DB2Driver** from the pull-down menu for Implementation Class.

   iii. Accept the default parameters for URL prefix and JTA enabled.

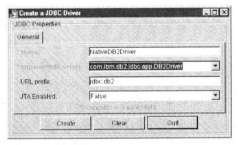

Figure 40. Configuring a JDBC driver

    e. Click the **Create** button.

    f. Click the **Types** tab, and right-click **DataSources**.

    g. Select **Create...** from the pop-up menu.

    h. Fill in the following parameters (see Figure 41):

- **Name**: This is the name of your data source. Enter `BankOneDataSrc`.

- **Database name**: This is the name of the database that you want to use for this data source. In our example, we use DB2 UDB for AS/400 on the same machine where we run the administration server. Enter `*local`. If you need to access the database located on the remote system, create a different JDBC driver using a different implementation class: `com.ibm.as400.access.AS400JDBCDriver`.

- **Driver**: From the pull-down menu, select **NativeDB2Driver**.

    i. Click the **Create** button.

Figure 41. Creating a data source

12. Install a driver. In the topology pane, follow these steps:

    a. Right-click **NativeDB2Driver**.

    b. From the pop-up menu, select **Install...**.

    c. In the new window, select a node on which you want to install a driver (AS20 in our case), and click the **Browse...** button to find the JAR file for the driver.

       The file you need is **/QIBM/ProdData/Java400/ext/db2_classes.jar**.

    d. Click the **Install** button.

13. You have configured the JDBC driver and data source. Now you need to point the EJB container to this data source. Expand the **BankOne** application server resource in the topology view. Click **BankOneContainer**.

   a. Click the **DataSource** tab in the EJBContainer: BankOneContainer pane.

   b. Click the **Change** button.

   c. Select **BankOneDataSrc** from pop-up window, and click **OK**. The window that appears is shown in Figure 42.

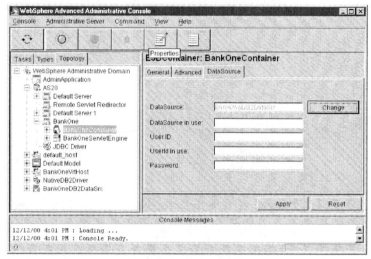

Figure 42. Specifying the data source for the EJB container

   d. Click the **Apply** button. *This is a very important step.* If you forget to click Apply, your change will not take affect.

14. Copy the presentation files for the Account and Transfer application, and modify some of them:

   a. Start Qshell on the iSeries by typing:

   ```
   strqsh
   ```

   b. Copy the presentation files by running two commands:

   ```
   cp /QIBM/ProdData/WebASAdv/WebSphereSamples/EJBs/Account/*.*
   /asp/hosts/BankOneVrtHost/BankOneWebApp/web
   ```

   ```
   cp /QIBM/ProdData/WebASAdv/WebSphereSamples/EJBs/Transfer/*.*
   /asp/hosts/BankOneVrtHost/BankOneWebApp/web
   ```

   c. For security reasons, do not enable serving servlets by class name. Change two of the files (use the EDTF command to modify the files):

   - **'/asp/hosts/BankOneVrtHost/BankOneWebApp/web/create.html**: Change one line in this file: `<form method="get" action="/servlet/com.ibm.ejs.doc.client.CreateAccount">` to `<form method="get" action="/banking/CreateAccount">`. Note that we used a virtual path that we defined in one of the previous steps (see Figure 39 on page 106).

- **/asp/hosts/BankOneVrtHost/BankOneWebApp/web/transfer.html**: Change one line in this file: `<form method="get" action="/servlet/com.ibm.ejs.doc.client.TransferFunds">` to `<form method="get" action="/banking/TransferFunds">`.

15. Up to this point, you have created an empty configuration for the application server. Now you need to provide resources (EJBs and servlets) that add some functionality to your server. First, you need to modify and then compile source files for EJBs and servlets. In this example, we used the Windows NT directory as a temporary placeholder for the JAVA and CLASS files.

   a. Map the Windows NT network drive to the root directory on the iSeries server.

   b. Copy the source files from /QIBM/ProdData/WebASAdv/EJBSamples/src/AccountAndTransfer to the newly created c:\asp directory.

   c. Modify the c:\asp\CreateAccount.java file. Search for **/servlet/com.ibm.ejs.doc.client.CreateAccount**, and change it to `/banking/CreateAccount`

   d. Modify the c:\asp\TransferFunds.java file. Search for **/servlet/com.ibm.ejs.doc.client.TransferFunds**, and change it to `/banking/TransferFunds`.

   e. Modify the c:\asp\ClientResourceBundle.java and c:\asp\Transfer.xml files if you use a port number to connect to administration server on the iSeries server other than the default (we used 1907 for this example). Change the port number in the following line:

      `"iiop://localhost:900"`

   f. Change the directory for the JDK_LIB and WAS_LIB environment variables in the c:\asp\createbeans.bat file. Specify a fully-qualified path to the location of the JDK jar file as well as the lib directory for WAS on Windows NT.

   g. Save all files.

   h. Run the c:\asp\createbeans.bat batch file.

   i. If you look at the c:\asp directory, you should see two JAR files (Account.jar and Transfer.jar) and a new subdirectory c:\asp\com.

   j. On the iSeries server, create a subdirectory for the JAR files. Run the following command:

      `md '/asp/deployableEJBs'`

   k. Copy c:\asp\Account.jar to the /asp/deployableEJBs/ directory on the iSeries server.

   l. Copy c:\asp\Transfer.jar to the /asp/deployableEJBs/ directory on the iSeries server.

   m. Copy the entire c:\asp\com subdirectory to the /asp/hosts/BankOneVrtHost/BankOneWebApp/servlets/com directory.

   n. After you complete all of these steps, you should see a directory structure on the iSeries server that is similar to the example in Figure 43 on page 110.

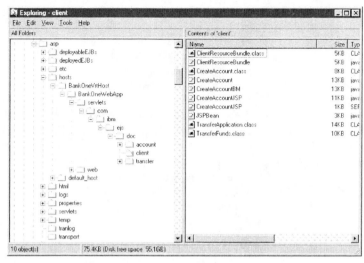

Figure 43. Directory tree after copying the sample files

16. Create two EJBs in BankOneContainer:

   a. Go back to the Administrative Console. In the topology view, expand the node tree up to the container to which you need to add the bean BankOneContainer.

   b. Right-click **BankOneContainer**.

   c. Select **Create...-> EnterpriseBean** from the pop-up menu.

   d. In the window that appears, click **Browse**, and navigate to /asp/deployableEJBs.

   e. Highlight **Account.jar**, and click the **Select** button.

   f. In the pop-up Confirmation dialog, click **Yes** to confirm addition of EJB to the container.

   g. Click the **Yes** button in the pop-up window that appears (see Figure 44). This should start the process of deploying EJB.

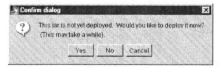

Figure 44. Confirmation dialog box for deploying an EJB

   h. After the process of deploying an EJB is over, you should see an Information dialog box (see Figure 45).

Figure 45. "EJB deployment completed" dialog box

    i. Go back to the window from where you started browsing for a JAR file (step d). Click the **Create** button.

       The new Information dialog window appears. It confirms that the EJB was added successfully.

    j. Repeat the process from step a to step i for Transfer.jar.

    k. Expand the **BankOneContainer** tree. You should see both EJBs as shown in Figure 46.

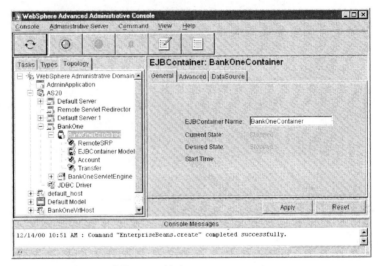

Figure 46. Verifying that EJBs were added

17. The last step before you can test your application is to add two servlets: CreateAccount and TransferFunds.

    a. Go to the Administrative Console, and select the **Tasks** tab.

    b. Expand the **Configuration** tree, and click **Add a servlet**.

    c. Click the **Start Task** button.

    d. Select **No** on this panel, and click **Next**.

    e. Expand the Nodes tree up to the Web application, and select **BankOneWebApp** (see Figure 47 on page 112).

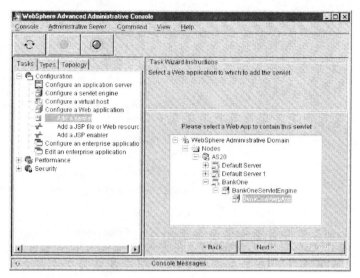

Figure 47. Adding a servlet to the Web application

   f. Click **Next**.

   g. Select **Create User-Defined Servlet** on this panel, and click **Next**.

   h. On this panel, provide information about the servlet you want to add. We
      provide information for the following parameters (see Figure 48):

- **Servlet Name**: CreateAccount

- **Web Application**: BankOneWebApp (should be the default)

- **Servlet Class Name**: com.ibm.ejs.doc.client.CreateAccount

- **Servlet Web Path List**: Click the **Add** button. In the pop-up window,
  type /banking/CreateAccount and click **OK**.

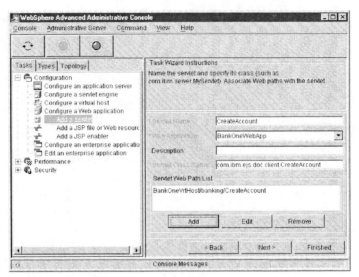

Figure 48. Specifying the servlet parameters

   i. Click **Next**.

   j. Click **Finished**.

   k. Repeat this task from step a to step j for the TransferFunds servlet. Use the same package name for Servlet Class Name, which is com.ibm.ejs.doc.client.

18. The resulting tree in the topology view should appear as shown in Figure 49 on page 114. Note that it shows two EJBs (Account and Transfer) under BankOneContainer, two servlets (CreateAccount and TransferFunds) under BankOneWebApp, and server Web paths under BankOneVrtHost.

Figure 49. Resulting topology tree

19. It is time to test your application! Select the application server **BankOne** in the topology view of the Administrative Console.

20. Click the **Start** button (with the green circle). It can take up to a minute for the application server to be started.

21. Open a Web browser, and point to `http://BankOne/banking/create.html`. You should see the window shown in Figure 50.

Figure 50. Create a new Account form

22. Enter the account number, choose the account type, enter a starting balance, and click the **Create** button (see Figure 51).

Figure 51. The account was successfully created

23. Create a few more accounts.

24. Point your Web browser to: `http://BankOne/banking/transfer.html`

25. In the new form, provide information for two accounts and enter the amount of money to transfer. Click the **Transfer** button.

The result of this operation will be similar to what is shown in Figure 52 on page 116.

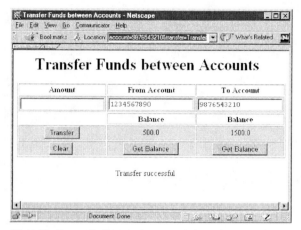

Figure 52. The result of transferring money between two accounts

26. The information about all accounts is persisted to the database by the EJB container.

3.11 Security and WAS Advanced Edition for AS/400

WebSphere Application Server's (WAS) unified security model enables the same security policies and task to apply to both Web resources, such as HTML, JavaServer Pages, and servlets, as well as Enterprise JavaBeans. Before delving into WAS specifics, let's examine the building blocks that form the product's security foundation as illustrated in Figure 53.

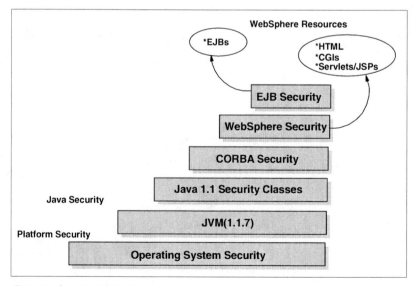

Figure 53. Security building blocks

Each of the blocks shown in Figure 53 is explained in the following list:

- **Operating system security**: The security infrastructure of the underlying operating system provides certain security services to the WebSphere Security Application. The WebSphere administrator can configure the product to obtain authentication information directly from the Local Operating System user registry – an iSeries server's user profile entry.

- **JVM 1.1.7**: The JVM security model provides a layer of security above the operating system layer.

  Note: For WAS 3.02, this could also be JVM 1.1.8. For WAS 3.5, it is JVM 1.2.2.

- **CORBA Security**: Any calls made among secure ORBs are invoked over a Secure Association Service (SAS) layer that sets up the security context and the necessary quality of protection.

- **WebSphere Security**: WebSphere security enforces security policies and services in a unified manner on access to Web resources and enterprise beans.

- **EJB Security**: The EJB server runs a security service. The security service handles authentication and authorization for the principals that need to access resources in an EJB server environment.

3.12 Security model

In general, the WebSphere security model consists of granting permissions to *principals* (a representation of a human user or a system entity such as a server process). This allows the principals to access resources within WebSphere Application Server (WAS). There are some important considerations about the WAS security model:

- Global security settings are specified at the WAS level and apply to all application servers running within this instance of the administration server (see 3.8, "Multiple instances of the WebSphere Administration Server" on page 97). You cannot specify a different security setting for an application server.

- By default, when the security is enabled, no EJBs access is permitted until you explicitly grant permissions to the principals.

- By default, when the security is enabled, all Web resources (HTML and JSP files, servlets) are accessible by everyone until you explicitly secure your Web resources.

The WAS security system provides the support to define permissions and assign these permissions to the principals. During runtime, the WAS security system is responsible for:

- Authenticating the principals
- Checking the principal's authorization to the WAS resources
- Delegating requests to run under another principal's identity

3.12.1 Authentication

Authentication is the process of providing the necessary proof that the principals are who they claim to be. WAS challenges the principal for authentication information.

3.12.1.1 Challenge types

The four different challenge types are:

- **None**: Specifies that clients will not be challenged for authentication information. If you have protected a resource within an application, selecting *None* will deny users access to that resource.

- **Basic**: Specifies that clients will be prompted for a user ID and password, usually acquired through a basic HTTP 401 challenge.

- **Certificate**: Specifies that clients must provide a digital certificate for authentication. If you additionally select the "Default to Basic" option, clients without certificates will be permitted to use the basic authentication scheme.

- **Custom**: Specifies that clients will log in using servlet-generated Web pages that you specify.

3.12.1.2 Challenge option

The Secure Sockets Layer (SSL) option specifies that an SSL connection is required between the client and Web server. That is, requests that do not arrive over SSL will be refused. This check box applies to the Basic, Certificate, and Custom challenge types.

3.12.1.3 Authentication information

Authentication information can consist of:

- User ID/password combination
- Certificate
- Lightweight Third Party Authentication (LTPA) token

WAS compares the authentication information received from the challenge against a user registry. A user registry is simply a list of principals (users) and distinguishing information (including a password). There are two mechanisms for managing a user registry:

- **Local Operating System**: The user ID and password are verified against the iSeries server's User Profile entry. This option, which is another example of WebSphere's security foundation as illustrated in Figure 53 on page 116, is the simplest to set up. However, it is somewhat restrictive if you plan to access more than one iSeries server.

- **Lightweight Third Party Authentication (LTPA)**: LTPA uses Lightweight Directory Access Protocol (LDAP). The LDAP directory service follows the client/server model. One or more LDAP servers contain the directory data. The LDAP client sends a request to an LDAP server. The server responds with a reply, or with a pointer, to another LDAP server. LDAP is a more flexible alternative to the Local Operating System register. However, its flexibility comes at the price of its setup and administer effort (see 3.12.4, "Configuring LTPA for use by WebSphere" on page 125).

3.12.1.4 Authentication model summary

Table 10 summarizes the different options available within the authentication model. Following a successful login, a set of credentials are generated to prove the principal's identity for the duration of the session.

Table 10. Authentication model summary

Challenge type	Authentication mechanism	User registry	Client support
Basic	LTPA	LDAP	Web, Java
	Native OS	Native OS	Web, Java
Certificate	LTPA	LDAP	Web

Figure 54 demonstrates an LTPA authentication sequence of events.

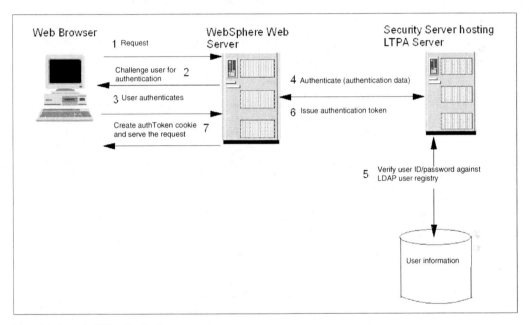

Figure 54. Example LTPA authentication sequence

The process flow shown in Figure 54 is explained here:

1. A user submits a request to the Web server for a resource. If the resource is protected, the Web server determines the authentication mechanism to use. The HTTP server generates a 401 response to the browser.

2. The Web server challenges the user for authentication information based on the specified challenge mechanism (user ID and password, or certificate).

3. The user responds by providing the authentication information.

4. The Web server contacts the security application (which wraps the LTPA server) and provides the authentication information.

5. The LTPA server uses the LDAP user registry to authenticate the user.

6. If the user's authentication data is authentic, the LTPA server issues an LTPA token to the client.

7. On successful authentication, the Web server receives the token issued to the user. The Web server then serves the requested resource to the authenticated user. The Web server also stores the token on the user's browser as an HTTP cookie.

3.12.1.5 HTTP Single Sign-On (SSO)

HTTP Single Sign-On extends LTPA capabilities by preserving the user's authentication across, not just multiple HTTP requests, but across multiple HTTP servers.

For example, if the domain is specified to be mycompany.com, then SSO will be effective with any Web server that serves the mycompany.com domain such as a.mycompany.com and b.mycompany.com. The Web server that processes the first request from the user created an SSO cookie. The cookie name is based on the SSO shared name. For example, if the shared name is MyCompaniesSSO, then a SSO cookie by name MyCompaniesSSOToken is created. The cookie contains an encrypted form of the user ID and password entered by the user for authentication. The contents can only be decrypted using the shared key with which the contents were encrypted.

When a user at an HTTP client (Web browser) that supports HTTP cookies requests a resource, the Web server creates the user's token credentials (LTPA token and SSO token) in the form of HTTP cookies. The domain part of the cookie is the network domain in which the cookie must be valid. For example, if the domain value is set to mycompany.com in the WebSphere configuration, the browser will present the cookie to any Web server residing in that domain. When a Web server in the domain performs authentication, it looks for the LTPA and SSO cookies. If the LTPA cookie is found, then the Web server extracts the LTPA token from the cookie and validates it. If the LTPA token is not found, but an SSO cookie is found, the Web server extracts the SSO token from the cookie. Then it extracts the user ID and password from the SSO token and performs authentication.

The WAS administrator can specify an expiration time for the LTPA token. By default, it is set to 30 minutes. After this period of time, the user might be required to re-authenticate. To ensure cookies are not persistent, the expiration time for the cookie is set to the browser's lifetime.

The secure field of the cookie is turned on if SSO is configured so that it is enabled only over secure sessions. This ensures that the cookie will flow only over SSL connections.

3.12.1.6 Programmatic login

Developers who do not want to either prompt the user with a 401 dialog window (in the case of a HTTP client Web browser) or a dialog box (in the case of a pure Java client) can log on programmatically based on a user ID and password retrieved through other means categorized as:

- Client side login
- Server side login

Client side login

The client side login pattern should be followed by pure Java clients that need to programmatically provide authentication data (logging in the user) and do not require authentication on the client side. The client programmatically sets up the authentication data (user ID and password) in the underlying security context (the "SecurityCurrent" in CORBA). The server processes a method request by pulling the authentication data out of the context and performing authentication.

A client side login example, the LoginHelper class, is shipped with WebSphere Application Server Version 3.02.

Server side login

The server side login pattern should be followed when a programmatic login is required to set up the security context and to perform the actual authentication. As with the client side login, CORBA security APIs provide the framework for programmatically providing authentication data, but in this case the framework is extended to force authentication to occur when required. The ServerSideAuthenticator helper class is available with WebSphere 3.02 and can be used to perform authentication on the server side.

3.12.2 Authorization

Authentication of a principal does not mean that principal is authorized to access specified object. Authorization is the step in which an authenticated principal is checked to see if appropriate authority exists to fulfill the request.

The WebSphere Application Server 3.0 Authorization model is based on the classic capability model, which is also adopted by the Java security manager (refer to Figure 53 on page 116). WebSphere Application Server 2.0 uses the access control model, which associates the principals and the operations they can perform with the resources. The capability model differs in the sense that it associates permissions required to perform operations on the resources with the principal.

The capability model is a cross-product of the following components:

- Resources
- Method Groups
- Permissions

3.12.2.1 Resources

What are the resources which, in WAS context, we call WebSphere resources? It can be any item or their combination from this list:

- Enterprise beans
- Web resources:
  - Servlets
  - JavaServer Pages (JSP files)
  - HTML files
  - Any WebSphere resource that is specified by a URL
- Web applications

To setup a security for WebSphere resources, you need to create an enterprise application. This application is a placeholder for all WebSphere resources that you want to protect. With the enterprise application configured, you can protect the collection of WebSphere resources as a whole. Adding a resource to the Enterprise Application is the only way to protect this resource.

> **Note**
>
> A Web application is not the same as an enterprise application. A Web application is a collection of servlets, JSPs, and HTML files managed as a group. To protect a Web application as a unit, it must be added as a resource to the enterprise application.

Web resource

A Web resource is a configuration that consists of:

- The path (Web path or Universal Resource Identifier (URI)), which users requesting a resource, such as a Web page, servlet, or JSP, entered in a Web browser.
- The virtual host by which the resource is hosted.

Web application

Servlets and other files can belong to a Web application. A Web application is comprised of one or more related servlets, JavaServer Pages (JSP) files, and Web pages that can be managed as a unit. The servlets and JSP files in a Web application share a servlet context, meaning they can share data and information about the execution environment. Web applications can also be started or stopped on an individual basis. Consider this example:

```
http://www.mycorp.com/WebSphereSamples/Account/CreateAccount
```

In the above example, *www.mycorp.com* represents the virtual host, */WebSphereSamples/Account/* represents the Web path, and *CreateAccount* represents the Web application name. Keep in mind that these values are simply aliases mapped to physical resources such as file locations and classpaths. We go into further detail in 3.14, "Implementing the ASP security model" on page 135.

3.12.2.2 Method groups

The security application bases authorization decisions on groups of methods in addition to enterprise applications. These methods are grouped by default based on their name or function. Even though default method groups are provided, there are no default associations of a resource's methods to method groups. Therefore, associating a resource's methods to method groups is a required step for protecting a resource.

WAS defines six default method groups:

- **ReadMethods**: For enterprise beans, any method that starts with "get" falls into this group when the default method groups are used. For example, getName(), getBalance(), and getType() would belong to this default method group. For Web resources, the HTTP_GET and HTTP_POST methods of the Web resource fall into this group when the default method groups are used.
- **WriteMethods**: For enterprise beans, any method that starts with "set" falls into this group when the default method groups are used. For example, setName(), setBalance(), and setType() would belong to this default method

group. For Web resources, the HTTP_PUT method of the Web resource falls into this group when the default method groups are used.

- **RemoveMethods**: For enterprise beans, the ejbRemove method falls into this group when the default method groups are used. For Web resources, the HTTP_DELETE method of the Web resource falls into this group when the default method groups are used.

- **CreateMethods**: For enterprise beans, the ejbCreate methods fall into this group when the default method groups are used. There are no corresponding Web resource methods that fall into this default method group.

- **FinderMethods**: For enterprise beans, the methods that start from "findBy" fall into this group when the default method groups are used. For example, findByPrimaryKey() and findByLastName() would belong to this default method group. There are no corresponding Web resource methods that fall into this default method group.

- **ExecuteMethods**: Any method that does not fall into one of the default method groups listed above, falls into this group when the default method groups are used. For example, retrieveUserPreferences(), updateNewUserFile(), and discardPendingChanges() would belong to this default method group. There are no corresponding Web resource methods that fall into this default method group.

With method groups, you can create your own method group and manually assign which methods in your application should belong to this group. As a result, you can assign different permissions to the methods in your method group.

You can see an example of working with method groups in 3.14, "Implementing the ASP security model" on page 135.

3.12.2.3 Permissions
Permissions, or capabilities, are granted to a user in the user registry. The permissions are given to a combination of enterprise applications and a method group.

As an example, consider a bank application that deals with customer accounts. Table 11 shows a sample registry for users who can access accounts.

Table 11. Sample user registry

User ID	Group ID
Sara	Manager
Anna	Teller
Steven	Internet User

All protected resources are grouped in the enterprise application named AccountEntApp. Using this enterprise application and the default method groups, you can assign permissions to the users from the registry. Table 12 shows these permissions.

Table 12. Account enterprise application method group permissions matrix

Permissions	Principals		
	Sara	Anna	Steven
AccountEntApp - CreateMethods	X	X	
AccountEntApp - RemoveMethods	X	X	
AccountEntApp - ReadMethods	X	X	X
AccountEntApp - WriteMethods	X	X	X
AccountEntApp - FinderMethods	X	X	X
AccountEntApp - ExecuteMethods	X		

From the scenario shown in Table 11 and Table 12, you can deduce that Sara is capable of performing all operations on the enterprise application. As a manager, she can look up, add, change, delete, and perform any other operations on an account. Anna, on the other hand, is capable of performing a lookup, add, change, and delete. And finally, Steven is only allowed to look up and change an account.

Please note that WebSphere does not provide any mechanism to limit permissions to a specific data. This would have to be performed at the application level. Therefore, in the above scenario, Steven would be capable of looking up and changing the data within any account record in the database.

3.12.3 Delegation and run-as

After an EJB client is authenticated, it can attempt to invoke methods on the enterprise beans. A method is successfully invoked if the principal associated with the method invocation has the required permissions to invoke the method. These permissions can be set by an application (an administrator-defined set of Web and object resources) and by a method group (an administrator-defined set of Java interface-method pairs).

In a case when one bean needs to invoke a method in another bean, WAS uses a process called *delegation*. This process goes along with the WAS security model, where WAS checks principal's authority to a WebSphere resource. To implement delegation, WAS uses a parameter called *run-as*. This parameter defines under which authority the downstream call will be made. For example, if methodA() in EJB_1 invokes methodB() in EJB_2, you, as the WAS administrator, can define that methodB() should be invoked with the same authority as methodA(). This run-as mode is called *client*.

There are three run-as modes available:

- **CLIENT**: The client run-as mode specifies that the user that is associated with the current method should be used to make the next method call. If "User A" is associated with this current method call, "User A" is associated with the next method call.

- **SYSTEM**: The system identity is used on downstream method calls. The system identity is specified on the User Registry page of the Security Specify Global Settings task.

- **SPECIFIED**: The specified user allows any identity known to the WebSphere domain to be used for downstream calls.

Note: When the user registry is specified as Local Operating System, the CLIENT and SPECIFIED run-as modes are ignored. All calls between WebSphere server instances have an effective run-as mode of SYSTEM.

3.12.4 Configuring LTPA for use by WebSphere

By default, when the security is enabled, WAS uses Local Operating System as its user registry. To use the Lightweight Third Party Authentication (LTPA) registry, the principal's information has to be added to the Lightweight Directory Access Protocol (LDAP) directory and the WAS configuration must be changed. The following sections explain how to configure the LDAP directory and use it for the WAS authentication.

3.12.4.1 Configuring an LDAP directory

This is a three-step task:

1. Configure the directory server on the iSeries server.

2. Create an LDAP Data Interchange Format (LDIF) file with the information about all principals to be added to the directory.

3. Import an LDIF file into the LDAP directory.

Configuring the directory server on the iSeries server
Follow these steps:

1. Start Operations Navigator.

2. Expand **Network** and **Servers**.

3. Click **TCP/IP**.

4. Right-click **Directory** in the left pane of the Operations Navigator.

5. Select **Configure** from the pop-up menu.

6. Follow the instructions on the wizard.

7. In the last wizard screen, click **Finish**.

The last screen should look like the example in Figure 55 on page 126. You can use the default value for Administrator DN (Distinguish Name) and specify DN for the root directory controlled by this directory server (in our example, the server controls the directory registry for the United States).

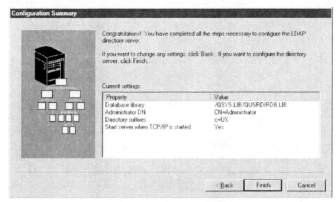

Figure 55. Configuring the directory server

By default, the only principal who can make changes to the directory is the administrator. All other principals have the authority to perform read, search, and compare operations. You can configure authority for any subdirectory in the registry and allow access for only specified principals or groups. However, it undermines the idea of LTPA. For more information about configuring directory server, see the *iSeries Information Center* at `http://www.as400.ibm.com/infocenter` (search for LDAP).

Creating the LDIF file

Now you are ready to create LDIF file. You can use iSeries EDTF utility or a text editor on your workstation to create the file and then save it in the iSeries Integrated File System (IFS).

If LTPA is run on the iSeries, each user entry in the directory must correspond to the ePerson schema definition. A simple entry in the LDIF file would look like the following example:

```
dn: cn=John Doe, ou=Rochester, o=IBM, c=US
objectclass: person
objectclass: inetOrgPerson
objectclass: top
objectclass: organizationalPerson
objectclass: ePerson
cn: John Doe
sn: Doe
uid: jdoe
userpassword: secretpass
```

This entry sets information for user John Doe with user ID (`uid`) `jdoe` and password `secretpass`. This person resides in the Rochester organizational unit (`ou=Rochester`), in the IBM organization (`o=IBM`) in the United States (`c=US`). All information related to the organizational unit, organization, and country has to be defined prior to using it for other entries in the LDIF file. As an example, we define the country:

```
dn: c=US
objectclass: top
objectclass: country
```

```
c: US
description: United States
```

With this country definition as the first entry in our example, we can define organization (IBM) as our second entry, organizational unit (Rochester) as our third entry, and so on.

Importing the LDIF file

When the LDIF file is ready, you need to import it to the LDAP directory. For this task, you can use Operations Navigator or the `ldapadd` command in QSH. Each of these two methods require the LDIF file to reside in IFS on the iSeries server.

To use Operations Navigator, select **Network->Servers->TCP/IP**, and right-click **Directory**. Select **Tools->Import File** as shown in Figure 56.

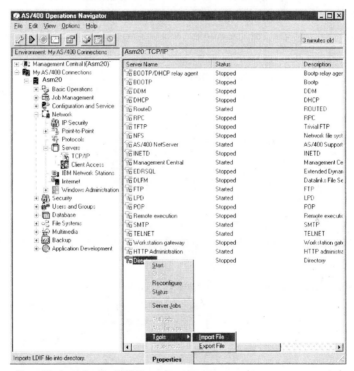

Figure 56. Importing the LDIF file

Find the LDIF file you want to import, and click **OK**.

To verify you settings before you configure WebSphere, follow these steps:

1. Start the directory server from Operations Navigator.

2. Go to the 5250 session window and start Qshell with the `STRQSH` command.

3. Run the command:

   ```
   ldapsearch -b 'c=US' -D CN=Administrator -w admin 'uid=jdoe'
   ```

   In this command statement, note the following explanation:

-b The DN for the root directory to search

-D Bind DN (you need to use this option only when the directory is protected and requires the DN and password of the principal with enough authority to perform this operation)

-w Password for the principal specified with option -D

The last parameter provides a search criteria (in our example, an entry with user ID jdoe).

All options and password are case sensitive. Any strings that you enter between single quotes are case insensitive.

If your LDAP is not protected (this means any user can perform read, search, and compare operations), you can omit options -D and -w.

If there is a need to add new users to the LDAP directory, you have to create a new LDIF file with the information about new users and import it to the existing directory.

3.12.4.2 Configuring WebSphere

At this point, you have a working LDAP registry and are ready to configure WebSphere to use LTPA.

The following steps explain the process for setting up security using LTPA:

1. In the WAS Administrative Console, select **Tasks**->**Security**->**Specify Global Settings**.

2. Click the **Start Task** button (with the green circle).

3. Select the **Enable Security** check box. You can modify the Security Cache Timeout value, but remember that WAS clears the security cache as soon as the timeout value is reached. Choosing a small value results in extra processing overhead and might be unacceptable. Choosing a big number creates a security risk because security information stays in the cache for a long time.

4. Click the **Application Defaults** tab.

5. Set Realm Name to the domain portion of the iSeries running LDAP. For example, if your iSeries Internet domain name is as20.itsoroch.ibm.com, then you would use itsoroch.ibm.com for this field.

6. Select **Basic** for the Challenge Type.

7. Click the **Authentication Mechanism** tab, and select the **Lightweight Third Party Authentication (LTPA)** radio button.

8. Click the **Generate Keys** button, and enter a password to be used to create the keys.

9. Click the **User Registry** tab and fill in the fields (see Figure 57):

   • **Security Server ID**: Specify a principal's LDAP user ID. This name, along with the Security Server Password field, have to be in the LDAP directory. If you enter invalid information, the Administrative Console will not start.

   • **Security Server Password**: Specify a principal's password as it exists in the LDAP directory.

- **Directory Type**: Select **SecureWay** from the pull-down menu. If your LDAP directory is not on the iSeries, you may need to select a different value.

- **Host**: Enter a fully-qualified TCP/IP host name on which the LDAP directory service is running, for example: as20.itsoroch.ibm.com.

- **Port**: The port number on which the LDAP directory is running. If you chose a default, non-SSL (Secure Sockets Layer) value while configuring the directory server on the iSeries, you can leave this field blank. WAS uses default port 389.

- **Base Distinguished Name**: Enter the DN for the root directory in which searches begin. In our example, we set this field to c=US (the United States directory). This is a required field for the iSeries.

- **Bind Distinguished Name**: Enter the DN of the principal who is allowed to perform searches on the directory. In many cases, this is the administrator of the directory, for example, CN=Administrator. This is a required field for the iSeries server.

- **Bind Password**: Enter the valid password for the principal specified in the Bind Distinguished Name field.

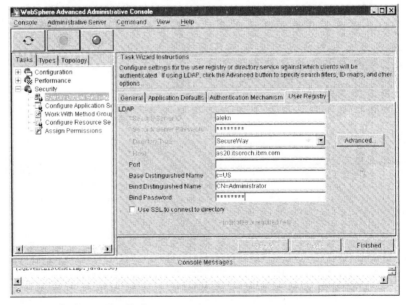

Figure 57. Configuring User Registry

10. Click the **Finish** button.

11. Click the **Topology** tab.

12. Right-click your node, and select **Restart** from the pop-up menu.

13. Choose **Yes** when prompted to close the Administrative Console.

14. Restart the Administrative Console.

3.12.5 Security model review

Now that you have all the components of your security model in place, let's look at a complete picture of WAS security.

To enforce security rules, WAS runs a security application. It is started by WAS when you enable security. The security application runs in a special application server instance called the *security server*.

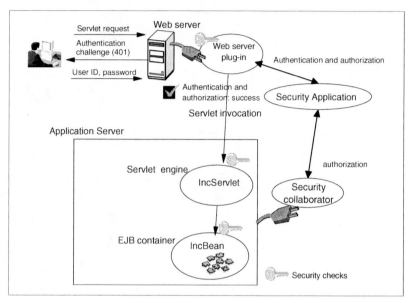

Figure 58. Web browser security scenario

The security application consists of two core components:

- **Security plug-in**: Is attached to a Web server. The plug-in helps make security decisions when users request Web resources (such as, HTML files, servlets) from Web clients (over HTTP).

- **Security collaborator**: Is attached to every application server. The collaborator makes security decisions on method calls on resources hosted by the application server.

Now let's turn our attention to the example shown in Figure 58.

When a user invokes the IncServlet by entering its URL in a Web browser, the target Web server receives the request. It determines that the URI representing the resource is a protected URI serviced by WAS. The Web server issues a 401 challenge back to the browser requiring the user to enter a user ID and password to access the servlet. The Web server plug-in performs authentication by delegating the task to the security application using the authentication data (user ID and password) received from the user. On successful authentication, the plug-in consults the security application to determine whether the user has the permissions that are necessary to access the URI. If authorization succeeds, the plug-in sets up a security context with the user's credential information and passes on the request to the servlet engine to service the request.

The servlet engine resides within an application server (for example, the default server). Servlets are viewed as object resources residing within an application server containing a servlet engine. Before invoking a method on the servlet, the security collaborator performs security checks. As a part of its security check, it extracts the user's credential information from the security context and verifies that the user has the authority to invoke the method on the servlet.

With this configuration, the IncServlet invokes a method on the IncBean. A method call from a servlet to an enterprise bean or another servlet is intercepted by the underlying security mechanism for authorization approval. Upon invoking the increment() method on the IncBean, the security collaborator is asked to perform security checks based on the security context set up by the servlet engine. If the user is authorized to invoke the method on the IncBean, the servlet runs successfully and sends the result to the user's browser.

The Java client scenario is illustrated in Figure 59.

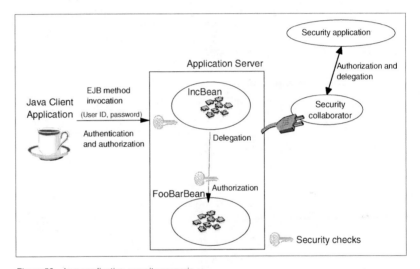

Figure 59. Java application security scenario

Only Java client applications (a servlet is a Java client too!) can invoke enterprise beans directly. A Java client that is configured to handle protected targets will prompt for a user ID and password when a request is made to invoke a protected method on a bean. Upon entering the user ID and password, the method invocation request is passed to the application server. The security collaborator authenticates the user ID and password against the user registry. On successful authentication, the security collaborator will consult the security application to make authorization decisions based on the permissions to the method. If the user is authorized to invoke a method, the security collaborator will consult the delegation policies and set up the appropriate security context.

For example, if the delegation policy is configured to use client identity, then the user's credentials are set up in the security context, and the method is invoked. If this invocation makes a downstream method call to another (hypothetical) bean, NextIncBean, that method call will be accessed under the user's identity (CLIENT run-as mode).

When the second method request is made on the NextIncBean, the security runtime will perform the security check based on the user's credential set in the security context. If this authorization check succeeds, the method call is executed as per the delegation policy.

3.13 Security tasks

You can perform the following security tasks in WAS:

- Specify Global Settings
- Configure Application Security
- Configure Resource Security
- Assign Permissions

3.13.1 Specify Global Settings

We already described the process of setting up the global security properties, and used LTPA as the authentication mechanism. If you want to use iSeries user profile information for authentication, you need to select **Local Operating System**. The rest of the process is the same (see 3.12.4, "Configuring LTPA for use by WebSphere" on page 125).

3.13.2 Configure Application Security

Besides setting up the global security, you need to secure all WebSphere resource (see 3.12.2.1, "Resources" on page 121).

1. As an example, you create an enterprise application using the resources in the default server.

   a. In the Administrative Console, click the **Tasks** tab.

   b. Expand **Configuration**.

   c. Select **Configure an enterprise application**.

   d. Start the task.

   e. Enter the name for the enterprise application (DefaultEnterpriseApp in our example).

   f. Add Hello EJB and two Web applications (default_app and examples) as the resources to the enterprise application.

   The last panel should like the example in Figure 60.

   g. Click **Finish**.

2. Setup a security for the resource associated with DefaultEnterpriseApp.

   a. Expand **Security**, and select **Configure Application Security**.

   b. Start the task.

   c. In the first panel, select **DefaultEnterpriseApp**.

   d. Click **Next**.

   e. Click the **Change** button to specify the user ID under which the application will run. The ID is used for delegation of the application's resources. Enter selection criteria for the used ID to look up. You may notice that, in this example, we search user profiles on the iSeries server. Global Settings affects what registry to search: Local Operating System or LTPA.

> **Note**
>
> If you click Finish on this panel, without modifying any parameter, the enterprise application security settings will default to the Global Security settings.

f. Enter a valid password for the user ID specified in the previous step.

g. Enter a realm name. Specify the security realm to which the application should belong. When a user at a Web client tries to access resources in a realm, this user is prompted to log into the realm. If the user tries to access a resource in a different realm, they are prompted to log into that realm. This applies even if Single Sign On (SSO) is used.

h. Leave Challenge Type as **Basic (User ID and Password)**.

i. Click **Finished**.

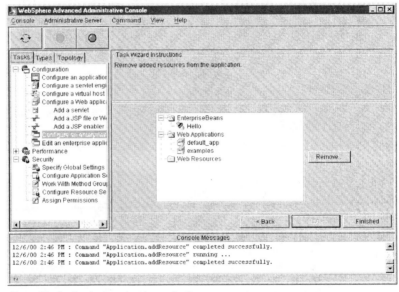

Figure 60. Configuring an enterprise application

3.13.3 Configure Resource Security

In the WebSphere security model, permissions are granted to a combination of the enterprise application and method groups. Method groups provide a way of grouping similar methods in a unit. This is a required step to set up a protection for WebSphere resources.

1. Select the **Tasks** tab.

2. Expand **Security**, and click **Configure Resource Security**.

3. Start the task.

4. Expand the **EnterpriseBeans** or **Virtual Host** tree to find the resource. We selected Hello bean.

5. Click **Next**.

6. If the resource is configured for the security for the first time, you should see a pop-up window as shown in Figure 61. If you select **Yes**, the default method groups will be assigned to each method in the bean. If you select **No**, during the next step, you will have to assign method groups to each method in the bean. In our example, we selected **Yes**.

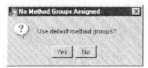

Figure 61. Method groups selection window

7. Select each resource's method, and click the **Add** button to add this method to the method group. If you want to remove a resource's method from the method group, select a method group name under the resource's method name and click the **Remove** button.

8. Click **Next**.

9. On the next screen, specify the delegation identity for the downstream calls. See 3.12.3, "Delegation and run-as" on page 124, for more information about the choices. We used default values for this example.

10. Click the **Finished** button.

11. Repeat this process for other resources in your enterprise application.

3.13.4 Assign Permissions

The last task you need to do to complete security enabling for WebSphere resources is to assign permissions. The permissions are given to an enterprise application/method group combination.

1. Select the **Tasks** tab.

2. Expand the **Security** tree.

3. Click **Assign Permissions**.

4. Assign permissions for each combination of application/method groups. Select the combinations, and click **Add** button.

5. On the next panel, select the principals that are eligible to access the method group in the specified enterprise application. Enter search criteria for either **Group** or **User**.

6. Click **Search**.

7. Select group/user from the list, and click **OK**.

8. Repeat this process for all enterprise application/method group combinations to which you want to assign permissions.

3.13.5 Summary of security tasks

In real life, a customer may want to set up different security parameters based on the part of the application being accessed. For example, consider a banking application. A customer is authorized to view the account details and to send instructions to the bank (send a payment, set up automatic payment, and so on).

A bank officer, on the other hand, is the one with authority to change the account details. You can use two different authentication mechanisms: LTPA for customers and Local Operating System for bank officers. As a result, you have to create and configure security for two enterprise applications: one with resources available for customers to use and another the bank to use.

In a case where you want to share the same authentication mechanism and user registry, you can still set up different security policies by changing the realm name and challenge type for each of the enterprise applications. Note that when a user at a Web client tries to access resources in a realm, they are prompted to log into the realm. If the user tries to access a resource in a different realm, they will be prompted to log into that realm. This applies even if Single Sign On (SSO) is used.

As you can see, WebSphere Application Server gives you the flexibility to achieve the security needs for your application.

3.14 Implementing the ASP security model

This section continues with the example that was started in 3.10, "Putting everything together" on page 103. In this section, we explain how to set up security for our sample application. To make it simpler, we use the Local Operating System authentication mechanism. If you would want to try LTPA, refer to 3.12.4, "Configuring LTPA for use by WebSphere" on page 125.

The sequence of steps to set up security in WAS is explained in 3.13, "Security tasks" on page 132. This section follows those steps for a sample application.

> **Important**
>
> Several files in your <root directory>/properties directory contain very sensitive information such as user IDs and passwords for WAS. To secure these files, you have to remove public access to all property files and directory, for example:
>
> ```
> CHGAUT OBJ('/asp/properties/bootstrap.properties') USER(*PUBLIC)
> DTAAUT(*EXCLUDE) OBJAUT(*NONE)
> ```
>
> However, the HTTP server has to access the <root directory>/properties directory and bootstrap.properties file in this directory. Therefore, you have to authorize the QTMHHTTP user to access the directory and file, for example:
>
> ```
> CHGAUT OBJ('/asp/properties') USER(QTMHHTTP) DTAAUT(*RX)
> CHGAUT OBJ('/asp/properties/bootstrap.properties') USER(QTMHHTTP)
> DTAAUT(*RX)
> ```

Enabling WAS security for Web resources
By default, the HTTP server is not configured to use WAS security for authorization service. To enable this feature, you need to change the bootstrap.properties file:

1. Open the /asp/properties/bootstrap.properties file.
2. Change `ose.security.enabled=false` to `ose.security.enabled=true`.
3. Save the file.

4. Restart the WAS administration server.

5. Restart the HTTP server.

If you have some Web resources that don't have to be secure, place them in a separate directory, and add a directive to the HTTP server configuration, for example:

```
Pass /images/* /nonsecure/images/*
```

With such a directive, the HTTP server doesn't have to use the authorization service to access non-secure resources.

Specifying Global Settings

Follow these steps to specify the Global Settings:

1. Click the **Tasks** tab in the Administrative Console.

2. Expand **Security**, and select **Specify Global Settings**.

3. Click the **Start Task** button (with the green circle).

4. Click the 'General tab, and select **Enable Security**.

5. Click the **Authentication Mechanism** tab.

6. Select **Local Operating System**.

7. Click the **User Registry** tab.

8. Provide data for Security Server ID and Security Server Password. This is the user ID and password you will use to log into the Administrative Console. This is also the user ID and password used for the SYSTEM run-as mode.

9. Click the **Finished** button.

Creating an enterprise application

Group all the resources you want to protect in an enterprise application. To do this, follow these steps:

1. Click the **Tasks** tab in the Administrative Console.

2. Expand **Configuration**, and select **Configure and enterprise application**.

3. Click the **Start Task** button (with the green circle).

4. Enter BankOneEnterpriseApp as the application name.

5. Click the **Next** button.

6. Expand the **EnterpriseBeans** and **Web Applications** trees. Select the **Account** EJB, and click the **Add** button. Repeat this operation for the Transfer EJB and BankOneWebApp Web application (see Figure 62).

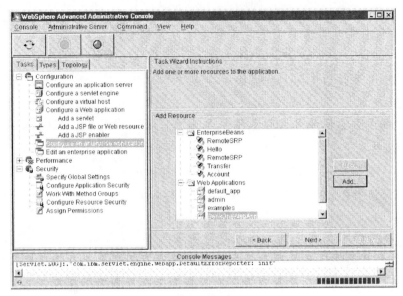

Figure 62. Adding resources to the enterprise application

7. Click **Next**. You can remove any resources on this panel.

8. Click **Finished**.

Configuring Application Security

With all the resources added to the enterprise application, you can configure security for all resources in the enterprise application.

1. Click the **Tasks** tab in the Administrative Console.

2. Expand the **Security** tree, and select **Configure Application Security**.

3. Click the **Start Task** button (with the green circle).

4. Expand the **Enterprise Applications** tree, and select **BankOneEnterpriseApp**.

5. Click **Next**.

6. Click the **Change** button.

7. In the pop-up window that appears, find a user ID you want to use for the delegation process for the resources in this application.

8. Click **OK**.

9. Type a password for the user specified in step 7.

10. Click **Finished**.

Configuring resource security

Follow these steps:

1. Click the **Tasks** tab in the Administrative Console.

2. Expand the **Security** tree, and select **Configure Resource Security**.

3. Click the **Start Task** button (with the green circle).

4. You should see a panel with two trees: EnterpriseBeans and Virtual Hosts. Expand the **EnterpriseBeans** tree, and select the **Account** bean as shown in Figure 63.

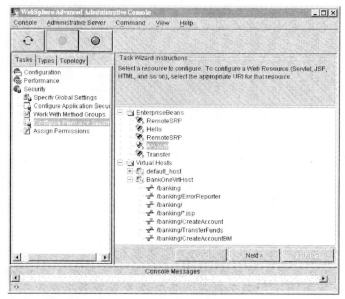

Figure 63. Configuring resource security: Available resources

5. Click the **Next** button.

6. Accept the default method groups by clicking **Yes** in the pop-up window that appears.

7. Click **Next**.

8. Accept the default value for Run-As Mode (it should be **SYSTEM**).

9. Click **Finished**.

10. Repeat these steps for Transfer EJB as well as for virtual paths: /banking/CreateAccount and /banking/TransferFunds. You don't have a Run-As Mode choice for virtual paths.

Assigning permissions

Follow these steps to assign permissions:

1. Click the **Tasks** tab in the Administrative Console.

2. Expand the **Security** tree, and select **Assign Permissions**.

3. Click the **Start Task** button.

4. Select an enterprise application/method group combination, and click the **Add** button.

5. In the Search pop-up window, click **Selection**, and specify a search criteria.

6. Select a user ID or user group, and click **OK** (see Figure 64).

Figure 64. Assigning permissions

7. You can assign permissions for multiple combinations at the same time. Press the Shift key, and click to highlight multiple combinations, and then click the **Add** button. Remember, all highlighted combinations will have the same set of permitted users.

Testing the application

You have completed the entire cycle of setting up WAS security. Now it's time to test it:

1. To be on a safe side, stop and start your HTTP and WAS administration servers.

2. Start the Administrative Console. With security enabled, you are prompted to enter a user ID and password as shown in Figure 65 on page 140. Type the user ID and password that were specified while configuring the security Global Setting.

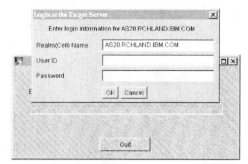

Figure 65. WAS login prompt

3. Click the **Topology** tab, and select **BankOne** as the application server.

4. Click the **Start** button.

5. Start your Web browser, and point it to `http://BankOne/banking/create.html`

6. Enter an account number and starting balance, and select the account type.

7. Click the **Create** button.

   You should see a login pop-up window as shown in Figure 66.

Figure 66. WAS requesting authentication information

8. Enter the user ID and password for a user that was authorized to access the CreateAccount servlet while configuring permissions. If you enter a user ID and password for a user with *SECOFR authority, WAS will not let you to access the servlet.

3.15 Accounting

WAS does not, nor does OS/400, give you a myriad of accounting and usage information for your direct billing efforts. But, is this necessary? On a practical level, many of the early ASPs are charging users on a less granular level. Some examples of this are:

- A flat monthly fee per user.
- The number of transactions per month.
- An ASP might charge a bank using its membership services a fee based on the number of accounts, for example: 0 through 500, *x* U.S. dollars (USD) per account, and 501 through 1000, *y* USD per account, independent of the actual usage.

The following sections highlight some of the options you have in WAS for keeping track of each account.

3.15.1 CPU usage

To enable the accounting features of the iSeries as described in 2.3, "Accounting and billing" on page 26, you have to separate the applications of each of your ASP customers by running them in a different application server. They can still share the same administration server instance. Accounting by using a different user profile (instead of the default QEJBSVR) to run the application server is not possible because the user profile is only used at a thread level, not at the job level which is used in accounting.

You can see all the jobs that WebSphere is using by entering the command:

```
WRKACTJOB SBS(QEJBSBS)
```

Figure 67 shows an example of how the screen will appear after you run WRKACTJOB command.

```
   .                      Work with Active Jobs                    AS26
                                                        04/12/00  14:02:47
 CPU %:     .0     Elapsed time:   00:00:00    Active jobs:   268

 Type options, press Enter.
   2=Change   3=Hold   4=End   5=Work with   6=Release   7=Display message
   8=Work with spooled files   13=Disconnect ...

 Opt   Subsystem/Job  User      Type  CPU %  Function        Status
       QEJBSBS        QSYS      SBS    .0                     DEQW
         JANADMIN     QEJB      BCI    .0                     JVAW
         JANMNTR      QEJB      BCH    .0   PGM-QEJBMNTR      EVTW
         JANSVR1      QEJB      BCI    .0                     JVAW
         JANSVR2      QEJB      BCI    .0                     JVAW
         JANSVR3      QEJB      BCI    .0                     JVAW
         QEJBADMIN    QEJB      BCI    .0                     JVAW
         QEJBMNTR     QEJB      ASJ    .0   PGM-QEJBMNTR      EVTW
         DEFAULT_SE   QEJB      BCI    .0                     JVAW

 Parameters or command
 ===>
 F3=Exit   F5=Refresh       F7=Find      F10=Restart statistics
 F11=Display elapsed data   F12=Cancel   F23=More options   F24=More keys
```

Figure 67. List of active jobs in the QEJBSBS subsystem

Each WebSphere instance has the following iSeries jobs associated with it:

- **Monitor job**: This job has the name used in the JOB() parameter of the SBMJOB command that we used to start the server (see page 99). We used JANMNTR in the example in this book. The default server uses QEJBMNTR.

- **Administration server job**: Uses the name of the mntr.admin.name property from the admin.properties file. In our example, its name is JANADMIN. The default name is QEJBADMIN.

- **Server job**: Has a default name DEFAULT_SE and actually uses the name of the application server truncated to 10 characters. You can have multiple jobs per node. We have been using JANSVR1, JANSVR2, and JANSVR3 in our examples.

For each of these jobs, the amount of CPU that is used can be tracked using the iSeries accounting features as described in 2.3.2, "iSeries accounting and billing in an ASP environment" on page 27. Unfortunately, there is no way to track the number of HTML, JSP, or servlet pages shown, unless you add logic for this to your own program.

3.15.2 Database transactions

The database transaction types that can be tracked at file level are: insert, modify, and delete. You can use the journal entries for these transactions as a starting point for accounting.

If you need more details like the number of database reads, you need to start the performance monitor using the Operations Navigator interface. This will collect more information such as the SQL statement, CPU usage, user profile, and so on.

If you only need to count the number of database transactions (reads), you should consider adding this to your application.

3.15.3 Disk space used

Accounting for disk space used by the application can be done fairly easily as long as you can differentiate the tables by name or place them in a different iSeries library (collection). Refer to 2.3.2.7, "Disk space accounting" on page 30.

3.16 Customizing WebSphere Application Server

WAS provides a great deal of flexibility when it comes to customizing its environment. This section discusses several features that you can use to facilitate the deployment of the application:

- XML Configuration Management tool (XMLConfig)
- Model/clone
- Different levels of JSP support

3.16.1 XML Configuration Management tool

XML Configuration Management allows you to export and import WAS configurations in XML format. A configuration "snapshot" from one system can be moved and imported to another system (with some modifications). Therefore, in a matter of minutes, you can create a duplicate WAS environment. In the ASP environment, you can create a duplicate WAS configuration from the existing one and then make it available for a new customer.

It is possible to perform a full or partial export. For example, you can do a full export for node AS20 as shown in Figure 68. Make sure the administration server is running, and then run the following command (all one line):

```
/QIBM/ProdData/WebASAdv/bin/XMLConfig -adminNodeName AS20 -export
/asp/xml/export.xml
```

Here, the options are:

- **-adminNodeName**: Provides a node name from the WAS topology to export
- **-export**: Specifies the file name to store the configuration

To import this configuration into another system, you need to modify the XML export file. If the new system is an iSeries and you want to create identical configuration, change the following parameters:

- Node name
- Aliases for the virtual hosts
- Class paths

There may be other parameters that you need to change. See the online documentation that comes with WAS, and search for XMLConfig.

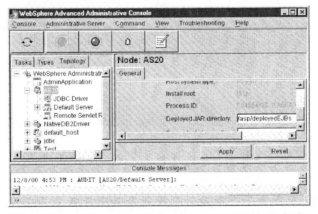

Figure 68. Specifying the node name as a line argument for the XMLConfig tool

After the XML file has been updated, you can import it into another system. Make sure the administration server is running. Use the following command (all one line):

```
/QIBM/ProdData/WebASAdv/bin/XMLConfig -adminNodeName AS20Duplicate -import
/asp/xml/export.xml
```

You can run this tool remotely. For example, let's execute the export command (all one line) from a Windows NT workstation (WAS has to be installed on the workstation):

```
C:\WebSphere\AppServer\bin\XMLconfig -adminNodeName AS20 -export
C:\asp\xml\export.xml -nameServiceHost as20.itsoroch.ibm.com -nameServicePort
1910
```

Here, the options are:

- **-nameServiceHost**: The fully-qualified domain name of the remote system
- **-nameServicePort**: The port number on which the administration server is listening

To export only part of your configuration, you need to create an input XML file where you specify which part of the configuration needs to be exported. For example, let's create an input XML file to export configuration for Default Server:

```
<?xml version="1.0"?>
<websphere-sa-config>
    <node name="AS20" action="locate">
        <application-server name="Default Server" action="export">
        </application-server>
    </node>
</websphere-sa-config>
```

Here, we start from the top most tag in the WAS configuration hierarchy, `<websphere-sa-config>`, and traverse the WAS hierarchy up to the resource that you want to export. For the resource that needs to be exported, change the action tag from `locate` to `export`.

Now you are ready to run the following command (all one line):

```
/QIBM/ProdData/WebASAdv/bin/XMLConfig -adminNodeName AS20 -export
/asp/temp/export.xml -partial /asp/temp/input.xml
```

Note the new option *-partial*, which is the name of the input file that specifies the resource in the WAS hierarchy that needs to be exported.

You will see messages that display the name of the resource being exported. They should look similar to this sample:

```
001.641 9f18a5e4 NodeConfig    A Processing Partial Export for Node: "AS20"
002.228 9f18a5e4 ApplicationSe A Processing Partial Export for Application Server: "Default
Server"
002.715 9f18a5e4 ApplicationSe A Exporting Application Server: "Default Server"
003.374 9f18a5e4 ContainerConf A Exporting Container: "Default Container"
004.133 9f18a5e4 EJBConfig     A Exporting EJB: "RemoteSRP"
004.311 9f18a5e4 EJBConfig     A Exporting EJB: "Hello"
004.445 9f18a5e4 EJBConfig     A Exporting EJB: "Increment"
004.743 9f18a5e4 ServletEngine A Exporting ServletEngine: "servletEngine"
005.533 9f18a5e4 WebApplicatio A Exporting Web Application: "default_app"
006.285 9f18a5e4 ServletConfig A Exporting Servlet: "snoop"
006.442 9f18a5e4 ServletConfig A Exporting Servlet: "hello"
006.603 9f18a5e4 ServletConfig A Exporting Servlet: "ErrorReporter"
006.770 9f18a5e4 ServletConfig A Exporting Servlet: "invoker"
006.952 9f18a5e4 ServletConfig A Exporting Servlet: "jsp"
007.055 9f18a5e4 WebApplicatio A Exporting Web Application: "admin"
007.625 9f18a5e4 ServletConfig A Exporting Servlet: "install"
007.783 9f18a5e4 ServletConfig A Exporting Servlet: "jsp"
007.938 9f18a5e4 ServletConfig A Exporting Servlet: "file"
008.095 9f18a5e4 ServletConfig A Exporting Servlet: "invoker"
008.250 9f18a5e4 ServletConfig A Exporting Servlet: "ErrorReporter"
008.333 9f18a5e4 WebApplicatio A Exporting Web Application: "examples"
009.099 9f18a5e4 ServletConfig A Exporting Servlet: "simpleJSP"
009.262 9f18a5e4 ServletConfig A Exporting Servlet: "error"
009.420 9f18a5e4 ServletConfig A Exporting Servlet: "ping"
009.580 9f18a5e4 ServletConfig A Exporting Servlet: "SourceCodeViewer"
009.737 9f18a5e4 ServletConfig A Exporting Servlet: "showCfg"
009.918 9f18a5e4 ServletConfig A Exporting Servlet: "HitCount"
010.078 9f18a5e4 ServletConfig A Exporting Servlet: "jsp"
010.238 9f18a5e4 ServletConfig A Exporting Servlet: "file"
010.637 9f18a5e4 SessionManage A Exporting Session Manager: "Session Manager"
010.945 9f18a5e4 UserProfileMa A Exporting User Profile Manager: "User Profile Manager"
$
```

Where can the XMLConfig tool be used? One example might be if you have an application in production mode servicing one customer. If you want to let the other customer use the same application, it is easy to run the XMLConfig tool and create a similar WAS configuration for the other customer (see Figure 69).

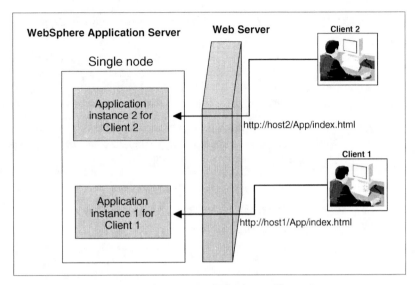

Figure 69. Hosting two instances of the same application for two different clients

You need to perform these steps:

1. Export the production version of your application using the XMLConfig tool.

2. Modify the virtual host names, aliases, application server name, class paths, and other parameters as needed.

3. Create a new virtual host for the second client. Its name has to be the same as the one that is specified in the XML file modified during the previous step.

4. Import the configuration file into WAS.

5. Create a new directory structure. If your production version is located in /asp/hosts/VirtualHostClient**1**, then the new directory structure will be located in /asp/hosts/VirtualHostClient**2**. The directory tree under /asp/hosts/VirtualHostClient1 and /asp/hosts/VirtualHostClient2 should be similar. This directory structure will host presentation files (HTML, IGF, and so on) and jar files for EJBs and servlets.

6. Copy the new version of the presentation and jar files to the new directory structure under VirtualHostClient2.

7. Start the application server, and point your Web browser to the new version of your application.

> **Note**
>
> The XMLConfig tool has some limitations:
>
> - It cannot export or import an enterprise application.
> - It cannot export or import security objects.
> - It does not save dependencies between models and their clones. Models/clones are exported and imported as stand-alone objects.

3.16.2 Models and clones

WAS supports a model and clone paradigm. The idea is very simple, but powerful: Create a model of a resource and test it. When the results of the test are satisfactory, make a copy of this model (clone) and deploy it. Before we explore the value of this concept, let's look at which resources in WAS you can clone. To check if a resource can be cloned, right-click that resource and a pop-up menu appears. If there is the option **Create...->Model...**, you can clone this resource.

The resources that can be cloned include:

- Application servers
- EJB containers
- Enterprise beans
- Servlet engines
- Web applications
- Servlets

WAS goes even further with this concept. It allows you to manipulate all clones under the model as a single unit. The changes you make to the model are propagated to the clones. You can start and stop the model, which starts all clones under that model.

The model and clone support makes it easier to balance the workload for a particular resource in WAS. By cloning a resource, you create multiple instances of this resource. When using an application server, each clone works with its own instance of the servlet and uses a separate instance of a class loader. Similarly, each JSP works with a separate instance of a class loader. As a result, you have the following advantages:

- You can better utilize the hardware and software resources of your system.
- With multiple clones on a single node, a single clone failure will not cause an application outage.
- With clones on multiple nodes, a single node failure will not cause an application outage.
- Makes it easy to scale your application.

For an example, create a model based on Default Server and then clone it:

1. In the Administrative Console, click the **Topology** tab.
2. Right-click **Default Server**.
3. From the pop-up menu, select **Create...->Model....**

4. Click the **General** tab, and fill in the properties as shown in Figure 70. We name our model Default Model. If you click **Make Default Server a Clone**, then the server is going to be the first clone for Default Model. If you don't select this check box, Default Server will be a stand-alone server. Make sure you select the **Recursively Model all Instances under Default Server** check box. This tells WAS to reproduce the exact hierarchy of all resources for Default Server under the model.

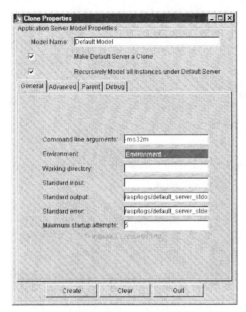

Figure 70. Configuration parameters for Default Model

5. Click the **Advanced** tab.

   Select **Workload management selection policy mechanism**. The default is Round Robin Prefer Local. This policy affects the way a clone is chosen for a new request for the resource.

6. Click the **Parent** tab.

   Expand the tree, and select **Models**. WAS uses the parent/child dependency for all resources. The root of this hierarchical structure is WebSphere Administrative Domain.

7. Click the **Create** button.

   Now you should see the Default Model resource in Topology view.

8. Right-click **Default Model**.

9. From the pop-up menu, select **Create...->Clone...**.

10.In the pop-up window, select the node, and enter the server name as shown in Figure 71 on page 148.

Figure 71. Creating a clone

11.Click the **Create** button.

You should see both of your servers in Topology view.

12.Right-click **Default Model**.

13.From the pop-up menu, select **Start**. After a while, you should see a confirmation window, which indicates that the command completed successfully. The icons for the application servers (clones) should change as shown in Figure 72.

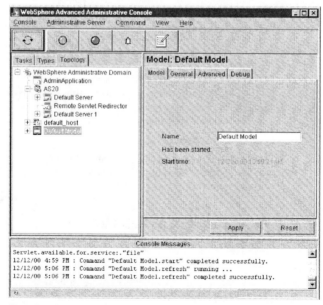

Figure 72. Starting the model

> **Note**
>
> There are some points you need to remember when you clone a resource. You need carefully examine the parameters for a cloned resource. For example, does a data source in the cloned EJB container point to the right database? It is possible to have a clone on the remote system, and if a model points to the local database, then your remote clone will not work properly.

3.16.3 Using different versions of JSP

WAS allows you to select the version of JSP to use. You can do this task while configuring an application server. One of the panels allows you to select the JSP version (shown in Figure 73). Select **Enable JSP 1.0** or **Enable JSP .91**. You cannot select both options simultaneously.

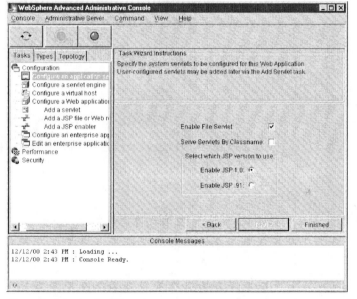

Figure 73. Selecting the JSP version

As a result of this step, WAS adds to the servlet engine either PageCompileServlet (JSP .91) or JSPServlet (JSP 1.0) as the JSP engine (see Figure 74 on page 150).

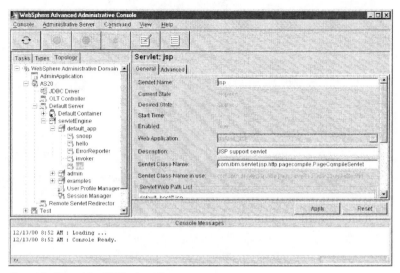

Figure 74. Support for JSP Version .91

3.17 WebSphere differences between Version 3.02 and 3.5

This section lists the differences between WebSphere Application Server Advanced Edition (WAS) 3.02 and 3.5. At the time this redbook was written, two fix packs were available: 3.5.1 and 3.5.2. The information in this chapter includes features and fixes from both fix packs.

The new features added to WAS 3.5 (above what is found in WAS 3.02) include:

- The new Version 1.2.2 of JDK.

- Usability enhancements throughout the product.

- Full support of JDBC 2.0 specifications.

- Changes to the administration repository format.

- Lotus Domino for AS/400 V5.0.5 HTTP Server Support. The Lotus Domino for AS/400 V5.0.5 HTTP server can now be used as a Web server with WebSphere Application Server for AS/400 V3.5.1 and V3.5.2. The Domino HTTP server can be used for serving both Domino and WebSphere Application Server Web content.

- Support of Servlet 2.2 and JSP 1.1 APIs.

- JNDI caching for lookup operation.

- The ability to redirect your standard output and standard error to another file.

- Downloadable documentation center. You can download it to your local machine.

- GUI changes. Some changes are described in the GUI interface, so you can follow the examples in this book using Version 3.5. The Administrative Console is shown in Figure 75.

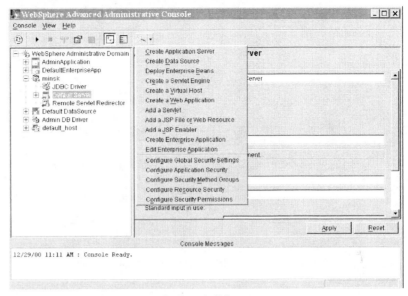

Figure 75. New look of the Administrative Console GUI

Some differences in the Administrative Console GUI are:

- As you can see, there are no tabs for Tasks, Types, and Topology. All tasks can be started from the wizards pull-down menu, which is the right most item on the tool bar (shown in Figure 75).

- The old buttons (Start, Stop, Ping, Properties, and Default Properties) have a different look.

- There are two new buttons: Topology View and Type View. They replace the Topology and Types tabs.

- The Create a JDBC driver option was removed. Now this task is part of the data source creation process.

The wizard's screens didn't change much. You can follow the examples from this book with slight modifications.

Chapter 4. Implementing Lotus Domino in an ASP environment

This chapter takes a closer look at various ways to implement Lotus Domino in an ASP environment. It also examines ASP implementation issues on Domino:

- Domino on iSeries: Hosting models, applications, and services
- Why Domino on the iSeries server
- Lotus ASP Solution Pack, including Lotus Host Management Services (LHMS)
- Clustering Domino servers
- Internet Cluster Managers (ICM) to support Web clients
- Partitioned Domino servers
- Lightweight Directory Access Protocol (LDAP)
- Large Scale Messaging Infrastructure
- Building a portal
- Security model

Note: In most implementation scenarios, we assume Domino R5 instead of 4.x.

We begin by introducing some of the key features of Domino running on the iSeries server in light of implementing an ASP.

There are very strong reasons why the iSeries is the most strategic platform for Domino, especially in an ASP environment:

- OS/400, the operating system of the iSeries server, is extremely stable:

  Domino for AS/400 is the most stable environment you can have for Domino. If you have more than one application running on an iSeries server and one of them crashes, it does not bring down the entire operating system.

- iSeries scales better than other platforms:

  You can host several Domino servers (called *partitioned servers*) on the iSeries server. You can separate each customer on a separate Domino server in the same box. You can allocate iSeries server resources to separate Domino partitions, a very unique features of Domino on the iSeries server. You can maintain each server separately, for example, by shutting it down, updating the Domino server, and turning it back on, without affecting other Domino servers in the same box. No rebooting of the machine is required, and there is no down time to all your ASP customers.

  For Domino R5, the iSeries server supports an unlimited number of partitioned servers that are subject only to the size of the system and the performance objectives of the installation.

- Ease of backup:

  The Domino server can be backed up as part of the regular backup schedule. In addition, Backup Recovery and Media Services for AS/400 (BRMS/400) has the unique ability to save and restore Domino data.

  QuickPlace for AS/400 Release 1.03 joins Domino for AS/400 Release 5.02a in supporting a true online backup capability with Backup Recovery and Media Services for AS/400 (with PTF SF60285). Online backup implies that QuickPlace, Domino, and other Lotus Server databases on the iSeries can be saved while they are in use, with no save while active synchronization points. This is true online backup support.

  Note: This function is supported in BRMS/400 release V4R4 and above.

You can direct your online backups to a tape device, an automated tape library device, save files, or a TSM server. It is critical that you do not replace your complete system backup with only online Lotus Server backups. The online Lotus Server backups only backup databases. There are other important Lotus Server pieces of data including libraries, files in the Lotus Server IFS directories, and other non-Lotus Server system data that should be backed up on a regular basis. An example may be QUSRSYS, QGPL, and so forth.

For more information, see the V4R4M0 *Backup Recovery and Media Services for AS/400*, SC41-5345.

- Integration with the iSeries:

  CL programs can be written to perform a variety of functions against the Domino server.

  In addition, many customers install Lotus Domino to serve as a "front end" or interface to the enterprise data they have on their iSeries server or other SQL database. Domino comes with a superb connection function, Domino Connection Services (DECS), which allows a developer to establish a link between a Domino database and live data stored on DB2, SQL, or any ODBC-enabled database. For a guide on how to implement DECS on the iSeries, see Technical Studio at `http://www.as400.ibm.com/tstudio/` and select the link **Access your AS/400 Data Using Domino Connection Services - DECS on AS/400** under Domino in the left navigation bar.

- Existing skill sets in the iSeries:

  If you already have strong AS/400 or iSeries skills, it is not necessary to develop new skills extensively or hire new people to support Domino on the iSeries. A short course on Administration training relating to Domino is sufficient.

4.1 Domino ASP on the iSeries: Hosting models, applications, and services

This section looks at the Domino hosting models for ASP, ASP services, and applications.

ASP hosting models

Some of the different hosting models that an ASP can provide are explained in the following list and highlighted in Table 13.

- **Shared Domino hosting on shared servers**: A shared server is also often referred to as a *virtual server*. Your customer will share the Domino server with a number of other customers. The services that are offered could include:

  - Limited size of disk storage (for example, 1 GB).

  - Options to access to the server via a Notes client or browser over the Internet.

  - Options to host customer mailboxes on Domino or forward e-mail to external e-mail addresses.

  - Options to access mailboxes via Notes, POP3, IMAP, or HTTP.

  - Customers can run restricted agents that are typically for normal data processing.

- Customers do not have administrative access including the Domino Directory.

- This package is often the most economical.

- **Partitioned Domino hosting on iSeries partitioned servers**: A customer has their own instance of the Domino server, on the iSeries server, that also has other Domino servers running. They also have their own unique Notes Domain, and users are certified in the /Company domain. The services offered are similar to Shared Domino Hosting, except the customer has complete administrative control including the Domino Directory, and they can run both restricted and unrestricted agents. The only restriction is that the customer does not have access to the base operating system.

- **Dedicated Domino Server**: A customer has a dedicated server and does not share it with anyone else. They can also install supplementary third-party programs on the server, provided they supply the licenses to do so. The server can be at the ASP's data centers, the customer's premises, or at a WSP.

- **Co-location hosting services**: The server is at a customer site, but it is managed by an ASP.

- **Any custom server configuration** for your customer.

Table 13. Various Domino hosting models

	Shared	Partitioned	Dedicated
Access to the base operating system	No	No	Yes
Group management	No	Yes	Yes
Domino directory access	No	Yes	Yes
Server document access	No	Yes	Yes
Unrestricted agents	No	Yes	Yes
Restricted agents	Yes	Yes	Yes
SSL	Yes	Yes	Yes
Update via replication	Yes	Yes	Yes
Notes, POP3, or IMAP or HTTP e-mail	Yes	Yes	Yes

ASP services

A Domino-based ASP also offers the following services to your customers:

- Security: Secure Service Access via SSL

- Data backup and restore: Daily backup, data restoration, and fireproof off-site storage

- Power backup: Power backup systems

- Integrated e-commerce

- Network connectivity: Multiple high-speed Internet connections

- Clustering

- Dial-in/dial-out access via phone lines

- System monitoring

- Help desk support

- Consultancy: Project management, analysis, and application development (that is: workflow application, security and networks, and Web page design)

- Enterprise integration with back-office systems and databases

ASP applications

As an ASP, you provide strategic applications to your customers. Such applications include:

- The customer's intranet (w3.company.com or www.intranet.company.com)

- The customer's Internet (www.company.com)

- Standard rentable Lotus Domino-based applications, such as LearningSpace and QuickPlace, which support all Domino platforms including the iSeries

- E-commerce, business-to-business (B2B), or extranet applications such as digital catalog sales support, project tracking, time and billing, and sales lead tracking

Figure 76 shows that the target market for Domino ASP is a shared server with multiple applications. The iSeries is quite strategic in this market segment too.

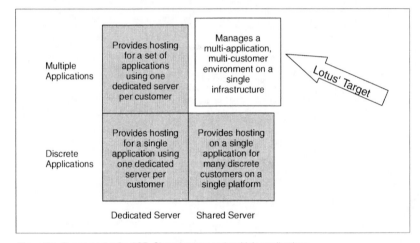

Figure 76. Target market for ASP: Shared server and multiple applications

4.1.1 Four phases of implementation: An overview

This section discusses the steps to setup the Domino server or servers in an ASP environment.

The IBM e-business process has four important stages:

- Transforming core business processes
- Building flexible, expandable e-business applications
- Running a scalable, available, safe environment
- Leveraging knowledge and information you gained through e-business systems

Based on this approach, we developed the following phases.

4.1.1.1 Phase 1: Gathering requirements, designing, and planning

This is probably the most important phase of all. In this phase, an ASP decides:

- Which hosting models to offer and the pricing levels
- What application hosting to provide
- What third-party application to provide
- Who the target customers are, and how many users there are per customer
- What the service level agreement is on support, network, application performance, and security
- How to keep track of user transactions as well as accounting and billing
- What technology to use, for example: Domino, iSeries, WebSphere, Lotus ASP Solution Pack
- What tools, methods, and APIs are necessary to facilitate integration

4.1.1.2 Phase 2: Setting up and configuring Domino servers

To set up and configure Domino servers, complete these steps:

1. Set up the first Domino server in the domain. Depending on your hosting model, you may have one domain in the Shared Model or several domains in the Partitioned and Dedicated Models.

2. Create a hierarchical name scheme, based on your company's or your customer's structure.

3. Create a Certification Log (CERTLOG.NSF) to record how you register additional servers and users.

4. Create organization certifier IDs and organizational unit certifier IDs, as required by the hierarchical name scheme.

5. Distribute certifier IDs to administrators at other sites, which could also be customer's administrators.

6. Add servers by registering them with the appropriate certifier ID.

7. Install and set up each server. This basically copies the software from the distribution medium (CD-ROM) to the iSeries disk storage using the Load Run (LODRUN) command. Setting up one or more servers creates environments on your system, and some basic configuration (CFGDOMSVR) is done at this time, for example, naming the server and specifying the data directory to be used.

8. Perform additional configuration procedures, based on the types of services, tasks, and programs that you want to run on the server.

9. Install additional software such as Lotus ASP Solution Pack, Lotus QuickPlace, and so forth.

> **QuickPlace on iSeries**
>
> For more information about Lotus QuickPlace, see the IBM Redpaper *Lotus QuickPlace for AS/400: Setup and Management Considerations*, REDP0045. You can find it on the ITSO home page at http://www.redbooks.ibm.com/ by searching for "quickplace".

10. Test all setups and configurations.

4.1.1.3 Phase 3: Running a scalable, available, and safe environment

In this phase, the environment is monitored and maintained.

In terms of server monitoring, the Domino server provides services and tasks that create and report information about the Domino system. The information comes in two forms: statistics and events.

- Statistics show the status of processes running on the system (that is, free disk space or server workload). To view statistics to monitor your Domino system, you can use the Collect task, which collects statistics and places the information into the Statistics database.

- The Domino server also provides monitor documents that you use to configure statistic thresholds. When the Collect task collects statistics and places them into the Statistics database, it compares each statistic to the threshold configured in the monitor document. An alarm is generated when a statistic has reached its threshold.

In terms of Domino server maintenance, the major tasks are:

1. The server is backed up regularly.
2. Users, both internal and external (ASP customers), can access the server quickly and consistently.
3. Mail is routed properly.
4. Administration Process requests are carried out.
5. Databases replicate correctly.
6. Server hardware is functioning.
7. Databases are active and maintained.

4.1.1.4 Phase 4: Leveraging the experience and returning to Phase 1

With the changes in the products and ASP marketplace, it is inevitable that a review phase is required to leverage experiences gained from previous phases to build a better system.

This is the phase to review the existing infrastructure and to further fine-tune the systems.

4.2 Clustering Domino servers to support Notes clients

This section provides information about the advantages of clustering in the Domino environment and why that is important for ASPs.

4.2.1 Overview

Clustered Domino servers are a group of servers that work together to provide workload balancing to improve performance and provide better scalability for your ASP customers.

How many servers?

The restriction on the number of servers that can make up a cluster was between two and six. This restriction has been removed. Now there is no architectural limit, but there is a realistic limit of how many servers can be in the cluster.

Domino clusters are extremely flexible:

- All supported Domino Server platforms support clustering, including the iSeries.

- It is possible to mix iSeries, UNIX, S/390, OS/2, and Windows NT Domino servers in one cluster.

How Domino clustering works

Domino clustering uses an advanced form of replication that is event-driven. This allows replicas of databases to be kept up-to-date within seconds of a change. When a request for a database on a specific server cannot be performed, there is automatic failover to another server within the cluster that has a replica of the database.

4.2.2 Why clustering is important for ASP

As an ASP, setting up a cluster provides several advantages to customers:

- **Failover support**: Clusters provide failover protection for your ASP business-critical databases and servers, including passthru server failover to other servers in the cluster. With failover, your ASP customers continue to have access to a database when a server goes down. Cluster servers fail over users by redirecting database requests to other servers in the cluster.

- **Workload balancing**: Server workload balancing ensures that heavily-used servers can pass requests to other cluster servers and that work is evenly distributed across the cluster. Server workload balancing helps you achieve optimum system performance for your ASP customers.

- **Continuous data synchronization**: A key to effective clustering is setting up replicas of databases on two or more servers in a cluster. Cluster replication ensures that all changes, whether to a database or to the cluster membership itself, are immediately passed to other databases or servers in the cluster. Databases are tightly synchronized to provide high availability of information.

- **Scalability**: Clusters let you grow your system as the number of users you support increases. You can distribute user accounts across clusters and balance additional workloads to optimize system performance. You can create multiple database replicas to maximize data availability and move users to other servers or clusters as you plan for future growth.

4.2.3 Components of clusters

Each server in a cluster runs cluster components that are installed with the Lotus Domino Advanced Services license. These components, with the help of the Administration Process, perform the cluster management and monitoring tasks that let you administer a cluster. These components are:

- **Cluster Manager**: This component tracks the state of all servers in a cluster. It keeps a list of which servers in the cluster are currently available and maintains information about the workload on each server. You can view this information by typing the Show Cluster command at the server console.

- **Cluster Administration Process**: This process (CLADMIN) is responsible for the correct operation of all cluster components. On clustered servers, the CLDBDIR and CLREPL processes run automatically at server startup and whenever the cluster membership changes.

- **Cluster Analysis**: You can analyze the configuration of a cluster and determine whether it has been correctly set up. The Cluster Analysis (CLUSTA4.NSF) database receives the results of the tests run by the Cluster Analysis tool. Test results are recorded in Cluster Analysis Results documents.

- **Cluster Database Directory**: This database (CLDBDIR.NSF) resides on each server in a cluster and contains information about all the databases and replicas within a cluster.

- **Cluster Database Directory Manager**: This task (CLDBDIR) keeps the Cluster Database Directory (CLDBDIR.NSF) up to date with the most current database information. It also manages databases with cluster-specific attributes such as databases marked out of service or pending delete.

- **Cluster Replicator**: This tasks is responsible for the tight synchronization of data among databases and their replicas in a cluster.

4.2.4 For more information

See Chapter 6 in *Lotus Domino for AS/400: Implementation*, SG24-5592, for good information on how to implement clusters in Domino on the AS/400 system.

4.3 Internet Clustering Manager to support Web clients

The previous section explained how to cluster Domino servers to support your ASP customers that use Notes clients. This section explains how Internet Cluster Manager (ICM) lets you use Domino clusters to provide failover and workload balancing to HTTP clients (Internet browsers) when they access Domino Web servers. This makes your Web servers and databases highly available to your ASP customers. For an ASP that provides strategic applications via a browser front end, ICM ensures that the applications are highly available to the customers.

You can run ICM on any server that is using the Domino Release 5 Enterprise Server license. You install and configure Domino clusters as you normally would, and then you configure the ICM. The ICM supports the HTTP and HTTPS protocols.

4.3.1 How ICM works

ICM acts as an intermediary between HTTP clients and Domino Web servers in a cluster. When Domino Web servers are running in a cluster, they generate URLs that direct HTTP client requests to ICM. ICM maintains information about the availability of servers and databases in the cluster. When ICM receives a client request, it redirects the client to the most available server that contains a replica of the requested database.

ICM sends periodic probes to the Web servers in the cluster to determine their status and availability. When ICM receives a client request, it looks at the information in the Cluster Database Directory to find a server that contains the requested database. ICM determines the most available server that contains the requested database, and then redirects the client to that server. This results in the client closing the session with ICM and opening a new session with the selected server. The user may see this as a change in the host name in the URL. The user may also see the path to the database change in the URL because the database may have a different path on the target server.

If the page that a Web server displays to a client includes links to other databases on the same server or to other databases in the cluster, the Web server includes the host name of ICM in the URLs to those databases. This ensures that users accessing those links go through ICM.

Figure 77 shows an HTTP client asking the ICM to open a database and ICM redirecting the client to the best server that contains the requested database, Server 2. The client then connects directly to Server 2.

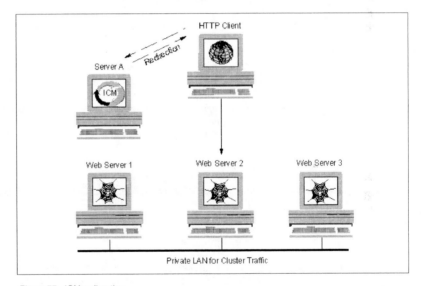

Figure 77. ICM redirection

ICM can run on a server in the cluster or outside the cluster. When ICM runs on a server in the cluster, it accesses the local copy of the Cluster Database Directory. When ICM runs on a server outside the cluster, it selects a server in the cluster and accesses the Cluster Database Directory on that server. If the server that ICM chooses becomes unavailable, this connection fails over to another server in the cluster.

ICM always uses its local copy of the Domino Directory. Therefore, ICM must be in the same Domino domain as the cluster.

In most cases, users will experience better performance when you use ICM. The overhead of using ICM is small, but the benefit to performance from workload balancing can be significant. In cases where the workload is already balanced, there will not be a significant increase or decrease in performance.

4.3.2 Planning to use the ICM

You should plan the cluster that the ICM will service, and then plan where to run ICM itself and how many ICMs to run.

You can add Web servers to an existing cluster, use existing servers in a cluster as Web servers, or create a cluster for Web traffic only. You plan the cluster by considering the same factors you consider when you create any Domino cluster. For example, you should consider the processing power of the servers available and how much traffic there will be in the cluster. If there is a lot of Web traffic on a server, consider dedicating the server to the Web traffic. You should also distribute databases and replicas in a way that balances the workload.

In general, you should consider the following factors:

- The number of servers to include in the cluster
- The number and placement of replicas in a cluster
- How to distribute databases across servers
- Whether to create a private LAN for cluster traffic
- Where to locate ICM

4.3.2.1 Determining how many servers to include in a cluster

In general, adding servers to a cluster increases the cluster's ability to balance the workload so that no server becomes overloaded and performance stays high. However, if servers contain too many server tasks, CPU-intensive applications, and replicas, adding servers can decrease performance because of the additional amount of cluster traffic that is required to keep databases synchronized on all servers.

If your organization is small, you can start with two servers and add servers as your enterprise grows, without affecting the performance to your users. Keep in mind that each server you add creates additional network traffic when it probes other cluster servers to find out their status and when it does cluster replication. Therefore, do not add servers to a cluster until you need the additional capacity or additional redundancy.

In a larger organization, you must decide whether to create large clusters or small clusters. A larger cluster can absorb the workload better when a cluster server fails. If you have a cluster with only two servers, for example, if one of server fails, the other server must absorb 100% of the failed server's workload. That means that you could run each server at only 50% of its capacity so that it has enough capacity available to absorb the workload of the other server. If the cluster has six servers, however, each of the remaining five servers must absorb only 20% of the failed server's workload. That means you could run each server at 80% of the capacity and they would still be able to absorb the workload if a server goes down. Of course, there are other factors that determine how the workload of a failed server is absorbed, such as the way you distribute replicas across the cluster servers.

Hardware considerations

The number of servers you decide to include in a cluster can be affected by the amount of disk space and the processing power of each server. Keep the following points in mind as you decide which hardware to use in your cluster:

- The more replicas you create, the more disk space you need and the more processing power you need for cluster replication.

- The Cluster Database Directory requires 2 MB of disk space, plus an additional 1 MB for every 2,000 databases in the cluster.

- The more servers that are in the cluster, the more processing power each server uses to communicate with the other cluster servers.

- The more server tasks and CPU-intensive applications you run on a server, the more processing power you need.

- Each server needs adequate processing power for the databases that it contains and for any databases that might fail over to the server.

- The more users a server has to handle concurrently, the more memory the server needs to keep performance high. You can use the following formula as a general indication of how much memory to install:

```
Recommended Domino memory + 1 MB for every three concurrent users
```

- If the recommended memory for Domino is 128 MB, for example, and you want to support 300 concurrent users on the server, you will need 256 MB of memory (128 MB + 300 / 3 MB). In this case, you would install 256 MB of memory, since that is, generally, the next largest configurable amount of memory.

- Table 14 on page 166 in the following section can help you determine how much memory is required for the databases in your cluster.

- When you have a large cluster or a cluster with a heavy workload, you might use multiple Cluster Replicators to improve performance during cluster replication. In a busy cluster, the number of Cluster Replicators you can use is one less than the total number of servers in the cluster. Install 2 MB of memory in addition for each Cluster Replicator you expect to use.

4.3.2.2 Determining the number and placement of replicas in a cluster

There are two major reasons to create a replica for a database in a cluster: to provide constant availability of the data and to distribute the workload between multiple servers because the database is so busy. Before you create replicas in a cluster, consider how frequently users access a database and their need for data redundancy. If a database is extremely busy or its availability is extremely important, you may want to create multiple replicas and locate them on your most reliable servers. For databases that are not very busy and whose constant availability is not important, you may not want to create any replicas at all. A server log file, for example, does not need to have a replica on another server.

In general, the more replicas there are of a database, the more accessible the data is. However, creating too many replicas can increase the overhead of maintaining a system and decrease performance. As you plan your cluster strategy, try to create a balance between your users' requirements for data availability and the physical ability of each server in your cluster to manage additional workload. More than three replicas of a database may not provide you with significant incremental availability. If users can adequately access a database from one or two servers with no problems, do not increase the number of replicas in the cluster.

When users require the constant availability of a specific database, consider placing replicas on every server in the cluster if you have adequate disk space and resources. If you are a public service provider, this configuration provides the highest possibility for redundancy of data.

In addition, try to distribute the busiest databases to different servers so that no server contains too many busy databases. If the servers in the cluster all have a similar amount of processing power, you can have an equal load on each server, including the processing power reserved for failover. If a server has significantly more or less processing power than the other servers, consider altering the number of databases on the server and the number of databases that can fail over to the server. Also, distribute mail files across a cluster, or set up separate servers or clusters for mail.

Because busy databases in a cluster can create a lot of replication events, it is a good idea to install these replicas on the fastest disk hardware available on the server. If possible, place these replicas where other processes are not in contention, for example, on a partition other than the one that contains the operating system swap file.

To view which databases and their replicas already exist in the cluster, open the Cluster Database Directory (CLDBDIR.NSF). Domino maintains a profile of all databases and replicas within a cluster in this directory.

Note that selective replication formulas work differently in a cluster.

How many replicas to create
The following list describes some factors to consider when determining how many replicas to create:

- The number of replicas of a database you create depends on how important the availability of that database is and the amount of use the database receives.

- You should create at least one replica of a database for which you want data redundancy. If a database becomes unavailable, users can then fail over to the replica.

- If you want to be sure that a database is available at all times, you can create more than one replica. The more important availability is, the more replicas you should create. Add multiple replicas for very important databases only. Unnecessary replicas can diminish cluster resources.

- For most databases, a single replica is adequate. More than three replicas are rarely needed, unless a database is truly mission-critical.

- Consider the power and bandwidth of your system when creating replicas. The busier a database is, the more network traffic and processing power it takes to keep replicas updated. If you have systems with limited power and bandwidth, you may want to create fewer replicas of busy databases than you would if you had more power and bandwidth. Or, you may want to add processors and other resources to the servers. In a cluster with limited resources, creating replicas of busy databases can be counterproductive because of the additional resources needed for cluster replication. Clustering is not a solution for inadequate resources. The less busy a database is, the less overhead it takes to keep that database updated.

- If you aren't sure how many replicas to create, start with one and track the cluster statistics. If the statistics show that performance becomes a problem, increasing the number of replicas may solve the problem.

- Do not create replicas for databases in which availability or workload balancing is not one of your goals.

Analyzing databases to determine the number of replicas

There are many factors to consider when deciding how many replicas to create. Some factors suggest creating more replicas and some suggest creating fewer replicas. These factors are outlined in the following list, which states how they might affect your cluster traffic and performance.

Prior to distributing databases in a cluster, it can be helpful to create a table of information about the databases and the cluster hardware. You can use the table to determine how important specific databases are and how adequate your resources are. You can include some or all the following factors in the table:

- Titles of the databases:

  This identifies each database.

- Size of each database:

  Large databases consume a lot of disk space. Depending on your disk capacity, you may want to create fewer replicas of larger databases to preserve disk space.

- Number and distribution of database users:

  If you have a large number of users, they may experience better performance if usage is spread across multiple servers. This requires multiple replicas. If the number of users is small, they may not notice a performance improvement from additional replicas.

- How often user transactions take place:

  If the transaction rate is high, creating multiple replicas may improve performance. To find out the rate of activity for a database, look in the Notes log file.

- Expected volume of new data:

  If you expect a large amount of new data in the database, additional replicas may slow down performance because cluster replication will cause a lot of additional traffic. If you have powerful servers and a lot of bandwidth, this may not create a problem.

- Capacity of Domino server hardware:

  The more powerful the servers are and the more disk space they have, the more replicas you can create without significantly affecting performance.

- Type of network connections between servers:

  Cluster replication can create a bottleneck on a network that does not have enough bandwidth. Therefore, the greater the bandwidth that exists, the more replicas you can create.

Example table
When you create a table of database information, include the factors that are most important to you. Table 14 uses a subset of the preceding information to determine the number of replicas needed.

Table 14. Determining the number of replicas needed

Database title	Size	Max active users	Trans-action rate	Growth rate	Need for availability	Suggested number of replicas
Product Discussion	2 GB	500	High	High	High	2
Sales Tracking	1 GB	200	Medium	High	Critical	2 or more
Classified Ads	800 MB	45	Medium	Medium	Low	0
Company Research	1.5 GB	20	Low	Medium	Medium	0 or 1

Table 14 helps identify which databases require high availability, which databases are the busiest, and how much additional disk space you will need in the future. In this example, two databases are very important and are growing rapidly. You should be sure that there are enough replicas of these databases so that they are always available. You should also be sure there is adequate disk space for growth on every server that contains a replica of these databases. One database is of medium importance and not growing as quickly. You should provide no more than one replica of this database, unless it would affect your business negatively if the database was not available for a while. One database is not very important and does not require a replica in the cluster.

The number of concurrent users helps you determine the need for workload balancing. In this example, two databases are very busy, and both are very important. Therefore, you should consider placing these databases on different servers to balance the workload. You should also be sure that the workload balancing parameters are set on the servers that contain these databases so that users will fail over to another server when these databases become busy.

4.3.2.3 Distributing databases in a cluster
The way you distribute databases significantly affects workload balancing, as well as the performance of your equipment.

Distributing mail databases
Clustering mail databases provides high availability to users. Some companies set up a cluster for mail only. This is not required but is one way to arrange your organization. Because mail is an important application, it is a good idea to have your mail databases in a cluster, whether the cluster is dedicated to mail servers only.

When you create a mail cluster, distribute the replicas for a server among the other servers in the cluster. This ensures that all the other servers share the load when a server fails, therefore, balancing the workload and keeping performance as high as possible.

It is a good idea to distribute the databases and replicas evenly across servers, as long as the servers are fairly equal in resources. If your mail cluster contains four servers and 1,200 users, for example, place 300 mail databases on each server; and place 100 replicas from each server onto each of the other three servers. When a server fails, 100 mail users fail over to each of the other three servers, increasing each server's work load by 33%. You might be tempted to place all 300 replicas from Server 1 onto Server 2 and all the replicas for Server 3 onto Server 4. In such a case, however, if Server 1 fails, all 300 users fail over to Server 2, increasing the workload on Server 2 by 100%, but not increasing the workload on Server 3 or Server 4 at all.

Figure 78 shows a mail cluster that contains four servers with 300 mail databases on each server. Replicas of the mail files are evenly distributed among all the other servers in the cluster, keeping the workload of the other servers as low as possible, even when failover occurs.

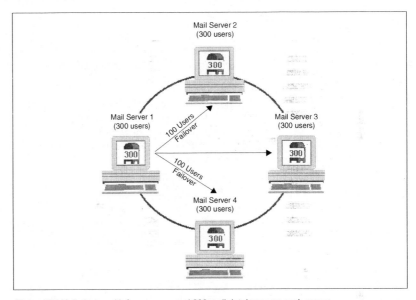

Figure 78. Mail cluster with four servers and 300 mail databases on each server

Figure 79 on page 168 shows a mail cluster that contains two servers with 100 mail files on each server. Because there are only two servers, each server must fail over to the other server. Therefore, each server contains replicas of all the mail databases on the other server.

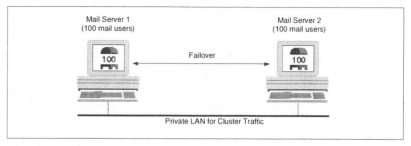

Figure 79. Mail cluster with two servers and 100 mail databases on each server

Since users often open the mail databases once a day and leave them open, distributing the mail databases is usually adequate for workload balancing. You do not usually have to use separate workload balancing settings, especially if you dedicate servers to mail only.

After failing over to a replica mail database, users automatically return to the mail database on their mail server the next time they start their Notes clients. This happens as long as the Location document that points to that mail database is the current Location document.

Note if you do not create a dedicated mail cluster, you should distribute mail databases equally among the cluster servers, if the cluster servers are approximately equal in power. If some servers are more powerful than others, distribute more databases to the more powerful servers. This distribution helps to keep the workload balanced.

Important

If you plan to create a cluster that includes some Release 5 servers and some Release 4 servers, keep the following points in mind:

- The Release 5 mail template does not work properly on Release 4 servers. If a user has a Release 5 mail database, do not create a replica on a Release 4 server.

- Because the Cluster Replicator always replicates the template design between replicas, a user's mail replicas should all use only the Release 5 mail template or only the Release 4 mail template.

Distributing application databases

When clustering applications, some applications need a higher level of availability than others. In addition, some databases are used much more frequently than others and some require more computing resources to run than others. You should consider all of these factors when distributing application databases. With application databases, workload balancing is more important than with mail databases.

As with mail, you should try to distribute the workload evenly across the cluster. However, consider the power of each server. If some servers are more powerful than others, be sure to increase their workload appropriately. Also, consider the amount of usage for each database.

Figure 80 shows a cluster with four servers of varying amounts of power. The databases in the cluster are distributed in a way that takes advantage of the resources of each server.

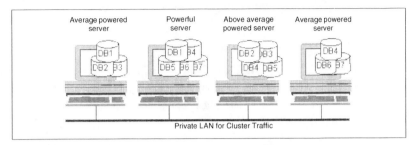

Figure 80. Distributing application databases: A cluster of four servers of varying amounts of power

Figure 81 shows a cluster with four servers that are equal in power. The databases in this example all receive a similar amount of use. DB1 is a critical database, so each server contains a replica.

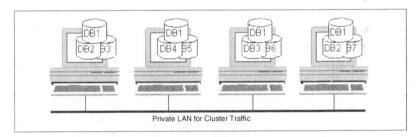

Figure 81. Distributing application databases: A cluster of four servers of equal amounts of power

4.3.2.4 Determining whether to create a private LAN for your cluster

To make a busy cluster more efficient, you can create a private network for your cluster. To do so, install an additional network interface card in each cluster server, and connect these network interface cards through a private hub or switch.

The main reason for creating a private LAN for your cluster is to separate the network traffic that a cluster creates with server probes and cluster replication. A private LAN can leave more bandwidth available on your primary LAN. If you anticipate a lot of cluster replication activity, you should create a private LAN.

You can also consider creating a private LAN for intra-cluster communication to ensure that cluster servers remain in communication with each other, even when certain network problems occur. By adding a private network, all servers in the cluster are connected by at least two distinct LAN segments. If a network board or a cable on one LAN segment fails, there is still network connectivity between all servers in the cluster. This assures you that cluster servers remain in contact with each other and that cluster replication continues to keep databases synchronized.

If you create a private LAN for your cluster, all cluster members must be connected to both the private LAN for intra-cluster communication, and to the primary LAN for client access.

Setting up a private LAN for a cluster

Setting up a private LAN for your cluster separates the server probes and cluster replication from the rest of your network traffic. This prevents the cluster traffic from slowing down your primary network.

Follow this procedure to set up a private network for your cluster:

1. Install an additional network interface card in each server in the cluster. These cards should be connected through a private hub or switch.

2. Configure the LAN to use TCP/IP.

3. Assign a second IP address to each server. In a cluster using two servers, for example, you could use the addresses 192.168.64.1 and 192.168.64.2.

4. Assign host names for the new IP addresses, and place entries in the HOSTS file or the DNS. In a cluster using two servers, for example, you could assign the host names ACME_CLU and ACME2_CLU. The entries in the HOSTS file might then be:

```
192.168.64.1   ACME_CLU
192.168.64.2   ACME2_CLU
```

5. Verify that the private LAN is operational by making sure that each cluster server can ping both the IP address and the host name of the other cluster servers. Also, be sure that other servers can still ping the cluster servers at their regular LAN addresses.

6. In the Ports - Notes Network Ports tab of the Server document of each cluster member, add and enable a new port for the private LAN. For example, add the following information:

```
Port=CLUSTER  Notes Network=Cluster Network  Net Address=ACME_CLU
Enabled=ENABLED
```

7. Assign each port an IP address from the corresponding subnets, and place this information in the Notes.ini file in the following form:

```
PORT1_TcpIPAddress=0,a.b.c.d:1352
PORT2_TcpIPAddress=0,e.f.g.h:1352
```

Here, *PORT1* and *PORT2* are the port names and *a.b.c.d* and *e.f.g.h* are the IP addresses for the ports.

If you have ports named TCPIP and CLUSTER, for example, these lines might be:

```
TCPIP_TcpIPAddress=0,192.114,32,5:1352
CLUSTER_TcpIPAddress=0,192.168.64.1:1352
```

8. Add the following line to the Notes.ini file:

```
Server_Cluster_Default_Port=Cluster Port
```

Here, *Cluster Port* is the port you created for the cluster. In this example, this line would be:

```
Server_Cluster_Default_Port=CLUSTER
```

Note: You can use a Server Configuration document to update the Notes.ini file on all the servers in the cluster.

9. Restart the server.

4.3.3 For more information

Please refer to the *Domino Administrators's Manual* on:

- Configuring the ICM
- Starting the ICM
- Failover and workload balancing
- Security
- Managing and Monitoring ICM

4.4 Partitioned Domino servers on a single iSeries environment

Domino for AS/400 supports multiple servers on a single iSeries server. This is referred to as *partitioned Domino servers*. This function allows you to operate multiple logically distinct servers, even representing different Domino domains, on the same iSeries server.

This is very strategic to ASPs:

- ASPs can host Domino servers for several customers in one iSeries server, with each one having a distinct identity, that is different domain names.

- ASPs can maintain each Domino server separately on one iSeries server, without affecting other Domino servers.

- ASPs can host customers with different workload schedules in one iSeries server. For example, customers from different time zones or countries can take advantage of the differences in working hours.

Note: Partitioned Domino servers are different from iSeries Logical Partitioning (LPAR). LPAR allows for the simultaneous running of multiple independent servers – each with its own processors, memory, and disks – within a single symmetric multiprocessing iSeries server.

4.4.1 Requirements

The requirements for partitioning Domino servers on a single iSeries environment are:

- A Lotus Domino Enterprise Server license is needed to use partitioned servers.

- Select **Advanced Services** (product option 7) when you run the Load and Run (LODRUN) command.

- Set up all Domino servers on the iSeries as partitioned servers.

- Before you start any of the partitioned servers for the first time, you may need to modify the Notes.ini file to define a port mapper server and the IP address and TCP/IP port where each Domino server partition is listening.

When you use the Configure Domino Server (CFGDOMSVR) command to set up a Domino server, you must specify either *ALL or *PARTITION for the Advanced services (ADVSRV) parameter. If you have already set up a single, non-partitioned server, you must reconfigure this server (CFGDOMSVR) to include support for partitioned servers.

If you see the LNT0109 message `Maximum number of servers exceeded`, this does not necessarily mean that you have already configured 16 servers. This message appears even if you did not configure partitioning support. To tell whether an existing server was configured as partitioned, check the server Notes.ini file for NPN=1.

Each partitioned server must have its own data directory. To avoid confusion, it is a good idea to use the name of the Domino server as the directory name in one level of the hierarchy. For example, using the convention /lotus/domino/<servername> places all the data directories under the main directory called /lotus/domino.

4.4.2 Deciding how many partitioned servers to install

For Domino on R5, the iSeries server supports an unlimited number of partitioned servers, subject only to the size of the system and the performance objectives of the installation.

We recommend that you follow these suggestions:

- Run partitioned servers on multi-processor iSeries servers.
- Plan your partitioned server configuration and your network configurations before you install and configure Domino for your customers.

4.4.3 Options for setting up partitioned servers

Two partitioned servers look like two different systems (two different IP hosts) to your ASP customers. As an ASP, this can be implemented in one of the following ways:

- Each server has its own IP address:

  If the servers use the same iSeries communication adapter, you assign more than one IP interface to the same line description. Each server must appear with its correct IP address on a name server (DNS) or in the clients' host tables.

- All servers have the same IP address but unique port numbers:

  Unique port numbers are used to distinguish between each partitioned server.

4.4.3.1 Each server has its own IP address

In this configuration, a unique IP address is assigned to each partitioned server and defined in the OS/400 TCP/IP configuration. Because the iSeries TCP/IP implementation supports multihoming, you can use the same line description for more than one IP interface. As an ASP, you may also have more than one communications adapter per iSeries, either for performance or for redundancy.

Follow these steps to assign a unique IP address to each partitioned server:

1. On the OS/400 command line, type the Add TCP/IP Interface (`ADDTCPIFC`) command.

2. Update the first three parameters of the Add TCP/IP Interface (ADDTCPIFC) screen:

   - Internet address: Enter the IP address
   - Line description: Enter the communications adapter
   - Subnet mask

3. Modify the Notes.ini file by adding the following statement:

```
TCPIP_TcpIpAddress=0,11.12.13.14:1352
```

The number *11.12.13.14* is the server's IP address, and *1352* is the standard port number used by Notes clients and Domino servers to connect to a server.

4. Restart the Domino server.

4.4.3.2 Each server has the same IP address but unique port numbers

In this configuration, each server has the same IP address, but different port numbers. This is called *port mapping* and works only for Notes Remote Procedure Call (NRPC) communication. TCP port mapping requires the assignment of a unique TCP port number to each partitioned server that shares an IP address and assigns one of these servers as the port mapper server.

The port mapper server listens on the default Lotus Domino TCP port 1352 and directs connection requests to other servers that share the same IP address. All other servers on this system that listen to the same IP address must use unique port numbers different from 1352. The port mapper server knows (using a definition in its Notes.ini file – the `TCPIP_PortMapping0x` statement) to which port each of the other servers is listening and redirects requests to the appropriate server.

The port mapper server must be running for the partitioned servers that share its IP address to receive new connections from workstations. If the port mapper server is down, new sessions cannot connect. However, existing sessions remain connected. The reason is that each Notes workstation maintains information in memory about recent server connections, including those redirected by the port mapper.

To assign the same IP address, different ports to each server, follow these steps:

1. Identify the ports to be used for other partitioned servers.

   A good approach is to use 5-digit numbers for port numbers for other partitioned servers since it is less likely that the number is already being used by other applications. In our example, we use port numbers 13521 and 13522.

2. Change the Notes.ini file for the port mapper server.

   Identify which server is the port mapper server, and modify the Notes.ini file for this server. The port mapper server must specify the shared IP address to be used for all servers, along with the standard NRPC port number (1352) on which the port re-direction takes place, for example:

   ```
   TCPIP_TcpIpAddress=0,11.12.13.14:1352
   ```

   In addition, add a *port mapping* statement for each of the other partitioned servers. Specify their names and port numbers, for example:

   ```
   TCPIP_PortMapping00=CN=Server01/O=Venus,11.12.13.14:13521
   TCPIP_PortMapping01=CN=Server01/O=Mars,11.12.13.14:13522
   ```

   This example specifies that the server for customer Venus is listening on port 13521 for IP address 11.12.13.14 and customer Mars is listening on port 13522 of the same IP address 11.12.13.14.

3. Change the Notes.ini file for each of the other partitioned servers.

The Notes.ini file for each of the other servers must specify its own IP address and port number. For example, for customer Venus, this would be:

```
TCPIP_TcpIpAddress=0,11.12.13.14:13521
```

Dedicating one server as the port mapper

You could have a dedicated server as the port mapper server so that it does not perform any functions other than routing clients to one of the other partitioned servers. In this case, you modify the Notes.ini file for the port mapper server, as described above, and disable all unnecessary tasks as explained here:

1. Edit the Notes.ini file. Change the ServerTasks setting to contain the very basic server tasks, for example (suggestion only):

```
ServerTasks=Replica,Router,Update,AMgr,Adminp
```

2. Remove large databases, such as the Help databases, from the data directory.

Configuration to support Web clients

If you want to set up IMAP, LDAP, NNTP, POP3, or HTTP to use unique ports for communication, the users must specify the port on which they want to communicate. For example, if you specify port 12080 for HTTP requests, users must enter the port number as part of the URL, for example:

```
http://servername.domain.com:12080/index.html
```

If a proxy or firewall system is placed between the Web client and the Domino server, which offers Network Access Translation/Protocol Address Translation (NAT/PAT) services, PAT services can be used to redirect the Web client access (port 80) to the given port on each Domino server.

It is also possible to allow for multiple IMAP, POP3, NNTP, and LDAP services to run on the default ports. This allows the service to listen on a specific address for connections. The Notes.ini variables are:

- IMAPAddress=*IP address or fully qualified domain name*

  Description: Specifies the IP address or fully qualified domain name (for example, server01.venus.com) of an IMAP server running on a partitioned server. To run an IMAP server on a partitioned server, you must add this setting.

- LDAPAddress=*IP address or fully qualified domain name*

  Description: Specifies the IP address or fully qualified domain name (for example, server01.venus.com) of an LDAP server running on a partitioned server. To run an LDAP server on a partitioned server, you must add this setting.

- NNTPAddress=*IP address or fully qualified domain name*

  Description: Specifies the IP address or fully qualified domain name (for example, server01.venus.com) of an NNTP server running on a partitioned server. To run an NNTP server on a partitioned server, you must add this setting.

- POP3Address=*IP address or fully qualified domain name*

    Description: Specifies the IP address or fully qualified domain name (for example, server01.venus.com) of an POP3 server running on a partitioned server. To run an POP3 server on a partitioned server, you must add this setting.

4.4.4 Connecting partitioned servers through the loopback interface

After you have configured multiple partitioned servers on the same iSeries server, you may need to replicate your databases or allow mail routing between those servers. Because these servers reside on the same iSeries server, it is obviously desirable to exchange information between them without going through an external communication network. This is done through a special TCP/IP function called the *loopback interface* in the iSeries server.

The loopback interface is a special virtual TCP/IP interface that allows socket connections without the use of a real hardware interface. The TCP/IP address of the loopback interface is 127.0.0.1. It is defined on every system using TCP/IP as a networking protocol.

If you set up two or more partitioned servers as described in the previous sections, either with unique IP addresses or using a port mapper, you can perform additional configuration to allow those servers to connect using the loopback interface.

4.4.5 For more information

Please refer to Chapter 6, "Advanced Domino Services for the AS/400 System", in the redbook *Lotus Domino for AS/400: Implementation*, SG24-5592.

4.5 Lightweight Directory Access Protocol (LDAP)

This section looks at LDAP and why it is important for ASPs.

4.5.1 What Lightweight Directory Access Protocol is

Lightweight Directory Access Protocol (LDAP) defines a standard method for accessing and updating information in a directory by a TCP/IP client. A directory contains information on the various users, applications, files, printers, and other resources accessible from a network.

Application-specific directory *versus* application-independent directory
An *application-specific directory* could be as simple as a set of editable text files, or it could be stored and accessed in an undocumented, proprietary manner. In such an environment, each application creates and manages its own application-specific directory. This quickly becomes an administrative nightmare. Keeping multiple copies of information up-to-date and synchronized is difficult, especially when different user interfaces and even different system administrators are involved.

What is needed is a common, *application-independent directory* that is based on an open standard that is supported by many vendors on many platforms. It must be accessible through a standard API. It must be extensible so that it can hold the types of data needed by arbitrary applications. It must also provide full functionality without requiring excessive resources on smaller systems. Since more users and applications will access and depend on the common directory, it must also be robust, secure, and scalable.

When such a directory infrastructure is in place, application developers can devote their time to developing an applicator instead of application-specific directories. LDAP is the protocol to be used to access this common directory infrastructure.

4.5.2 Why LDAP is important for ASP

LDAP offers a common, application-independent directory, supported by many vendors on many platforms. LDAP allows users or applications to find resources that have the characteristics needed for a particular task.

For example, LDAP can be used to look up a person's e-mail address or fax a number. A directory could be searched to find a nearby PostScript color printer. Or a directory of application servers could be searched to find a server that can access customer billing information.

The directory as part of the infrastructure

A directory that is accessible by all applications is a vital part of the infrastructure supporting a distributed system, much especially true for ASPs. A directory service provides the ASP and ASP customers a single logical view of the users, resources, and other objects that make up a distributed system. This allows ASP customers and applications to access network resources transparently. That is, the system is perceived as an integrated whole, not a collection of independent parts. Objects can be accessed by name or function without knowing low-level identifiers such as host addresses, file server names, and e-mail addresses.

For example, an ASP may offer various Domino, WebSphere, and other *directory-enabled applications* to customers. LDAP allows different applications to share a common directory infrastructure. A directory-enabled application uses a directory service to improve its functionality, ease of use, and administration.

When applications access a standard common directory that is designed in a proper way, rather than using application-specific directories, redundant and costly administration can be eliminated, and security risks are more controllable. New uses for directory information will be realized, and a synergy will develop as more applications take advantage of the common directory.

4.5.3 Directory services in Domino

In addition to the Domino Directory itself, Domino provides three directory service features:

- Directory catalog
- Directory assistance
- LDAP service

These features help users find user names, e-mail addresses, and other information in the Domino Directory.

The directory catalog consolidates key information about users and groups from one or more Domino directories into a small, lightweight database. Notes users who use a local copy of the directory catalog (a mobile directory catalog) can quickly address mail to users throughout the organization, even if the organization uses a large directory or multiple directories. In organizations with multiple Domino directories, a directory catalog on a server combines these directories into a single database so that a server can look up names in one database rather than in multiple Domino directories.

Directory assistance is a feature that helps manage name lookups in organizations that use multiple Domino directories or third-party LDAP directories. A directory assistance database associates each Domino directory/LDAP directory with specific hierarchical names so that when it looks up a hierarchical name, Domino first searches the directory that contains names in that hierarchy.

You can set up a Domino server to run the LDAP service to enable LDAP clients to search for and modify information in the Domino Directory. The Domino LDAP service is LDAP v3 compliant.

Related to Domino-based directory services on the iSeries is the feature that allows you to synchronize the iSeries System Distribution Directory (SDD). If you are an ISV that is considering migrating from an OfficeVision/400 (OV/400) or systems network architecture distribution services (SNADS)-based e-mail solution to a Domino-based solution (which is a good and common step), this feature allows you to migrate your users to the Domino directory with ease.

4.5.4 Domino LDAP service features

The Domino LDAP service supports these features:

- LDAP v3 and v2
- Anonymous access to fields that you specify, name and password authentication, SSL and x.509 certificate authentication, Simple Authentication and Security Layer (SASL) protocol
- LDAP searches extended to secondary Domino directories
- LDAP client referrals to other LDAP directories
- Use of a third-party, LDAP-compliant server (such as the Netscape Enterprise Web server) to authenticate users that have name and passwords or x.509 certificates stored in the Domino Directory on a Domino server running the LDAP service. For information on setting up a third-party server to do this, see the server's documentation.
- Use of LDAP clients to add, modify, and delete directory entries
- Schema publishing, schema checking, and schema extension
- Searches based on alternate languages

Domino also supports these features that don't require the LDAP service:

- Command-line utility for searching LDAP directories
- Migration tool that lets you import entries from another LDAP directory and register the entries in Domino

Although Domino Release 5 doesn't provide an LDAP API toolkit, you can use standard LDAP C, Java, and JNDI libraries that are available on the Internet to customize the Domino LDAP API.

4.5.5 Setting up the LDAP service

Before you set up the Domino LDAP service, be sure you:

- Understand TCP/IP concepts, including DNS host names and IP addressing.
- Set up the Domino server, and set up security for the server.

Then, perform these steps:

1. To allow clients to connect to the LDAP service over the Internet, connect the server that runs the LDAP service to an Internet service provider (ISP), and register the server's DNS name and IP address with the ISP.

2. Create a full text index for the replica of the Domino Directory on the server that runs the LDAP service. We strongly recommend that you create a full text index, unless LDAP users search only for names.

3. Start the Domino server, and then start the LDAP task.

4. If your organization uses more than one Global Domain document, you must specify the one that the LDAP service uses to return users' Internet addresses to LDAP clients. Open the Global Domain document. In the Use as default Global Domain field, choose **Yes**.

5. Set up LDAP clients to connect to the LDAP service.

6. (Optional) Customize the default LDAP service configuration. In most cases, the LDAP service functions correctly when you use the default settings.

7. To check whether you set up the LDAP service correctly, use an LDAP client or the lsearch utility to issue a query to the LDAP service.

4.5.6 Setting up users to use the LDAP service

To use the Domino LDAP service, each LDAP user, whether Notes or non-Notes, must set up the client to connect to the LDAP service.

4.5.6.1 Setting up non-Notes LDAP users

To set up a non-Notes LDAP user to connect to the LDAP service, in the LDAP client configuration, specify the host name of the Domino server running the LDAP service, for example ldap.acme.com, or the IP address for the server. If you want an LDAP user to connect using a name and password or client certificate authentication, the user must have a Person document in the primary Domino Directory used by the LDAP service that includes the user's password or client certificate.

By default, LDAP users that connect to the LDAP service using name and password security can use any name in the FullName (User name) or ShortName (Short name) field in the Person document as the LDAP client user name, as long as the name is unique in the directory. However, to require that instead these users specify their fully qualified distinguished names as specified in RFCs 2251 through 2254, use the Notes.ini setting LDAP_Strict_RFC_Adherence.

4.5.6.2 Setting up Notes users to connect to the LDAP service

To set up Notes users to connect automatically to the LDAP service, you need to create or modify a User Setup Profile. If you do not use a User Setup Profile to set up users, each Notes user who wants to use the LDAP service must create an account to connect to the server.

1. From the Domino Administrator, in the server pane on the left, select a server. If you do not see the server pane, click the servers icon.
2. Click the **People & Groups** tab.
3. Expand **Domino Directories**, and then choose **Setup Profiles**.
4. Choose one of the following tasks:
   - To modify an existing User Setup Profile, select the profile, and then click **Edit Setup Profile**.
   - To create a new User Setup Profile, click **Add Setup Profile**, and enter a name for the profile in the Profile name field.
5. Click the **Accounts** tab. Then complete the Default Accounts to Internet Servers as shown in Table 15.

   Note: To create accounts for multiple Internet services, enter multiple values in each field, and separate the values with commas (,).

Table 15. LDAP settings

Field	Enter
Account Names	A descriptive name for this LDAP service account. Users see this name when they're prompted to select an LDAP service to search. If you specify more than one account, for example, an account for another Internet service, separate the account names with commas (,).
Server Addresses	The host name of the server running the LDAP service, for example, ldap.acme.com.
Protocols	Choose LDAP.
Use SSL Connection	Enter Yes to use SSL. Otherwise, enter No.

6. Complete the other fields in the User Setup Profile, as desired, and then click **Save and Close**.

4.5.7 Interoperability of Domino with other LDAP directories

Depending on the circumstances, an ASP may or may not use Domino Directory as the primary enterprise directory.

The Domino Directory can pass LDAP referrals and mail addressing requests. It supports LDAP v3. For example, you can read and write information, not just read. The Domino Directory could be the best general-purpose directory for any application to use, not just the Notes application. It allows non-Notes applications to read and write, and to store their own application information in the Domino Directory.

The Domino HTTP server can authenticate clients using a different directory. You can set up an LDAP directory that contains such information as passwords and X.509 certificates for a set of people who may not be Notes users. You can point the Directory Assistance database to reference that particular "foreign" LDAP directory for lookups. This solves the problem of people having to put names in the Domino directory when they're already elsewhere. It also works in the opposite direction. You can enable other servers, such as the Netscape Enterprise Server, to authenticate users in the Domino Directory through LDAP.

4.5.8 For more information

Please refer to *Understanding LDAP*, SG24-4986. The Domino 5 Administration Help database also offers good information related to:

- Setting up the LDAP service
- Setting up users to use the LDAP service
- Customizing the LDAP service configuration
- Monitoring the LDAP service
- Using the Isearch utility to search LDAP directories

4.6 Building a portal

This section explains what a portal is and why it is important to an ASP.

4.6.1 What is a portal

A *portal* is an application or device that provides a *personalized* and *adaptive* interface for people to discover, track, and interact with other relevant people, applications, and content.

As an ASP, you may concentrate on the following portals:

- **Commercial portal**: To provide an electronic catalog applications to your ASP customers

- **Personal portal**: To provide online bill paying applications

- **Corporate portal**: To provide intranet applications to your corporate customers

4.6.2 Implementing a portal

The BlueNotes Office Portal creates a sample set of Lotus Notes Welcome Pages (a portal) as a basis for the creation of a consistent and manageable user interface to corporate and departmental intranets, extranets, and Internet sites and to personal and workgroup applications. The workgroup page is designed to include the Notes and Domino function (Mail, Calendar, Directory, Document Library), which replaces the function from the OfficeVision/400 menu. Therefore, it is now easier for former OV/400 users to locate their usual function. Office Portal can be customized further by administrators and developers using the Lotus Notes Release 5 Portal Builder and can be distributed automatically to end users.

This sample Domino portal is available as a free download from:
http://www.bluenotes.com/

4.6.3 For more information

Please refer to *Building a Portal with Lotus Domino R5*, REDP0019, which is available from the IBM Redbooks Web site (http://www.redbooks.ibm.com/). This redpaper describes the techniques to create an effective, customizable portal for both Lotus Notes clients and Internet browser clients using the Domino R5 platform.

4.7 Domino and WebSphere

IBM WebSphere is a Web application server and is a key product offerings for ASPs. It offers a standards-based Java server run-time environment and a set of Java development tools. This section talks about the preliminary work on Domino and WebSphere integration. Much of the information in this section is from the Notes.net article "The Highs and Lows of Domino/WebSphere Integration" with guest John Banks-Binici.

For a practical side of Domino and WebSphere integration, see the IBM Redbook *Domino and WebSphere Together*, SG24-5955.

4.7.1 Three different editions of WebSphere

Currently, there are three different server editions in the WebSphere product family:

- **Standard Edition**: WebSphere Application Server Standard Edition for AS/400 3.5 is shipped as an iSeries licensed program option (LPO) 5733-AS3 Product and uses North American Encryption (128 bit).

- **Advanced Edition**: Builds on the Standard Edition by having an Enterprise JavaBeans (EJB) programming environment. This environment allows you to write portable Java component-based applications with easy-to-use builder tools. With these tools, an ASP can build commercial applications that take advantage of complex server features, like two-phase commit transactions, which are critical to many applications, especially customer-to-business and business-to-business applications. Advanced Edition also includes a Java Object Request Broker for building networked Java objects.

- **Enterprise Edition**: Adds the Component Broker C++ ORB, which allows you to write and deploy C++ based server objects as well. The Enterprise Edition is not available on the iSeries.

4.7.2 Positioning WebSphere with Domino

WebSphere is a Java server platform and provides a set of platform extensions that allow you to write truly portable applications abstracted by the Java Virtual Machine (JVM). For example, an ASP can write Java programs to access the directory via a standard API such as the Java Naming and Directory Interface (JNDI). An ASP can also use WebSphere to leverage the EJB programming model to distribute highly scalable transactional applications to their customers.

WebSphere and Domino offer different capabilities. There is ongoing work within IBM and Lotus to leverage the strength of both products so that these two products work together. For example, if Domino has been deployed in your ASP environment, you would want WebSphere to leverage your existing Domino Directory, security, and administrative infrastructure.

Which product is the right one?
In short, if you are building Web applications that focus on collaboration, Domino is the right choice. If you are building a Web site that needs to handle a lot of transactions or requires the use of Enterprise Java components, WebSphere is the right choice. If you need to build a site that needs both of these capabilities, Domino and WebSphere work together over the same HTTP stack to deliver the best of both worlds.

For example, one customer built an application that uses a Domino workflow infrastructure to implement content management for their Web site catalog. Domino-based workflow and collaboration software is used to manage the content generation and content approval process for catalog entries and prices. The highly scalable transaction services of WebSphere are used in tandem to implement the actual catalog site. Domino messaging is used to send confirmation information to the customer and to maintain the dialog with the customer.

4.8 Billing

In the ASP market, the term *billing* refers to charging customers for the ASP services and resources provided. The billing tool maintains a list of all the registered ASP users and services, and uses a predefined model to track charges for services.

Domino Enterprise Server R5 for AS/400 has a billing feature. It can be used to collect information about the activity in the enterprise. Then using the information that billing collects, users can be charged for the usage of the system, usage trends can be monitored, resource planning can be conducted, and it can be determined if clustering would improve the efficiency of the system.

> **A word of caution**
>
> The Domino billing feature might have a short life with the arrival of the Lotus Hosting Management System (LHMS) (see 4.12, "A common framework for Domino ASPs: Lotus ASP Solution Pack" on page 211).
>
> Billing via the billing feature can be done. However, we recommend that you either go directly to LHMS or use the flexibility of Domino in which a variety of billing models can be supported. The final decision about how to approach billing is up to the ASP and the ISV. Payment by the end customer does not have to be tied to a per user model. For example, pricing could be based on the occurrence of particular events or on a flat price with a cap on the number of users.

When you enable billing, Lotus Domino collects information about client and server activity and places this information in the billing message queue. Periodically, the billing task polls the message queue and moves the billing information to a specified destination – a Lotus Notes database, a binary file, or both.

To create billing reports, an application is written to access the billing information. If the information is collected in a Lotus Notes database, a Notes application can be written to create the billing reports needed. If the information is collected in a binary file, a third-party program is used to analyze the data and create the billing reports.

Appropriate settings in the Notes.ini file can be used to tell Lotus Domino which types of billing information to collect. Table 16 explains the seven classes of billing information that can be collected.

Table 16. Billing information

Billing class	Tracks
Agent	When users and servers run agents on the billing server, as well as the running time of the agents
Database	When users and servers open and close databases, and the duration of use
Document	Read and write activity for specified documents
HTTPRequest	Web server requests
Mail	When the mail router on a billing server transfers messages to another Lotus Domino server
Replication	When a billing server initiates replication with another server or client
Session	When users and servers start and end sessions with a billing server and when network-related activities, such as document creation and editing, occur during the session

The billing task provided with Lotus Domino or the Lotus Notes C API can also be used to design a custom billing task that includes billing classes and collects information that Lotus Domino does not.

4.8.1 The Billing database

When billing information is recorded in a Lotus Notes database, Lotus Domino creates a database named Billing.nsf on the server. The database contains these views:

- Agents by user name
- Document by user name
- HTTP requests
- Mail by originator
- Replication by server
- Sessions/Database Open by user name
- Sessions/Network Traffic by user name

A Notes API program can be created to access the information in the database.

Setting up billing

To set up billing, you edit the Notes.ini file. Within the Notes.ini file, you enter commands to start the billing task, to specify which billing classes to track, and to specify where to store billing records.

You can tell Domino to store billing records in a Notes database, in a binary file, or in both. If you specify a Notes database, Domino uses the template Billing.*ntf* to create the database and names it Billing.*nsf*. The billing task transfers billing records from the message queue to documents in the Billing database. If you specify a binary file, Domino creates the Billing.*nbf* file. The billing task transfers billing records from the message queue to Billing.nbf in stream format. Because each billing record begins with the length and structure type, the program you use to read the billing records can easily parse the file.

1. Edit the ServerTasks setting in the Notes.ini file to include the billing task. For example, the line might read:

   ```
   ServerTasks=Replica,Router,Update,Stats,Billing
   ```

2. Add this line to the Notes.ini file to specify which billing classes to track:

   ```
   BillingClass=list
   ```

   Here, *list* contains one or more of the following options:

   - Agent
   - Database
   - Document
   - HTTPRequest
   - Mail
   - Replication
   - Session

3. Add this line to the Notes.ini file to specify where to store the billing information:

   ```
   BillingAddinOutput=n
   ```

   Here, *n* is one of the following values:

   - 1 to store the records in a Notes database
   - 2 to display the records on the server console
   - 8 to store the records in a binary file
   - 9 to store the records in both a database and a binary file

You can add "2" to each of the other numbers to combine that choice with displaying the records on the server console. For example, "3" stores records in a Notes database and displays records on the server console.

4.8.2 Starting billing manually

Enter this command on the console:

```
Load billing
Set configuration BillingClass= list
```

Here, *list* contains one or more of the following options:

- Agent
- Database
- Document
- HTTPRequest
- Mail
- Replication
- Session

4.8.3 Stopping billing

To stop all instances of the billing task for the current session, enter this command at the console:

```
tel billing quit
```

Disabling the task stops it from transferring billing records from the message queue to the Billing database or the binary file. If you still have the BillingClass setting in the Notes.ini file, Domino continues to write billing records to the message queue. When you restart the billing task, it transfers the records from the message queue to the Billing database or the binary file.

4.8.4 Optimizing billing performance

As an ASP, running billing tasks for all your customers could be a resource-intensive exercise. You can improve the performance of billings by adjusting how often billing performs certain tasks.

4.8.4.1 Changing the frequency of adding records to the message queue

You can control how often Domino adds session stamp records and database DBStamp records to the message queue. During times of peak usage, if system performance decreases or the system runs out of virtual memory, add records to the message queue less frequently. If performance is not a problem and you want to generate more billing records, add records more frequently.

By default, Domino creates records every 15 minutes. To change this default, add the BillingSuppressTime setting to the Notes.ini file. To determine the best amount of time for your system, try various amounts of time, and track the performance for each.

4.8.4.2 Controlling the transfer of records from the message queue

The billing task may use a lot of system resources to transfer records from the message queue to the Billing database or the binary file, especially when your system is busy. There are three ways to control this process. You can change how often the billing task runs, you can change the length of time the billing task runs, and you can run multiple billing tasks.

By default, the billing task starts running once every minute and runs for 10 seconds each time. To adjust these default behaviors, edit the settings shown in Table 17 in the Notes.ini file.

Table 17. Notes.ini settings for billing task

To change	Edit this setting in the Notes.ini file
How often the billing task runs	BillingAddinWakeup
How long the billing task runs	BillingAddinRuntime

If you have system performance problems, adjust these settings so that the billing task runs less frequently or runs for less time. As with BillingSuppressTime, the best way to find out which settings are best for your system is to test various settings and track the performance.

Another way to control the transfer of records from the message queue is to run more than one billing task. Multiple billing tasks work simultaneously to process records in the billing message queue. Do not run more billing tasks than the number of processors that are in your computer because this could impede performance.

4.8.4.3 Running multiple billing tasks

Perform one of the following tasks:

- To run multiple billing tasks at server startup, edit the ServerTasks setting in the Notes.ini file to include multiple instances of billing, for example:

  ```
  ServerTasks=Cldbdir,Clrepl,Router,Repl,AgentMgr,Billing,Billing,Billing
  ```

- To run multiple billing tasks from the console, enter this command one or more times at the console:

  ```
  load billing
  ```

4.9 Domino security model

Setting up security is the act of making information available to selected users, while denying access to other users. How you implement security depends on whether you are setting up security for Notes and Domino or Internet and intranet clients. Internet and intranet clients do not use ID files. Therefore, the Domino server cannot enforce server security the same way that it does for Notes users and Domino servers.

You can think of security as consisting of several layers. Once a user or server passes through one security layer, the next layer of security is enforced. The following sections offer a brief description of the security layers that you set up to protect the Domino system.

4.9.1 Physical security

Physically securing servers and databases is just as important as preventing unauthorized user and server access. Therefore, we strongly recommend that you locate all Domino servers in a ventilated, secure area, such as a locked room. If servers are not secure, unauthorized users might circumvent security features (for example, access control list (ACL) settings) and access application on the server, use the operating system to copy or delete files, or physically damage the server hardware itself.

4.9.2 Network security

Network security is beyond the scope of this book, but you must set it up before you set up Notes and Domino security. Network security prevents unauthorized users from breaking into the network and impersonating an authorized Notes user and from eavesdropping on the network where the Domino system resides. Eavesdropping can occur only if transactions are not encrypted. Therefore, to prevent eavesdropping, encrypt all Domino and Notes transactions. Then eavesdroppers cannot understand the transactions they receive.

4.9.3 Server security

This is the first level of security that Domino enforces after a user or server gains access to the server on the network. You can specify which users and servers have access to the server and restrict activities on the server. For example, you can restrict who can create new replicas and use passthru connections.

If you set up servers for Internet and intranet access, set up SSL and name and password authentication to secure network data transmitted over the network and to authenticate servers and clients. In addition, set up a firewall server to protect

Internet servers from unauthorized access from outside the organization's network.

4.9.4 Application security

After users and servers gain access to another server, you can use the database ACL to restrict access that specific users and servers have to individual applications on the server. You can also provide data privacy by:

- Encrypting the database with an ID so unauthorized users cannot access a locally stored copy of the database
- Electronically signing or encrypting mail messages users send and receive
- Signing the database or template to protect workstations from formulas.

4.9.5 Application design element security

Although a user may have access to an application, the user may not have access to specific design elements in the application, for example, forms, views, and folders. When designing a Domino application, an application developer can use access lists and special fields to restrict access to specific design elements.

4.9.6 ID security

A Notes or Domino ID uniquely identifies a user or server. Domino uses the information in IDs to control the access that users and servers have to other servers and applications. One of the responsibilities of the administrator is to protect IDs and make sure that unauthorized users do not use them.

Some sites may require multiple administrators to enter passwords before gaining access to a certifier or server ID file. This prevents one person from controlling an ID. In such cases, each administrator should ensure each password is secure to prevent unauthorized access to the ID file.

4.9.7 The Domino security team

A typical Domino security team includes administrators and database managers who are responsible for implementing and managing specific aspects of the Domino security system.

4.9.7.1 Server administrators

Server administrators are responsible for one or more Domino servers. Major responsibilities of a server administrator include defining and managing server access lists and server restrictions, both for Notes clients and Web users. In small organizations, a server administrator might serve as the Domino certification administrator and the database manager for system databases, such as the Domino Directory and the log file (LOG.NSF). A server administrator might also be responsible for creating and maintaining File Protection documents for HTTP access, and other Web-related security measures.

4.9.7.2 Database managers

Database managers are responsible for one or more applications. The major responsibilities of a database manager include defining and managing database ACLs.

4.9.7.3 Domino certificate authorities

Domino certificate authorities have access to certifier ID files, which are the binary files that the administrator uses to create user and server IDs. The Domino certificate authority issues certificates that are signed by the organization or organizational unit certifier ID. These certificates are stored in the ID file. The Domino certificate authority creates a public/private key pair while registering the user. The user can later replace this key pair, if desired, and submit the new public key to the Domino certificate authority for certification. Certificates contain the user's public key (from the public/private key pair in the ID file) and ensure that the information in the certificate – that is, user name, public key, expiration date, and so on – is accurate.

Domino certificate authorities can also issue Internet certificates to Notes users, Internet clients, and Internet servers. The Domino certificate authority issues signed x.509 format certificates that uniquely identify the requesting client or server. Internet certificates are required when sending encrypted or electronically signed Secure Multipurpose Internet Mail Extensions (S/MIME) mail messages and when using SSL to authenticate a client or server.

Certificate authorities are responsible for adding new Notes users and Domino servers to the system, as well as for recertifying existing IDs. Since certification is the cornerstone of Notes and Domino security, delegate responsibility for it with the utmost care.

4.10 User management for ASP customers

As an ASP, you will provide a front-end tool called the *provisioning tool*. This tool provides two key functions: a front end for users to log into the ASP and a dashboard for administrators to perform administrative tasks. If you are an ASP for Domino applications, your provisioning tool could be a Lotus Notes client or a Web browser.

All registered users log in into the ASP via the provisioning tool's front end. The tool checks the service-level access permissions of each user and makes the applications available. The front end usually allows users to handle basic administration on their accounts such as viewing the account balance, changing the password, and managing other account details.

The provisioning tool also presents a dashboard for ASP administrators to perform administrative tasks. That is, the tool could be the Lotus Notes Client, Domino Designer Client, or Domino Administrator Client. Using the dashboard, administrators can create new user accounts and assign service-level privileges, add services to existing user accounts, apply credits, temporarily disable or permanently close accounts, plus all other user-level administrative functions.

Provisioning tool and operating costs
The operating cost of the ASP largely depends on the provisioning solution. Delegating as many tasks as possible to customer-level administrators and users reduces operating costs. Providing users the means to perform basic administration decreases the number of requests to the ASP administrator and that, in turn, reduces costs. A well-design and powerful provisioning solution also results in higher customer satisfaction by facilitating easy user access to the service and quick responses to administrative requests.

4.11 Capacity planning for Lotus Domino for AS/400

A basic way to implement Domino in an ASP environment is to implement one Domino server instance per customer. Using this method, you can host an unlimited number (depending on the type of workload and size of the iSeries server, of course!) of customers on one iSeries server, reducing the cost of ownership and the number of footprints in your server farm significantly compared to an Intel or UNIX-based scenario. That is, in the past, you were restricted to no more than 30 or 99 Domino partitions running on one AS/400. Now this restriction has been eliminated. Before you start to implement an unlimited number of partitions on your iSeries server, please read this section on capacity planning.

The outline that we develop in the following paragraphs is not intended to be a complete "how to" guide on installing, administrating, sizing, and tuning Domino. If you need further specific information on these topics, we strongly recommend that you read these redbooks:

- *Lotus Domino for AS/400: Implementation*, SG24-5592
- *Lotus Domino for AS/400: Performance, Tuning, and Capacity Planning*, SG24-5162

You should also review the documentation found at the IBM Workload Estimator for iSeries 400 Web site at: `http://as400service.ibm.com/estimator`

4.11.1 Scenario description

This scenario looks at a business case in which the ASP is tasked with providing Domino server functionality to a set of five Small and Medium Business (SMB) customers with 5 to 500 users each. These SMB customers usually do not have any significant IT resources of their own to implement a solution such as Domino and will, therefore, be a likely target for an externally provided solution.

The transport medium used to connect the customers to the data center will be the Internet. Connection security will be provided by using secure socket layer (SSL) encryption for the clients, which delivers sufficient security for a low to middle secure environment.

The workload mix in this scenario is 80% mail users (for example, mail or calendaring) and 20% Lotus Domino applications (for example, discussion databases). Within each of the two groups of mail and Lotus application users, we will expect a mix of 10% casual, 70% moderate, and 20% heavy usage. Extensive DB2 UDB integration and legacy application workload on the iSeries server is not a part of the scenario (but can be easily added using the online Workload Estimator).

Other assumptions made in this scenario include using RAID-5 for DASD storage protection and two Domino partitions for *each* ASP customer. One partition will serve the applications, and the other partition is for a hot-backup of their data.

The ASP's initial customer mix in this example is shown in Table 18.

Table 18. ASP example customer mix

Customer	Mail users	Domino application users	Type of client	Common assumptions
Cust1	200	50	Notes	RAID-5, two Domino partitions for each customer, mix of concurrent users and percent casual, moderate and heavy as defaulted in the IBM Workload Estimator for iSeries 400 Web site.
Cust2	30	7	Web	
Cust3	400	100	Notes	
Cust4	128	32	Web	
Cust5	5	1	Notes	

4.11.2 Sizing the solution

The first step toward finding a good value proposition is to find the right server size. The determining factors are basically the number of users you want to serve, the number of server instances you want to run, and the type of Domino applications you are serving.

The IBM Workload Estimator for iSeries 400, a publicly available sizing tool for Domino on the iSeries server, is especially nice because it allows you to mix other types of workloads such as Java, WebSphere Commerce Suite (formerly called Net.Commerce), traditional, WebSphere, HTTP, and a generic application model. You can access the Workload Estimator for iSeries 400 at:
`http://as400service.ibm.com/estimator`

Using the IBM Workload Estimator for iSeries 400, you can establish workload estimations for a proposed iSeries ASP system. Follow these steps:

1. Use the high-level planning information that is available in Table 18 to update the Type of Workload to *Domino* for all five of our customers (Name of Workload Cust1 through Cust5).

   a. Click the **Operational Assumptions** button on the bottom of the form (as shown in Figure 82).

   b. Change the Base Calculation Defaults for RAID Support to `RAID5`.

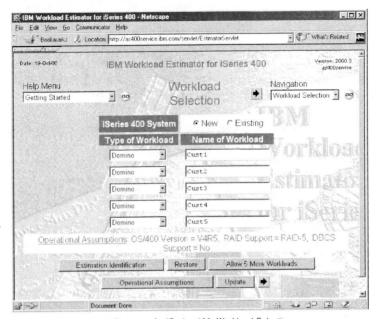

Figure 82. IBM Workload Estimator for iSeries 400: Workload Selection

2. Click the right arrow (->) button to move forward through the series of panels so you can further define the workloads for your five customers. You can click the left arrow (<-) to review or change any values on the previous panels. The panel for our first customer Cust1 is shown Figure 83. For this scenario, nothing needs to be changed on this panel.

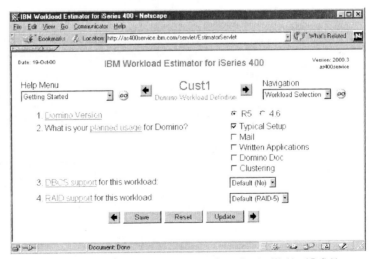

Figure 83. IBM Workload Estimator for iSeries 400: Cust1 Domino Workload Definition

3. Click the right arrow (->) button to move forward to the panel shown in Figure 84 on page 192. On this panel, you estimate the Domino mail workload for the

first customer Cust1. As estimated in Table 18 on page 190, there will be 200 mail users using a Notes client to access their mail with an expected mix of 10% casual, 70% moderate and 20% heavy usage.

a. Update the fields as necessary.
b. Change the Number of registered users that are mail users field to 200.
c. For high-availability and security, you should have two Domino partitions per customer. This is done by specifying 2 for the Number of partitions for MAIL in this instance of the Domino Workload field.

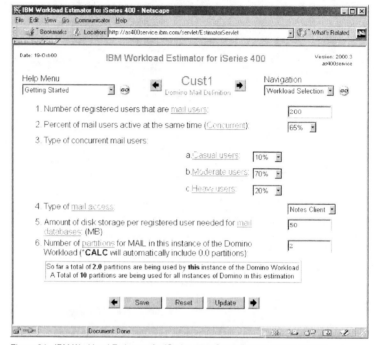

Figure 84. IBM Workload Estimator for iSeries 400: Cust1 Domino Mail Definition

4. When you are done with the Domino mail workload estimation, click the right arrow (->) to move forward to the panel shown in Figure 85. Here is where you estimate the Domino application workload for the first customer Cust1. As estimated in Table 18 on page 190, there will be 50 application users using a Notes client.

Notice that the Number of partitions for MAIL in this instance of the Domino Workload field is set to *CALC because two Domino partitions are already defined as part of the mail workload estimation.

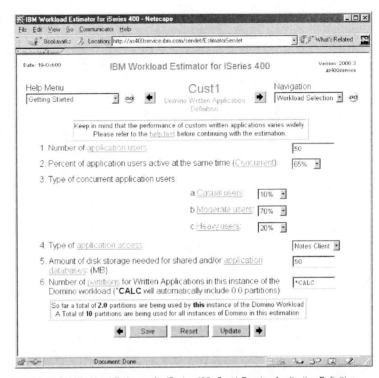

Figure 85. IBM Workload Estimator for iSeries 400: Cust1 Domino Application Definition

5. When you are done with the Domino application workload estimation, click the right arrow (->) to move forward to repeat the process for customers Cust2 through Cust5. Remember to refer to Table 18 on page 190 for the estimated numbers of mail and Domino application users.

It is important to correctly change the Type of application access field (Figure 85) to reflect whether these clients will access the Domino server as Notes clients or Web clients.

When you are done, you should see the IBM Workload Estimator for iSeries 400 Selected System result panel as shown in Figure 86 on page 194.

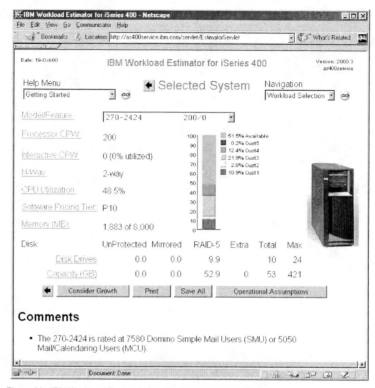

Figure 86. IBM Workload Estimator for iSeries 400: Selected System

In this case, the Workload Estimator has selected Model 270-2424.

6. You may want to click the **Consider Growth** button. This button allows you to select a one-time growth estimate in the terms of a percentage. Leaving room for growth is a very important part of the total ASP solution. Consider this example where you click the Consider Growth button; enter 20%, for example, in the Growth Solution field; and then click Calculate. If you do this, you will see the panel shown in Figure 87.

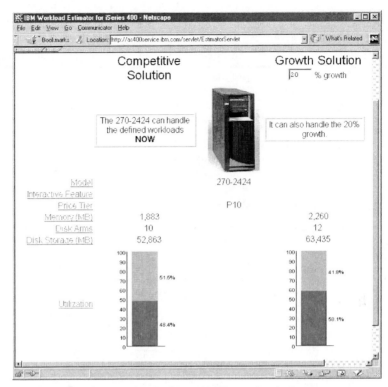

Figure 87. IBM Workload Estimator for iSeries 400: 20% growth estimate

It is sometimes difficult to plan for growth, especially in an ASP where so many factors are outside your control. Born out of the ASP business model is Capacity Advantage, a newly announced feature for the iSeries Model 840. What if your business does too well, that is, you have more customers jumping on your solution than you can handle with the sub-second response time you have agreed to? Would it be helpful to have a hot-spare processor already in the machine that you could simply "turn on"? Vertical Capacity Upgrade defines such a solution. Vertical Capacity Upgrade on Demand ensures fast, non-disruptive growth by including extra processors held in reserve in your server. Customers also have the opportunity to "try out" the standby capacity for a number of days without charge. The vertical approach is ideal when changing workload requirements dictate an increase in capacity on the server. For more information about this feature, see: `http://www-1.ibm.com/servers/eserver/introducing/capacity.html`

4.11.3 Pre-installation considerations and prerequisites

Before moving on to the actual installation of Domino on your system, there are a few points you need to consider.

First, you have to make sure that you've finished your Network (IP) planning. The IP addresses we use in our example are shown in Table 19.

Table 19. Example IP configuration

Customer (server)	IP	Subnet mask
Customer 1 (Cust1)	10.5.92.42	255.255.255.0
Customer 2 (Cust2)	10.5.92.43	255.255.255.0
Customer 3 (Cust3)	10.5.92.44	255.255.255.0
Customer 4 (Cust4)	10.5.92.46	255.255.255.0
Customer 5 (Cust5)	10.5.92.51	255.255.255.0

We show you how to configure these IP addresses on your server in 4.11.4, "Network setup" on page 197.

To use TCP/IP on your iSeries server, please ensure that you have the TCP/IP Utilities for AS/400 (5769-TC1) installed.

The minimum OS/400 release you need for this scenario is V4R3M0. Note that the end-of-life for V4R3M0 is 31 January 2001. However, using a DSD model for implementation will give you a release level of V4R4M0.

To look up the latest required PTFs for Domino, please check the Web site: http://www.iseries.ibm.com/domino/support/

Make sure you have all the PTFs you need installed on your iSeries server before you proceed.

For a fully featured Domino environment on your iSeries server, you need to install the software listed in Table 20 on your iSeries server.

Table 20. iSeries software for fully featured Domino environment

Feature code	Description	Why
5769-SS1 option 12	OS/400 host server	Enables you to use Operations Navigator.
5763-XD1 or 5769-XE1	Client Access or Client Access Express	With Operation Navigator installed, gives you the ability to easily start, stop, and configure your Domino servers from your PC desktop.
5769-CX2	AS/400 ILE C compiler	Compile Notes C APIs on your iSeries.
5769-CX4	Visual Age C++ for OS/400	Compile Notes C APIs on your desktop.
5769-SS1 option 30	Qshell interpreter	Enables you to run 5769-JV1.
5769-JV1	AS/400 developer Kit for Java	Needed to run Java Domino agents.

To administrate your Domino Server, you need to setup a Notes client. The Domino for AS/400 server can connect to Lotus Notes Release 5 (R5), Domino Designer R5, and Domino Administrator R5 clients that run on the following operating systems:

- Microsoft Windows 95, Microsoft Windows 98, or Microsoft Windows NT Version 4.0

- Macintosh PowerPC

The Domino for AS/400 server can connect to Lotus Notes Release 4.6 clients running on the following operating systems:

- AIX 4.1.5 or 4.2.1
- HP-UX 10.20
- Sun Solaris Intel Edition 2.5.1 or Sun SPARC Solaris 2.5.1
- Microsoft Windows 95, Microsoft Windows 98, or Microsoft Windows NT Version 4.0

Earlier versions of Notes Release 4 clients can also connect to the Domino server. These earlier versions support additional operating systems, in particular OS/2 and Microsoft Windows 3.1. However, some iSeries administration functions require a Notes 4.6 client or later. To manage a Domino server on the iSeries from a Notes client, you must have a workstation connected to the iSeries server. The software requirements for that workstation depend on which administrator functions you use to manage the server.

We recommend that you use an R5 Domino Administrator client to administer a Domino R5 server. If you plan to use the Web administration functions, you must have a Web browser on the workstation.

If you plan to use the AS/400 Operations Navigator to manage the Domino server, you must have the following software on the workstation:

- A Microsoft Windows 95, Microsoft Windows 98, or Microsoft Windows NT Version 4 operating system

- IBM AS/400 Client Access for Windows 95/NT or IBM AS/400 Client Access Express for Windows

- TCP/IP configured

- Domino Administrator R5

For a good source of information to install and get started with a Domino server on the iSeries, consult *Up and Running with Domino for AS/400*, SC41-5334, and other Lotus Domino for AS/400 manuals, redbooks, and release notes on the Web site: http://www.iseries.ibm.com/domino/support/

You should also refer to the document *Installing and Managing Domino for AS/400* located at: http://www.notes.net/doc

4.11.4 Network setup

The Domino for AS/400 server uses TCP/IP to connect to Notes clients, the Web, or other Domino servers.

From the Notes client PC point of view, two partitioned servers look like two different systems. Since they reside in the same iSeries, you have to configure

TCP/IP to differentiate the partitioned servers. You can choose from two different ways to differentiate the partitioned servers on your iSeries server:

- Assign each server its own IP address (recommended). This is the simplest and recommended method of setting up partitioned Domino for AS/400 servers. That is, if the servers use the same iSeries communication adapter, you need to assign more than one IP interface to the same line description. Each server must appear with its correct IP address on a name server (DNS) or the clients' host table.

- As an alternative, you could use port mapping to assign all servers the same IP address. This is a more involved way of setting up multiple partitioned servers. In port mapping, all servers running on the iSeries server use the same IP address. Unique port numbers are used to distinguish between each partitioned server. However, due to severe limitations in availability and performance, this method is not recommended for use in an ASP environment and will not be further discussed here.

4.11.4.1 Configuring a unique IP address for each server

In this step, you assign a unique IP address to each partitioned server and define that IP address to your iSeries TCP/IP configuration. Since the iSeries TCP/IP implementation supports multihoming, you may use the same line description for more than one IP interface.

In our example, we assign the names and IP addresses to five partitioned servers as shown in Table 19 on page 196.

Assuming you want to use the same physical token-ring line of the iSeries server, you need to add all three interfaces to the appropriate line description. Follow these steps:

1. On the OS/400 command line, type the Configure TCP/IP (CFGTCP) command, and press the Enter key. The Configure TCP/IP screen appears as shown in Figure 88.

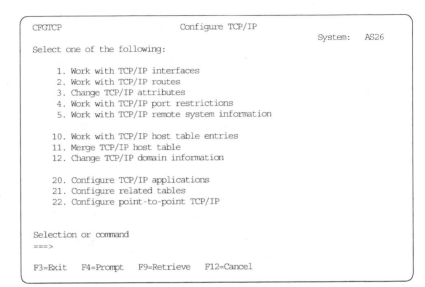

```
CFGTCP                          Configure TCP/IP
                                                        System:    AS26
  Select one of the following:

        1. Work with TCP/IP interfaces
        2. Work with TCP/IP routes
        3. Change TCP/IP attributes
        4. Work with TCP/IP port restrictions
        5. Work with TCP/IP remote system information

       10. Work with TCP/IP host table entries
       11. Merge TCP/IP host table
       12. Change TCP/IP domain information

       20. Configure TCP/IP applications
       21. Configure related tables
       22. Configure point-to-point TCP/IP



  Selection or command
  ===>

  F3=Exit    F4=Prompt   F9=Retrieve    F12=Cancel
```

Figure 88. The CFGTCP menu

2. On the OS/400 command line, type 1, and press the Enter key. The Work with TCP/IP Interfaces screen appears as shown in Figure 89.

```
                     Work with TCP/IP Interfaces
                                                        System:    AS26
  Type options, press Enter.
    1=Add    2=Change    4=Remove    5=Display    9=Start    10=End

        Internet          Subnet              Line       Line
  Opt   Address           Mask                Description Type

   _
        9.5.92.41         255.255.255.128     TRNLINE     *TRLAN
        9.5.92.47         255.255.255.128     TRNLINE     *TRLAN
        127.0.0.1         255.0.0.0           *LOOPBACK   *NONE

                                                                  Bottom
  F3=Exit       F5=Refresh    F6=Print list    F11=Display interface status
  F12=Cancel    F17=Top       F18=Bottom
```

Figure 89. Work with TCP Interfaces

3. Take note of the existing Line Description name in the column labeled "Line Description." (for example TRNLINE, ETHLINE, TOKENRING, and ETHERNET). Ignore the line that reads *LOOPBACK.

4. Enter 1 in the Option field to add an interface as shown in Figure 90 on page 200.

```
                     Work with TCP/IP Interfaces
                                                      System:    AS26
     Type options, press Enter.
       1=Add   2=Change   4=Remove   5=Display   9=Start   10=End

           Internet          Subnet            Line        Line
     Opt   Address           Mask              Description  Type
     1
           9.5.92.41         255.255.255.128   TRNLINE      *TRLAN
           9.5.92.47         255.255.255.128   TRNLINE      *TRLAN
           127.0.0.1         255.0.0.0         *LOOPBACK    *NONE


                                                                  Bottom
     F3=Exit      F5=Refresh    F6=Print list   F11=Display interface status
     F12=Cancel   F17=Top       F18=Bottom
```

Figure 90. Selecting option 1 to add a new TCP/IP logical interface

5. Press the Enter key. The Add TCP/IP Interface screen appears as shown in
   Figure 91.

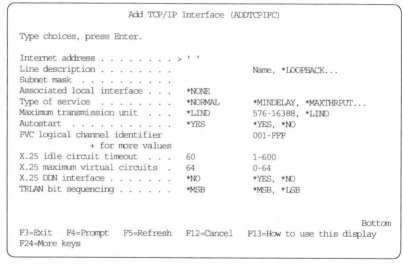

Figure 91. Add TCP/IP Interface (ADDTCPIFC)

6. Change each of the parameters listed in Table 21 to the values you
   determined for each server.

Table 21. ADDTCPIFC parameters

Parameter description	Example value
Internet address	The iSeries IP address for this new server. In our example, it's 10.5.92.42.
Line description	The name of the line description for your LAN adapter. In our example, the line description name is TRNLINE. Yours may be different.

Parameter description	Example value
Subnet mask	The same subnet mask address as the one held by the existing interface. In our example, it's 255.255.255.0. for a C class subnet.
All other parameters	Keep the default values.

7. Press the Enter key. A message appears at the bottom of your screen stating `TCP/IP interface added successfully.`

8. Repeat this process to assign an IP address for each of your partitioned servers.

You have now successfully configured the TCP/IP logical interfaces for your partitioned servers. You still have to define a specific IP address for each Domino server on your iSeries server by modifying their Notes.ini file. For a detailed "how to" guide, see the following section.

4.11.5 Installation

Installing and running a Domino server on iSeries involves a combination of tasks.

4.11.5.1 Using the LODRUN command to install the Domino software
This installation process takes between 20 and 30 minutes, plus about five minutes to upgrade any existing servers. Follow this process:

1. Place the Domino for AS/400 CD into the iSeries CD-ROM drive. Enter the following OS/400 command:

   `lodrun dev(*opt) dir('/os400/')`

2. Type 1 beside each product option that you want to install. Make sure that you also select the Advanced Services option.

3. If you previously installed Domino for AS/400 on your system, you must select each option that you already installed. If you want clustering, billing, and partitioning you *must* install the Advanced Services option. Also, you must have the Enterprise or Advanced Enterprise Server licenses to use these options.

4. Press Enter to install the product options that you selected.

5. The system loads the Domino for AS/400 programs to the appropriate AS/400 libraries and /QIBM directories. You see status messages as the system installs each option that you selected.

6. If you already have Domino servers on the iSeries, the system copies updated data files to the data directory for each server. During this process, you see a status message for each server that the system upgrades.

7. Use the Display Software Resources (DSPSFWRSC) command to determine whether Domino for AS/400 installed successfully (see Figure 92 on page 202).

```
                        Display Software Resources
                                                System:    AS26
   Resource
      ID      Option   Feature   Description
   5769LNT    *BASE    5050      Lotus Domino For AS/400
   5769LNT    *BASE    2924      Lotus Domino For AS/400
   5769LNT    1        5050      AS/400 Integration
   5769LNT    1        2924      AS/400 Integration
   5769LNT    3        5050      C API
   5769LNT    4        5050      C++ API
   5769LNT    5        5050      LotusScript Extension ToolKit
   5769LNT    6        5050      HiTest C API
   5769LNT    7        5050      Advanced Services
   Press Enter to continue.


   F3=Exit   F11=Display libraries/releases   F12=Cancel
   F19=Display trademarks
```

Figure 92. Display Software Resources (DSPSFWRSC)

4.11.5.2 Using CFGDOMSVR to set up the first server in a domain

Follow these steps:

1. On any OS/400 command line, type:

   cfgdomsvr

2. Press the F4 key.

3. On the resulting display shown in Figure 93, provide these details:

   - For *Server name*, type the name of the Domino server. While the cursor is on this field, you can press the F1 key to display more information about what you can specify for the name. For our example, we used the information from Table 22.

Table 22. CFGDOMSVR setup values

Customer	Server name	Domain
Cust1	custserv1	cust1
Cust2	custserv2	cust2
Cust3	custserv3	cust3
Cust4	custserv4	cust4
Cust5	custserv5	cust5

```
                    Configure Domino Server (CFGDOMSVR)

Type choices, press Enter.

Server name  . . . . . . . . . .   custserv1



Option . . . . . . . . . . . .    *FIRST         *FIRST, *ADD, *REMOVE

                                                                     Bottom
F3=Exit    F4=Prompt   F5=Refresh   F10=Additional parameters   F12=Cancel
F13=How to use this display         F24=More keys
```

Figure 93. Configure Domino Server (CFGDOMSVR) (screen one)

- Choose *FIRST to indicate that you are setting up the first server in a Domino domain. Press Enter.

4. The display expands to request more details about the server. Press the Page Down key to display additional fields.

5. You must provide information for the following fields:

- Data directory (for example, /NOTES/CUST1)
- Organization name
- Administrator name and password
- Time zone (press the F4 key to display a list of valid values)

For information about what to specify for each field, position the cursor on the field and press the F1 key.

Make sure that you specify *http on the Web browsers line and *partition and *billing in the Advanced services line.

6. When you have completed all fields, press Enter to set up the server.

7. While the CFGDOMSVR command is running, you see messages that indicate what is happening during the process. Then, the iSeries opens a terminal session and displays a series of messages that describe the setup activities. When the setup is complete, a message tells you to press Enter to end the terminal session.

8. Repeat this process for each server you want to set up.

> **Note**
>
> If you plan to set up more than one server in a single customer's domain, you will be forced to install and configure an additional server which is not documented here. In this case, refer to the online document *Installing and Managing Domino for AS/400*, to guide you through this task. Start with the "Overview of setting up an additional Domino server on AS/400".
>
> You can view the document online or download it from the library at:
> http://www.iseries.ibm.com/domino/support/

9. To work with your newly created Domino servers, enter the WRKDOMSVR command on the OS/400 command line as shown in Figure 94 on page 204.

```
                    Work with Domino Servers
                                                       System:    AS26
  Type options, press Enter.
    1=Start server      2=Change server   5=Display console   6=End server
    7=Submit command    8=Work console    9=Work server jobs
   11=Change current directory   12=Work object links   13=Edit NOTES.INI

        Domino                              Domino
  Opt   Server                 Subsystem    Status
        CUSTSERV1              DOMINO05     *ENDED
        CUSTSERV2              DOMINO06     *ENDED
        CUSTSERV3              DOMINO07     *ENDED
        CUSTSERV4              DOMINO08     *ENDED
        CUSTSERV5              DOMINO09     *ENDED

                                                               Bottom
  Parameters or command
  ===>
  F3=Exit      F4=Prompt    F5=Refresh    F9=Retrieve    F11=Display path
  F12=Cancel   F17=Top      F18=Bottom    F22=Display entire field   F24=More keys
```

Figure 94. Work with Domino Servers (WRKDOMSVR)

10. Using separate IP addresses, you can have multiple partitioned servers on an iSeries, depending on the iSeries server size and processing load. See 4.11, "Capacity planning for Lotus Domino for AS/400" on page 189, for information that can guide you as to how many partitioned servers you can successfully run on your iSeries server.

You can use the Change Domino Server (CHGDOMSVR) command to set a separate IP address for each partitioned server. The TCP/IP port options parameter (TCPOPT) is used to specify the IP address, for example (should all be on one line):

```
CHGDOMSVR SERVER(CUST1) TCPOPT((TCPIP NETWORK1 *NOENCRYPT '10.5.92.42'
*YES))
```

The effect is to add this line into your Notes.ini file for CUST1 (shown in Figure 95):

```
TCPIP_TcpIpAddress=0,10.5.92.42:1352
```

You can also choose to edit the Notes.ini file manually. Enter 13 in the Opt field in the Work with Domino Servers (WRKDOMSVR) screen (Figure 94). Then you see a screen like the example in Figure 95.

```
Edit File: /notes/cust1/NOTES.INI
Record . :      50 of     78 by  10                           Column:
Control  :


CMD ....+....1....+....2....+....3....+....4....+....5....+....6...

    ServerName=custserv1/cust1
    TCPIP=TCP, 0, 15, 0
    TCPIP_TcpIpAddress=0,10.5.92.42:1352
    Timezone=6
    DST=1
    $$HasLANPort=1
    Ports=TCPIP
    SPX=SPX, 0, 15, 0
F2=Save  F3=Save/Exit   F12=Exit   F15=Services   F16=Repeat find
```

Figure 95. Editing the Notes.ini file

11. To verify that the Domino server was set up successfully, try to start the server and display its console. You can do both from the Work with Domino Servers display.

12. To start the server, type 1 in the Opt field on the line containing the server name and press Enter. Once you issue the request to start the server, display the server console by typing 8 in the Opt field and pressing Enter.

The Domino server setup is complete. However, you still have to set up an administrator workstation for the server.

To use a Lotus Notes client to administer a Domino server on your iSeries, you must connect a Notes client workstation to your iSeries through TCP/IP. You also need to copy the server's Certifier ID and administrator ID from your iSeries to the workstation.

You must manually copy at least the Certifier ID file to the workstation. You must also copy the administrator ID file to the workstation if you specified that the administrator ID should be stored only in a file (not in the Domino Directory) when you set up the server.

The following procedure assumes that the Notes client is not installed on the workstation. If Notes is already installed, skip the tasks that are already done.

1. If you want to take advantage of the Operations Navigator graphical interface for managing Domino servers on the iSeries, install and set up AS/400 Client Access on your iSeries server and the workstation.

   For details, see *AS/400 Client Access for Windows 95/NT - Setup*, SC41-3512, or *Client Access Express for Windows - Setup*, SC41-5507.

   Make sure you have installed the iSeries Integration option of the Domino for AS/400 software.

   Add the Lotus Domino plug-in to Client Access.

2. Verify the TCP/IP connection to the iSeries server.

   a. Open a command window on the workstation.

   b. If the name of the Domino server is different from the TCP/IP host name for the iSeries, also enter:

```
ping servername
```

Here, *servername* is the name of the Domino server.

If the PING is successful, the workstation is communicating with the server and the iSeries. If the PING is not successful, review the steps you followed to set up TCP/IP on the workstation and the iSeries.

Note: If you are using a firewall, the PING technique most likely will not work. However, you may still be able to communicate with the server.

3. Install the Lotus Notes client software on the workstation. Make sure you install the full set of administrative functions (called Notes Designer for Notes 4.6 or the Domino Administrator for Notes 5).

   Do *not* start Lotus Notes yet.

4. If you already have a \NOTES\DATA directory on your workstation that contains a Certifier ID (CERT.ID) or administrator ID (USER.ID) file, take precautions to avoid replacing those files.

   a. Create a separate directory for the ID files that you will copy from the iSeries. For example, create this new directory:

   ```
   \notes\idfiles\servername
   ```

   Here, *servername* is the name of the Domino server you just set up on the iSeries.

   b. As needed, copy the Certifier ID (CERT.ID) and the administrator's user ID (USER.ID) files from the Domino server to the workstation. Copy the files in binary format. Use any method that you typically use to copy files between the iSeries and a workstation. For example, you can copy the files by using:

   • The Windows Network Neighborhood in combination with either AS/400 Client Access or AS/400 Net Server support to map a network drive between the workstation and iSeries. Then you can copy the file by using any method that copies files from one directory to another on the workstation.

   • In Operations Navigator, choose **File Systems-> Integrated File Systems-> Root**, and select the server's data directory, which is usually /NOTES/DATA or /Servername/NOTES/DATA. Then copy (or drag) the ID files to a local directory on the workstation.

   To use any of these methods, you must have TCP/IP communications set up and active between the workstation and the iSeries.

5. Start Lotus Notes on the workstation and fill in the information requested:

   a. Indicate how the workstation is connected to the Domino server, for example, network configuration via LAN.

   b. If the administrator ID is in a file that you copied to the workstation, click the box that indicates the user ID is in a file. Also specify the location of the ID file on the workstation, for example:

   ```
   c:\notes\data\user.id
   ```

   c. Provide the password for the administrator. You specified the password when you set up the Domino server.

   d. Indicate that the Domino server is your home server, and specify it by name.

You have completed setting up a Domino server and an administrator workstation for the server. At this point, the Notes workspace should appear.

A common pitfall that is actually quite simple to avoid when installing Domino on an iSeries is conflicts between the iSeries HTTP server and Domino.

The iSeries operating system (OS/400) includes several TCP/IP application servers, including an HTTP server that is known as the IBM HTTP Server for iSeries. This HTTP server processes HTML documents, CGI scripts, and Java scripts for home pages. Domino for AS/400 also provides an HTTP server capability, which enables Notes databases to be seen as HTML documents on the Web.

You can have both HTTP servers installed and running. However, the Domino HTTP server and the Internet Connection Secure Server are both set up to use TCP/IP port 80. Because both HTTP servers use the same port, the second server that is started will have a problem accessing the port. To eliminate this problem, configure each server to listen on port 80, but at a different IP address:

1. End the TCP/IP HTTP server by entering the following command:

   ```
   endtcpsvr *http
   ```

2. Use the `BindSpecific` and `HostName` directives in the Work HTTP Configuration (WRKHTTPCFG) command to change the TCP/IP server so that it binds to a specific IP address.

3. Enable the Bind to host name field in the Server document in the Domino Directory. Specify an IP address that is different from the IP address used for the TCP/IP server.

4. Change the Domino HTTP server so that it uses a port number other than port 80. You change the HTTP server port number in the server document of the Domino Directory for the Domino server.

For more information, see *Internet Connection Server and Internet Connection Secure Server for AS/400 Web Master's Guide*, GC41-5434.

Domino Plug-in to the HTTP server

Domino R5.0 contains the Domino Plug-in for the HTTP Server for iSeries. This allows Domino databases (*.NSF) to be served through the IBM HTTP Server for iSeries instead of the Domino HTTP Server. That is, it allows you to select built-ins for HTTP or iSeries HTTP so you don't need to configure both.

4.11.6 Basic operation and administration concepts

There are many ways to manage a Domino server on the iSeries, but not all of them fit an ASP scenario. When you are offering ASP services on a small scale, you may want to offer administration as a chargeable service to your customers. However, in a bigger ASP scenario, it is almost inevitable that you enable your customers to do their own administration.

Typically, you manage a Domino server from a Notes client. The Notes client interface provides the full set of Domino administration functions. Because the Domino server on the iSeries does not have a local Notes client, you use a remote Notes client on a workstation to manage the Domino server. The iSeries also supports the Domino Web Administration tool. This tool allows you to perform a subset of the Domino administration tasks from a Web browser. The Domino Web administration Tool provides a way of enabling browser-based customers to administrate their Domino server.

4.11.7 Backup and restore

A Domino server often contains important business information that may not exist elsewhere in your organization. For example, users may rely on e-mail for important communications that are not documented anywhere else. Similarly, an on-line customer service application might contain records that do not exist in printed form.

To protect the data from disasters (such as a site loss or hardware loss) and from human error, such as accidentally deleting a critical database, develop a good strategy for regularly backing up the information on your Domino server. Make a plan to back up:

- Objects that change infrequently, such as programs for the Domino product
- Objects that change regularly, such as Domino databases

Domino for AS/400 takes advantage of the iSeries single-level store architecture. Domino databases and programs are spread across all the iSeries disk units, along with other iSeries objects. The OS/400 operating system automatically manages the allocation of disk space so that you do not need to. To back up information on the iSeries, you back up logically (by library or directory), not physically (by disk unit). To plan a backup strategy, you need to understand the logical location of your Domino for AS/400 databases and programs.

4.11.7.1 Libraries and directories for the Domino for AS/400 product

iSeries libraries contain programs for the Domino for AS/400 server product, programs that are available for your Domino developers to copy to their workstations, and customization information such as subsystem descriptions. Table 23 lists the Domino libraries.

Table 23. Domino libraries

Items	iSeries library	Library path
Domino for AS/400 product	QNOTES	/qsys.lib/qnotes.lib
Directory synchronization	QNOTESINT	/qsys.lib/qnotesint.lib
C APIs	QNOTESAPI	/qsys.lib/qnotesapi.lib
C++ APIs	QNOTESCPP	/qsys.lib/qnotescpp.lib
Lotus Script Extensions	QNOTESLSKT	/qsys.lib/qnoteslskt.lib
Customization information (such as subsystem descriptions and job descriptions)	QUSRNOTES	/qsys.lib/qusrnotes.lib

Directories in the iSeries Integrated File System contain product information, customization files, and databases. Table 24 lists the Domino directories.

Table 24. Domino directories

Item	Path
Product information	/QIBM/ProdData/Lotus/Notes
Customization information	/QIBM/UserData/Lotus/Notes
Directory for databases on the server	Specified when you set up the server (in our example, /NOTES/CUST1)

Develop a plan to back up all Domino databases, including users' mail databases and system databases, such as the Domino Directory.

When you configure a Domino server, you specify the directory for that server, such as /NOTES/CUST1. By default, all the databases for the server are in that path. Use a combination of policies and security to keep all Domino databases within the default directory (path) for the Domino server.

The following process shows you the steps to back up the data directory for your Domino for AS/400 server and the directory with customization information. Substitute the name of your tape device for TAP01 and the name of your Domino server data directory for /NOTES/DATA.

1. To ensure that you obtain a complete copy of your server, stop the server before you start the save operation. Use the following command:

   ```
   enddomsvr server(servername)
   ```

   Here, *servername* is the actual name of your Domino server.

2. To back up the directories, use the following command. Substitute your directory name for /NOTES/CUST1:

   ```
   sav dev('/qsys.lib/tap01.devd') obj(('/notes/cust1/*')
   ('/QIBM/UserData/Lotus/Notes/*'))
   ```

One of the disadvantages of saving Domino objects this way is that you actually have to end the Domino server you want to save. If you want to offer a 24x7 operation to your customers, you have to implement two Domino server instances per customer and cluster these two server instances. This ensures that you can end one server for backup and the other server is still available to your customer for use. However, this implementation limits you to 15 customers per iSeries server.

Another interesting feature of the iSeries that might be useful when implementing ASP is the auxiliary storage pools.

ASP versus 'ASP'

If you mention ASP to somebody who works with the iSeries server, most likely their first thought would be "auxiliary storage pools", and not "application service provider". Since this IBM Redbook is primarily about *application service providers*, we spell out *auxiliary storage pools* to avoid any confusion.

Normally, all disk units attached to an iSeries server are treated as a single logical disk unit. The operating system places data across the disk units to optimize performance and disk utilization. However, an iSeries administrator has the option to create logical groupings of disk units, called *auxiliary storage pools*. Auxiliary storage pools provide several possible benefits, for example:

- Auxiliary storage pools provide the option for different strategies for backup and disk protection. For example, you might have large history databases that do not change very often. By segregating them in a separate auxiliary storage pool, you can easily set up a less frequent backup schedule. You might also choose not to use RAID-5 disk units for this auxiliary storage pool if availability of the information is not time-critical.

- Auxiliary storage pools provide the option to isolate database journals from the databases both for protection from data loss and for performance.

- If you want to place your Domino data directory in a user auxiliary storage pool, you need to create a user-defined file system (UDFS) to map the integrated file system directory to the correct auxiliary storage pool.

You can read more about auxiliary storage pools and creating user-defined file systems in *OS/400 Backup and Recovery V4R5*, SC41-5304. Or, consult the AS/400 Technical Studio for Domino information at:
http://www.as400.ibm.com/techstudio

One possible setback about using auxiliary storage pools in an ASP scenario is granularity. The minimum size of an auxiliary storage pool is one disk unit.

4.11.7.2 BRMS/400 to provide online Lotus server backup

Domino for AS/400 Release 5.02a supports an online backup capability with Backup Recovery and Media Services for AS/400 (BRMS/400). Online backup implies that Domino, QuickPlace, and other Lotus Server databases on the iSeries can be saved while they are in use, with no save while active synchronization points.

Note: This function is provided with PTF SF60285. It is supported in BRMS/400 release V4R4 and above.

You can direct your online backups to a tape device, an automated tape library device, save files, or a Tivoli Storage Manager (TSM) server.

It is critical that you do not replace your complete system backup with only online Lotus server backups. The online Lotus server backups only back up databases. There are other important Lotus server types of data including libraries, files in the Lotus server IFS directories, and other non-Lotus server system data that should be backed up on a regular basis. Such examples include QUSRSYS, QGPL, and so forth.

For more information, see the V4R4M0 BRMS manual *Backup Recovery and Media Services for AS/400*, SC41-5345.

4.12 A common framework for Domino ASPs: Lotus ASP Solution Pack

This section takes a close look at the Lotus ASP Solution Pack.

4.12.1 Architecture

The Lotus ASP Solution Pack is a comprehensive hosting platform and a core set of ready-to-rent applications.

The Lotus ASP Solution Pack combines products and technologies from both Lotus and IBM into a single platform for ASPs and ISVs to target the quickly growing application hosting market. It provides a critical mass of server platforms, starter-applications, and infrastructure services to help both ISVs and ASPs. ASP customers will typically access the hosted Domino applications via Web browsers over the Internet. The architecture of the Lotus ASP Solution Pack is shown in Figure 96.

The foundation of the solution is built upon three application servers: Domino, WebSphere, and Sametime. With each application server's strengths, the ASP Solution Pack can be leveraged for hosted solutions ranging from Domino-based Web-collaborative applications (for example, mail, online workflow, document sharing, and virtual teams) to WebSphere transactional-based Web applications.

The next layer in the environment is Lotus Hosting Management System (LHMS) middleware. LHMS provides the tools for comprehensive user, group, application, and license management, plus integration to an ASP's back-end billing system. Layered on top of LHMS is a Community Desktop User Interface (UI). This interface allows for secured access, directory services, information alerts, synchronous chat capabilities, and a dynamic list of applications that the authenticated user is authorized to access. Lotus will include a few horizontal "starter" applications with the ASP Solution Pack: Domino-based Web Mail & Calendar, QuickPlace Collaboration, and links to Sametime Meeting Center whiteboard and application sharing services.

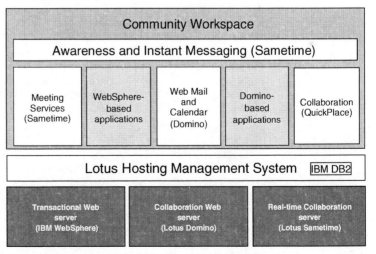

Figure 96. Architecture of Lotus ASP Solution Pack

While many of the initial ASP hosting models require dedicated servers and significant application customization, the architecture for the Lotus ASP Solution Pack handles multiple applications for multiple customers on a single infrastructure environment. In addition, the Lotus platform provides for the self-registration and subscription of a business to a set of applications in a low or no-touch method for the ASP. Delegation of user and group administration to the SMB offloads an even greater amount of work from the ASP and provides the SMB the ability to have better control of their environment (see Figure 97).

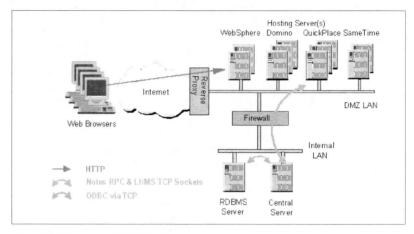

Figure 97. Recommended LHMS environment

4.12.2 Lotus Hosting Management System (LHMS)

LHMS, previously named Domino Instant! Host, provides the framework for a developer to create a Web-based application that can be hosted in a single, common infrastructure for use by several independent end customers. This middleware delivers much of the same functionality as its predecessor, Domino Instant! Host. However, it supports the WebSphere and Sametime servers and applications as well as Domino-based hosting.

The components of LHMS are:

- **Community Desktop**: A Web desktop that end users log into. It becomes their central location for launch all applications. The Community Desktop provides a dynamic list of applications based on what the authenticated users have access to:
  - Community Directory
  - Community Welcome
  - Community InfoAlerts
  - URL Links at a User
  - Community and Service Provider level
  - Sametime Place Awareness for Instant Messaging to members who are also online

  A key development goal was for the Community Desktop to have a "replaceable design" that would allow for a third party or Raven Portal Technology in future releases.

- **Community Manager Workspace**: The Web interface for managing Users, Groups, and Applications:
    - Add/Modify/Delete Users
    - Add/Terminate Applications
    - Create Groups
    - Add/remove users to/from groups
    - Assign Groups to Application Roles
    - Create Community Links.

- **License Manager**: Tracks application licenses for both Lotus and non-Lotus applications on a monthly high-water mark of users per application. Each application's high-water mark is recorded in a License database that has multiple views for displaying licenses by ISV, Application, or Community.

- **Warehouse**: The application available to the Service Provider Administrator to manage the environment. The functions include:
    - Register ISV Applications (AppKits)
    - Create Syndicates (offers)
    - Create Storefronts
    - Publish Syndicate (Offer) to Storefronts
    - Publish Application Templates to Hosting Servers
    - Manage Hosting Servers

- **Storefront**: The external catalog of applications available from the Service Provider. This is broken up into the Offer Storefront (Community or stand-alone applications) and the Community Application Storefront (for adding applications within the Community).

- **Help Desk**: A Web-based tool geared for the first line support organization. The tools provide the support staff with view status of Users, Applications, and Communities, plus the ability to change an end user's password.

- **Admin Console**: A Web-based Service Provider Management Tool, which provides the same functionality as Help Desk tool. It also provides the ability to suspend or terminate individual users or applications and move application instances between the different hosting servers (if needed for load balancing).

- **Application/Community Registration Tool**: Provides the application/community owner the ability to self-register and subscribe to the application/community. It helps to integrate the Service Provider's preferred payment option and account clearance.

- **Reverse Proxy**: The component that front ends all of the LHMS hosting servers, providing a single sign-on solution for all Domino applications within the LHMS environment. Additionally, the reverse proxy provides name decoration to expand a user entered ID "Brian Jones" to the FQN "Brian Jones/SMB1" for uniquely identifying a user.

- **Central Server, Primary Hosting Server, Hosting Server, Extended Hosting Server**: Different LHMS servers in the environment. The Central Server maintains the connection to the RDBMS and has the Warehouse application to manage the whole environment. The Primary Hosting Server has the Storefront and Application/Community Registration Tool. The Extended Hosting Server is used for QuickPlace and WebSphere application hosting servers.

- **LHMS Software Development Kit (SDK)**: Available for ISVs to create both Domino- and WebSphere-based applications for the hosting environment.

ISVs build AppKits of their Web Applications for easy installation within the Service Provider LHMS environment. The LHMS API is available to perform User, Group, and Instance calls to lookup information with the private space of the community. The Application Event API is available for the ISV to directly write out an application event important for the Service Provider to track (that is, an application event signaling the ASP to bill an additional fee for the download of a white paper).

LHMS comes with Community Manager Workspace that issued to manage community applications, community members, and special groups that define the access community members have to individual copies of an application.

The Community Manager can perform these functions:

- Add, modify, and delete users.
- Create groups and assign members to them.
- Create (instantiate) community applications, and for each copy of an application, select which of its user roles (such as Manager versus member) to assign a group.
- Notify new members (by e-mail or by mail-merging an exported list of members) of their membership in the online community and invite them to register.
- Monitor the overall state of the community: the number of members by status (newly added, registered, notified, and removed) and the number of active applications.
- Perform routine maintenance on the membership list and groups. As the community membership changes, add and remove members. As member access privileges change, adjust the group membership. As new members are added, notify them by e-mail or mail-merge.
- Perform routine maintenance on applications. As access privileges change for a group, re-assign that group to a different role in each affected application. As new applications are needed, add them and assign groups to them. As applications are no longer needed, delete them.

4.12.3 User management

Typically, Domino applications share the Domino Directory. However, that is not appropriate in an ASP environment where it is important to separate users and data. Therefore, LHMS blocks applications from directly accessing the Domino Directory and instead uses a virtual directory.

A community can grow to accommodate a large number of community members because of the way that users and groups are stored:

- Groups are stored within the primary Domino Directory (and group names are modified to prevent duplicates).
- Users are stored within the cascaded Domino Directory.
- Only users associated with instances on a hosting server will appear within that server's cascaded Domino Directory.

4.12.4 LHMS Software Developer Kit (SDK)

The LHMS Software Developer Kit facilitates the development of *hosting-ready* applications by ISVs. Developers will be able to write an AppKit for their Domino applications for the ASP Solution Pack. The LHMS provides the framework for a developer to create a Web-based application that can be hosted in a single, common infrastructure for use by several independent end customers. By creating an AppKit, ISVs can write the application once and deliver the AppKit to any service provider using the LHMS environment.

4.13 References

This section guides you to common points where you can obtain more information about Domino for AS/400.

4.13.1 Commonly used Domino for AS/400 commands

Table 25 lists some commonly used Domino for AS/400 commands.

Table 25. Commonly used Domino for AS/400 commands

Command	Description
CFGDOMSVR	Configure a Domino server.
DSPDOMCSL	Display a Domino console. This can be run by multiple users at once.
WRKDOMCSL	Display a Domino console and submit server commands. This can only be used by one user at a time.
ENDDOMSVR	End a Domino server.
SBMDOMCMD	The Submit Domino Command (SBMDOMCMD) command submits a Domino server command to run on a Domino server on the iSeries.
STRDOMSVR	Start a Domino server
WRKDOMSVR	Shows the status of all your Domino servers, assigned subsystem, and the assigned data directory.

4.13.2 Domino and iSeries Web site sources for information

The following sites offer a good starting place for searching the Web for information on Domino and the iSeries:

- http://www.lotus411.com
- http://www.searchdomino.com
- http://search400.com

From the creators of SearchDomino.com is an iSeries-specific search engine and portal site: http://notes.net

Good links for developers are:

- Lotus Developer Network: http://www.lotus.com/developer
- Webinar/Webcast Schedule: http://www.lotus.com/developertraining
- Masters Broadcast information: http://www.lotus.com/masters
- Lotus Dev-Net site: http://www.lotus-dev.net/
- Iris Sandbox: http://www.notes.net/sandbox
- IBM DeveloperWorks: http://www.ibm.com/developer

- To register for the Developers e-Newsletter: `http://www.lotus.com/lwm`
- DevCon 2000 Information: `http://www.lotus.com/devcon`

To take a quick survey of what other companies are doing in the area of Domino and ASP, look at the following sites. Note, these sites may or may not be powered by an iSeries server.

- `http://www.bsky.net`
- `http://clk.net`
- `http://co-learn.net`
- `http://dominohost.net`
- `http://www.eapps.com`
- `http://www.interliant.com`
- `http://www.riverwatch.com`
- `http://www.prominic.net`

Appendix A. Security study: ScotSystems' StoreReport

Do not be fooled into thinking that ASP means complexity. There are many ways to serve your application to your customers. The ScotSystems' way follows the tried and true enterprise-out for customers that would generally be categorized as Small and Medium Businesses (SMB). These customer do not want and cannot afford, complex systems to help manage their business. They demand turn-key solutions that are often tailored to their individual business needs. ScotSystems' home page is shown in Figure 98, along with the StoreReport.com home page.

Figure 98. ScotSysytems on the Web: www.scotsystems.com (upper), www.storereport.com (lower)

A.1 Scenario overview

In this case, ScotSystems focuses on a complete set of menu-driven, integrated computer programs for the oil marketer and convenience store operator. Convenience stores, in the USA, generally sell gasoline and other goods and services. They are either individually owned and operated, or a network of stores may be owned and operated by a single company covering a wide area (sometimes measured in many hundreds of miles).

This geographical nature of the industry has created an environment consisting of hundreds of isolated businesses, often located hundreds of miles from a central office, and often having little or no contact with their employers and the company's administrative employees. Whether the main office is an oil marketing operation, or simply a central location for independent stores, logistically speaking, they may as well be located on another planet. Paperwork sometimes takes three days or longer through the mail to reach its destination. Poorly prepared, but precious company information, such as sales, purchases, and bank deposits, is severely limited in value by the time it arrives at the central office and is processed.

In 1992, ScotSystems began taking steps to address this problem. For many years, they marketed a product called ScotSystem Satellite, which ran on stand-alone PCs at the stores. Satellite collected store information and sent it back to the office through personal computer communications programs. From there, it was transferred to the company's AS/400 computer, using PC Support and later Client Access. The system worked beautifully, but it required a sizable investment. In addition, workers at the stores received little help from their office peers when simple personal computer problems occurred.

The solution provided with StoreReport.com that we study in the following pages started by taking back the screens and data captured by the PCs located at the stores to the central AS/400. The interface and data was now using the 5250 data stream. Finally, ScotSystems used SecureWay Host On-Demand (HOD) to dynamically convert the 5250 data stream to Java-based host access. More information about HOD can be found at:
http://www.ibm.com/software/network/hostondemand/

Amazingly so, this ASP solution is rented to customers starting at just $180 (as the lowest of a three-tier pricing system of $180, $199 and $225) per month and written by just one individual — Bill Scott, CED of ScotSystems, Inc.

If you have more questions about ScotSystems Inc, StoreReport.com, or this case study, you can contact Bill Scott by telephone at (601) 638-6989 or via e-mail at: billscott@storereport.net

AS/400e servers used
ScotSystems' has two AS/400e servers that are used to ASP StoreReport.com as shown in Table 26.

Table 26. ALLTEL's AS/400 systems used for ASP

AS/400 Model	Processor	Main Store	DASD	OS Version
720	206A	768 MB	50 GB	V4R4M0
150	2269	128 MB	8 GB	V4R4M0

Both systems are physically located in Vicksburg, Mississippi.

A.2 Application overview

StoreReport is a set of integrated computer programs, accessible via the Internet. It offers convenience store operators and oil marketers an alternative to having expensive and troublesome computer equipment installed in their stores and offices:

- Accounts Receivable
- Accounts Payable

- General Ledger
- Inventory
- Convenience Store Operations
- Payroll
- Taxes

StoreReport is Year 2000 compliant and based on the latest state-of-the-art technology, but StoreReport is not new. In the traditional enterprise-out sense, the system has gone through 19 years of exhaustive testing at hundreds of locations due to the fact that it is a solution that has been created, modified, and tested over the years.

Network

The server side of ScotSystems' network is powered by two AS/400e servers. The Model 720 runs the Storereport.net application, while the smaller Model 150 serves the Web pages found at http://www.storereport.com and http://www.scotsystems.com. These are connected to the Internet via a Cisco router using a fractional T1 line.

The clients are connected to the Internet too, using a means that is more cost effective for them.

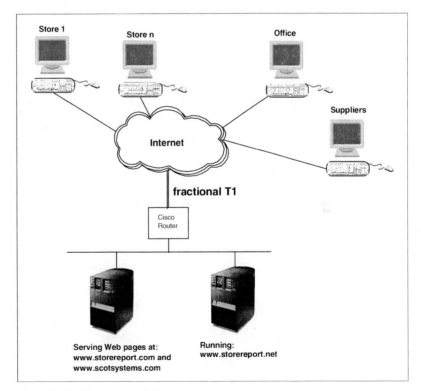

Figure 99. ScotSystems network diagram

Accounting and billing

The billing model is quite simple. Generally, the price includes a fixed setup price along with a flat fee per month. For example, for each remote convenience store location, there is a one time setup fee of $199 and an average monthly charge of $199 that would include the following services:

- Secure logon user ID and password
- Assistance in setting up convenience store files
- Manual available online and delivered on CD-ROM
- Nightly backups
- Convenience store Profit and Loss Statements daily
- Various history reports and fuel logs
- Convenience store transactions available in ASCII format
- Purchase analysis by store and vendor
- Assistance and advice in entering and handling transactions
- Printing at your location
- Telephone support during normal business hours. 24-hour support prices available on request and subject to the three-tier pricing system.

Usage above a limit of 10,000 gallon transactions per month is charged an additional 0.0025 cents per transaction. This is ascertained by looking at the number of records in a transaction file.

User registration

New users are registered by making a phone call to ScotSystems. ScotSystems then sets up the user profiles, output queues, and printers and builds their databases.

Security

Within the StoreReport application, security is provided by OS/400 with a user ID and passwords.

Refer to Figure 100 for the following discussion.

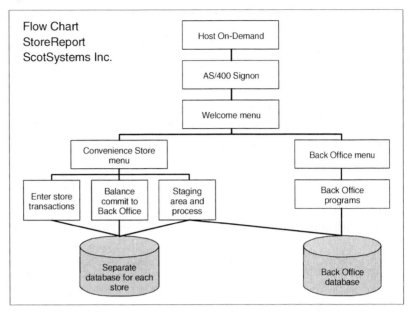

Flow Chart
StoreReport
ScotSystems Inc.

Host On-Demand

AS/400 Signon

Welcome menu

Convenience Store menu

Back Office menu

Enter store transactions

Balance commit to Back Office

Staging area and process

Back Office programs

Separate database for each store

Back Office database

Figure 100. ScotSystems' StoreReport layout and security

When a user signs on, the Welcome menu allows them to select the back office or a single store. The current library in their user profile points them to the proper store if they are a store employee. A store employee would be denied access to the back office. Usually the data in the store's library is good for a single day. There may be multiple shifts in that day. Once all the shifts are entered, a program is run by the store manager to combine the shifts into a single day's "StoreReport". The manager okays the day's StoreReport and commits that day's data to the back office. Data from multiple days may be passed to the back office (that is, Friday, Saturday, and Sunday). Someone in the back office, validates the store's data and processes in the company library database.

Throughout the day, other company business is transacted at the office level. At least once each day, a batch process is run at the office level to update the master files. The store's data is processed along with other office business. Store history is retained in the store libraries.

The table is maintained at the user lever. Each unique user ID is listed in this table with the Command Languages (CLs) to which they may have access.

ScotSystems maintain a table (SSSECURE) at the user level. Each unique user ID is listed in this table along with the CL program or programs that the user is authorized to use. Menu changes are called through CLs and are checked. The security program SEC100CL is called from every CL program to check the user authorities. If the user is not authorized to use the CL, they are denied access, and the event is logged. The user is denied access to command line functions and the use of the attention key. Details of this center-point of security are shown in A.5.1, "SEC100CL CL security program" on page 224.

StoreReport sets up a simple tree in which XXX00 is the "holding company", XXX01 is the first company within the holding company, and XXX01.0001 is the first store in company '01'. This way, they can support 99 companies in a holding company, and 9,999 conveniences stores in each company.

For example, the databases you would use with your signon are AAF00, AAF01.0000, and AAF01.0001. In this example, the Holding Company Identity Code is AAF, the Corporation Identity Code is 01, and the Store Identification Code is 0001. StoreReport puts common tables in QUSRSYS and can insert customized programs at any level in the user's library list.

SecureWay Host On-Demand (HOD) is used to both dynamically convert the 5250 data stream to one that can be used by any remote client using a Web browser capable of running a Java applet and to provide end-to-end security via SSL Version 3.0.

A.3 Administration

All programs are located in a library located at the farthest user-level library. Modified programs or databases, such as unique tax tables, can be placed at the holding company level, the company level, or the convenience store level that will supersede the standard programs and tables.

StoreReport.Net consists of three separate, but integrated systems. These are referred to as the Remote Store, the Back Office, and the Staging Area (which is an interface between the Back Office and the Remote Store). StoreReport supports 9,999 stores per company. Therefore, there may be multiple Remote Stores and Staging Areas feeding a single Back Office. Further, there may be 99 separate companies in a single holding corporation.

In a StoreReport convenience store environment, the store employees use the Remote Store functions to enter their daily sales information or to integrate point-of-sale (POS) equipment to StoreReport. Someone that works in an office capacity would use the Staging Area to check their work, print store reports, correct errors and commit the store reports to the Back Office for processing.

The Back Office functions are used for more complicated tasks such as paying bills, making journal entries, handling incoming fuel invoices, and running payroll. Limited Back Office functions are available to small operators running one or two stores.

A.4 SecureWay Host On-Demand

SecureWay Host On-Demand allows full and complete access to the 5250 applications running on the AS/400 ASP server at ScotSystems business from any place connected on the Internet. This includes an interactive 5250 host session that dynamically converts the 5250 data stream to a Java-based host access. That is, from most any Web browser, you can have an "IBM Personal Communications" quality look-and-feel including the ability to print reports directly to your local PC printer. Figure 101 shows a sample of the interactive 5250 session as presented by a Web browser on the customer's local PC.

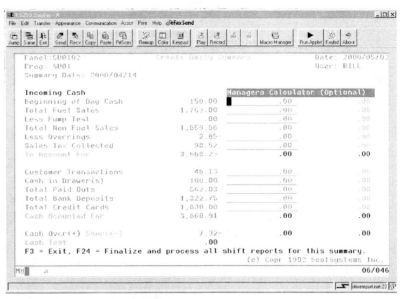

Figure 101. ScotSystems: Sample HOD screen

Host On-Demand provides the following functions for 5250 host printing:

- **Host Print key**: Available in a 5250 display session. It is the key that tells the host to print the contents of the presentation space as text.

- **Host Print Transform (HPT)**: Converts the AS/400 print data stream just before it is sent from the AS/400 to the printer spooled file. Because the AS/400 does the conversion, the host does most of the print processing instead of the workstation.

  Many printers, including IBM printers, support the ASCII print-data stream. The ASCII data stream uses AS/400 system objects that describe the characteristics of a particular ASCII printer. When you configure a printer session, you select the printer from the list provided.

  By default, Host On-Demand uses the SCS-to-ASCII transform, but you can configure the AS/400 to perform an AFP-to-ASCII transform, which Host On-Demand also supports. The ASCII data stream is passed through the emulator using the SCS ASCII Transparency (ATRN) command. Host On-Demand deletes the ASCII Transparency command and passes the ASCII data stream to the workstation printer.

  For more information about Host Print Transform, refer to *Printer Device Programming Version 4*, SC41-5713.

When you ask ScotSystems what benefits SecureWay Host On-Demand gives their customers, the answer is:

- They have the ability to review their entire previous business day from home, before they get ready for work in the morning.

- It speeds up the point-of-sale to bookkeeping process by several days, and in some cases, even weeks.

- It reduces labor expense by 40% to 50%.

- Employees can now work from home, when they have personal matters to attend.

- They can communicate with their office and retail outlets regardless of where they might be located.

- They know what they owe today, who owes them what, and how much money they have available.

- They have the ability to close the month on the first instead of the tenth or the fifteenth.

- It provides the ability for their CPA, accounting firm, and themselves to extract data from their database to include in PC spreadsheets, databases, and word processing programs.

- They can print reports from anywhere to any printer located on their network.

- They do not have to wait for software upgrades; they occur daily.

- Hardware upgrades too are no longer their problem.

- They save a lot on local computer support.

- ScotSystems can run queries for them for a fraction of the cost required to pay their own staff to do it and in less time.

- ScotSystems can see immediately what problems they are having and may even fix the problem if it can be done in a reasonable amount of time.

- ScotSystems can make changes to their software, watch the effects, and remove those changes if ScotSystems has concerns or doesn't like the results. This benefits customers because ScotSystems can enhance their product much faster.

- The customers don't need to remember to make a backup. They don't need any storage at all.

- So far, it's been faster than what they have been using.

For more information about SecureWay Host On-Demand, see:
http://www-4.ibm.com/software/webservers/hostondemand/

A.5 Security program samples

The following sections show you three different security program sample written by ScotSystems for StoreReport.

A.5.1 SEC100CL CL security program

This is a sample of an OS/400 CL security program written for StoreReport. The purpose of the program is to check each and every client (based on the OS/400 user profile) menu request against a table of authorities.

It uses a Local Data Area (*LDA) to pass information to and from the calling CL program. The layout of the *LDA is shown in the comment lines.

```
SEQNBR*...+... 1 ...+... 2 ...+... 3 ...+... 4 ...+... 5 ...+... 6 ...+... 7 -
  100 /* ------------------------------------------------------------ */
  200 /* SEC100CL - System Initialization, Processing Status, and     */
  300 /*            Security Processing.                               */
  400 /*                                                              */
```

```
 500 /* Woodrow W. Williams, Jr.  March 12,2000                          */
 600 /* StoreReport Inc.                                                  */
 700 /* **************************************************************** */
 800 /* LDA Layout for System                                             */
 900 /* ---------------------------------------------------------------- */
1000 /* 0001 499 Previously used by ScotSystems   RESERVED                */
1100 /*                                                                   */
1200 /* 0500 001 &PASSED      Passed Security 'Y'=YES  'N'=NO             */
1300 /* 0501 070 &ERRMSG      Error Message                               */
1400 /* 0601 001 &SSMODL      Module '0'=Backoffice '1'=C-Store           */
1500 /* 0611 001 &BYPASS      ByPass Security Check 'B'                   */
1600 /* 0621 001 &ADMINUSER   Administrative Access and Privilege 'Y'     */
1700 /* 0626 001 &FIRSTPASS   ADMINUSER First Pass Setup                  */
1800 /* 0631 001 &MAINTAUTH   Maintenance Authority 'M'=Maintenance       */
1900 /* 0641 ...  ..........  ...........................                 */
2000 /* 0651 010 &HLDLIBR     Holding Company Library                     */
2100 /* 0661 010 &CORLIBR     Corporation Library                         */
2200 /* 0671 010 &STRLIBR     Store Library                               */
2300 /* 0681 010 &CURLIBR     Current Library                             */
2400 /* 0691 010 &GLOLIBR     Global Library for ALL Hld, Corp, Str Usrs  */
2500 /* 0701 010 &USER        System User                                 */
2600 /* 0711 010 &USERDTA     User Data Area  IE USER(Not Currently Used) */
2700 /* 0721 010 &USERDTALIB  User Data Area Library                      */
2800 /* 0731 010 &SECFILE     Security FIle                               */
2900 /* 0741 010 &SECLIBR     Security Library                            */
3000 /* 0751 010 &SECDDSLIBR  Security DDS Library                        */
3100 /* 0761 010 &SSSEC       Sys Appl Security Data Area 'Y'=Active      */
3200 /* 0771 010 &SSSECLIBR   Sys Appl Security Data Area Library         */
3300 /* 0781 010 ..........   ...........................                 */
3400 /* 0791 010 ..........   ...........................                 */
3500 /* 0801 010 &QSYS        System Serial Number                        */
3600 /* 0811 010 &QUSR        System User                                 */
3700 /* 0821 010 &QCON        System Console                              */
3800 /* 0831 010 &QSYSP       System Printer                              */
3900 /* 0841 010 &QWSD        Workstn ID                                  */
4000 /* 0851 010 &QCLP        CL Pgm Executing                            */
4100 /* 0861 010 &QMNU        Menu CL Executed From                       */
4200 /* 0871 006 &QNBR        Job Number                                  */
4300 /* 0881 006 &QDAT        Job Date                                    */
4400 /* 0891 006 &QTIM        Job Time                                    */
4500 /* 0901 001 &QTYP        Job Type ' '=Interactive ' '=Batch          */
4600 /* 0911 008 &QSWS        Job Switches                                */
4700 /* 0921 010 &QPRT        Job Default Printer Device                  */
4800 /* 0931 010 &QOUQ        Job Default Outq                            */
4900 /* 0941 010 &QOUL        Job Default Outq Library                    */
5000 /* 0951 049 &SSMODLNM    'ScotSystems, Inc. Backoffice System'       */
5100 /* 0951 049 &SSMODLNM    'ScotSystems, Inc. C-Store System'          */
5200
5300 /* **************************************************************** */
5400 /* - R E C E I V E   &QCLP  &  D E C L A R E   V A R I A B L E S - */
5500 /* -  &QCLP is the name of the call CL program                   - */
5600 /* ---------------------------------------------------------------- */
5700          PGM       PARM(&QCLP)
5800
5900          DCL       VAR(&QCLP) TYPE(*CHAR) LEN(10) /* Proc ID   */
6000
6100 /* System information:                                              */
6200
6300          DCL       VAR(&QSYS) TYPE(*CHAR) LEN(10) /* System +
6400                    Name */
6500          DCL       VAR(&QCON) TYPE(*CHAR) LEN(10) /* System +
6600                    console */
6700          DCL       VAR(&SYSP) TYPE(*CHAR) LEN(10) /* System +
6800                    printer */
6900          DCL       VAR(&QTIM) TYPE(*CHAR) LEN(06) /* System +
7000                    Time */
7100
7200 /* Job information: name, number, date, type, switches, etc.       */
7300
7400          DCL       VAR(&QWSD) TYPE(*CHAR) LEN(10) /* Workstn ID */
7500          DCL       VAR(&QNBR) TYPE(*CHAR) LEN(06) /* Job Number */
7600          DCL       VAR(&QDAT) TYPE(*CHAR) LEN(06) /* Job Date   */
7700          DCL       VAR(&QTYP) TYPE(*CHAR) LEN(01) /* Job Type   */
7800          DCL       VAR(&QSWS) TYPE(*CHAR) LEN(08) /* Switches   */
7900          DCL       VAR(&QPRT) TYPE(*CHAR) LEN(10) /* Print Dev  */
8000          DCL       VAR(&QOUQ) TYPE(*CHAR) LEN(10) /* Out Que    */
8100          DCL       VAR(&QOUL) TYPE(*CHAR) LEN(10) /* Out Que Lib*/
8200
```

```
 8300 /* Session attributes:                                                 */
 8400
 8500              DCL          VAR(&QCLB) TYPE(*CHAR) LEN(10) /* Current Lib*/
 8600              DCL          VAR(&QMNU) TYPE(*CHAR) LEN(10) /* Menu Name  */
 8700              DCL          VAR(&QUSR) TYPE(*CHAR) LEN(10) /* User ID    */
 8800
 8900 /* User attributes:                                                    */
 9000
 9100              DCL          VAR(&USRCLS) TYPE(*CHAR) LEN(10)
 9200
 9300 /* RPG program SEC100R    variables:                                   */
 9400
 9500              DCL          VAR(&PASSED)  TYPE(*CHAR) LEN(01)
 9600
 9700 /* General interactive messages:                                       */
 9800
 9900              DCL          VAR(&ERRMSG)  TYPE(*CHAR) LEN(70)
10000
10100 /* Activity Security Flag from 'SSADMN'    Data Area                   */
10200
10300              DCL          VAR(&ASECURITY) TYPE(*CHAR) LEN(1) VALUE(' ')
10400
10500
10600 /* ------------------------------------------------------------------- */
10700 /* ScotSystems Variables for LDA Storage & Usage                       */
10800 /* ------------------------------------------------------------------- */
10900
11000              DCL          VAR(&SSMODL)      TYPE(*CHAR) LEN(001)
11100              DCL          VAR(&BYPASS)      TYPE(*CHAR) LEN(001)
11200              DCL          VAR(&ADMINUSER)   TYPE(*CHAR) LEN(001)
11300              DCL          VAR(&FIRSTPASS)   TYPE(*CHAR) LEN(001)
11400              DCL          VAR(&MAINTAUTH)   TYPE(*CHAR) LEN(001)
11500              DCL          VAR(&HLDLIBR)     TYPE(*CHAR) LEN(010)
11600              DCL          VAR(&CORLIBR)     TYPE(*CHAR) LEN(010)
11700              DCL          VAR(&STRLIBR)     TYPE(*CHAR) LEN(010)
11800              DCL          VAR(&CURLIBR)     TYPE(*CHAR) LEN(010)
11900              DCL          VAR(&GLOLIBR)     TYPE(*CHAR) LEN(010)
12000              DCL          VAR(&USER)        TYPE(*CHAR) LEN(010)
12100              DCL          VAR(&USERDTA)     TYPE(*CHAR) LEN(010)
12200              DCL          VAR(&USERDTALIB) TYPE(*CHAR) LEN(010) +
12300                             VALUE('SSLIB')
12400              DCL          VAR(&SECFILE)     TYPE(*CHAR) LEN(010) +
12500                             VALUE('SSSECURE')
12600              DCL          VAR(&SECLIBR)     TYPE(*CHAR) LEN(010) +
12700                             VALUE('SSLIB')
12800              DCL          VAR(&SECDDSLIBR) TYPE(*CHAR) LEN(010) +
12900                             VALUE('QDDSSRC')
13000              DCL          VAR(&SSSEC) TYPE(*CHAR) LEN(010) VALUE('SSSEC')
13100              DCL          VAR(&SSSECLIBR)   TYPE(*CHAR) LEN(010) +
13200                             VALUE('SSLIB')
13300
13400              DCL          VAR(&SSLOCK)      TYPE(*CHAR) LEN(001)
13500
13600              DCL          VAR(&HLDID)       TYPE(*CHAR) LEN(003)
13700              DCL          VAR(&CORID)       TYPE(*CHAR) LEN(002)
13800              DCL          VAR(&STRID)       TYPE(*CHAR) LEN(004)
13900
14000              DCL          VAR(&OBJFND)      TYPE(*CHAR) LEN(001)
14100              DCL          VAR(&TEMP)        TYPE(*CHAR) LEN(015)
14200
14300              DCL          VAR(&SSMODLNM0) TYPE(*CHAR) LEN(049) +
14400                             VALUE('ScotSystems, Inc. - Backoffice +
14500                             System')
14600              DCL          VAR(&SSMODLNM1) TYPE(*CHAR) LEN(049) +
14700                             VALUE('ScotSystems, Inc. - C-Store System')
14800 /* ------------------------------------------------------------------- */
14900 /* ScotSystems Variables LDA input to this procedure "PREVIOUS"        */
15000 /* ------------------------------------------------------------------- */
15100
15200              DCL          VAR(&PSSMODL)     TYPE(*CHAR) LEN(001)
15300              DCL          VAR(&PBYPASS)     TYPE(*CHAR) LEN(001)
15400              DCL          VAR(&PADMINUSER)  TYPE(*CHAR) LEN(001)
15500              DCL          VAR(&PFIRSTPASS)  TYPE(*CHAR) LEN(001)
15600              DCL          VAR(&PMAINTAUTH)  TYPE(*CHAR) LEN(001)
15700              DCL          VAR(&PHLDLIBR)    TYPE(*CHAR) LEN(010)
15800              DCL          VAR(&PCORLIBR)    TYPE(*CHAR) LEN(010)
15900              DCL          VAR(&PSTRLIBR)    TYPE(*CHAR) LEN(010)
16000              DCL          VAR(&PCURLIBR)    TYPE(*CHAR) LEN(010)
```

```
16100            DCL       VAR(&PGLOLIBR)    TYPE(*CHAR) LEN(010)
16200            DCL       VAR(&PSSMODLNM)   TYPE(*CHAR) LEN(049)
16300
16400 /* -------------------------------------------------------------- */
16500 /* Addition/Modification WWW 10.24.2000   USER DTAARA             */
16600 /*  Add variable to test dtaara of ADMINUSERs to see if libl change */
16700 /*  should be performed at end of this CL as regular user         */
16800 /* -------------------------------------------------------------- */
16900
17000            DCL       VAR(&ADMINLIBL)   TYPE(*CHAR) LEN(001)
17100
17200 /* -------------------------------------------------------------- */
17300 /* ScotSystems Prompt Screen for Access to libraries/companies    */
17400 /* -------------------------------------------------------------- */
17500
17600            DCLF      FILE(*LIBL/SEC101PMT)
17700
17800 /* ************************************************************** */
17900 /* -----   R E T R I E V E   S Y S T E M   V A L U E S    ---- */
18000 /* -------------------------------------------------------------- */
18100            CHGJOB    LOGCLPGM(*YES)
18200
18300 /* Retrieve system network attribute:                            */
18400
18500            RTVNETA   SYSNAME(&QSYS)
18600
18700 /* Retrieve system console id:                                   */
18800
18900            RTVSYSVAL SYSVAL(QCONSOLE) RTNVAR(&QCON)
19000
19100 /* Retrieve system printer:                                      */
19200
19300            RTVSYSVAL SYSVAL(QPRTDEV) RTNVAR(&SYSP)
19400
19500 /* Retrieve system time:                                         */
19600
19700            RTVSYSVAL SYSVAL(QTIME) RTNVAR(&QTIM)
19800
19900 /* Retrieve job attributes:                                      */
20000
20100            RTVJOBA   JOB(&QWSD) USER(&QUSR) NBR(&QNBR) +
20200                        OUTQ(&QOUQ) OUTQLIB(&QOUL) DATE(&QDAT) +
20300                        SWS(&QSWS) TYPE(&QTYP) CURLIB(&QCLB) +
20400                        PRTDEV(&QPRT)
20500
20600 /* Retrieve user attributes:                                     */
20700
20800            RTVUSRPRF USRPRF(*CURRENT) USRCLS(&USRCLS)
20900
21000 /* Retrieve *LDA &BYPASS parm to only perform security verification */
21100 /*  will not alter environment or library list (P for PRINT)     */
21200
21300            RTVDTAARA DTAARA(*LDA (0611 01)) RTNVAR(&BYPASS)
21400
21500 /* -------------------------------------------------------------- */
21600 /* -----   R E T R I E V E   ScotSystem Values (Previous)    ---- */
21700 /* -------------------------------------------------------------- */
21800
21900            RTVDTAARA DTAARA(*LDA (0601 01)) RTNVAR(&SSMODL)
22000            RTVDTAARA DTAARA(*LDA (0601 01)) RTNVAR(&PSSMODL)
22100
22200            RTVDTAARA DTAARA(*LDA (0611 01)) RTNVAR(&PBYPASS)
22300            RTVDTAARA DTAARA(*LDA (0621 01)) RTNVAR(&PADMINUSER)
22400            RTVDTAARA DTAARA(*LDA (0626 01)) RTNVAR(&PFIRSTPASS)
22500            RTVDTAARA DTAARA(*LDA (0631 01)) RTNVAR(&PMAINTAUTH)
22600            RTVDTAARA DTAARA(*LDA (0651 10)) RTNVAR(&PHLDLIBR)
22700            RTVDTAARA DTAARA(*LDA (0661 10)) RTNVAR(&PCORLIBR)
22800            RTVDTAARA DTAARA(*LDA (0671 10)) RTNVAR(&PSTRLIBR)
22900            RTVDTAARA DTAARA(*LDA (0681 10)) RTNVAR(&PCURLIBR)
23000            RTVDTAARA DTAARA(*LDA (0691 10)) RTNVAR(&PGLOLIBR)
23100            RTVDTAARA DTAARA(*LDA (0951 49)) RTNVAR(&PSSMODLNM)
23200
23300 /* ************************************************************** */
23400 /* -- T E S T   F O R   S S L O C K  -  F U L L   S Y S T E M  -- */
23500 /* -------------------------------------------------------------- */
23600
23700     /* Test For System Wide SSLOCK FLAG */
23800
```

```
23900   SSLOCKALL:   RTVDTAARA   DTAARA(QSYS/SSLOCK (01 01)) RTNVAR(&SSLOCK)
24000
24100                IF          COND(&SSLOCK *EQ 'Y') THEN(DO)
24200                SNDBRKMSG   MSG('Attempted Log On by ' *BCAT &QUSR +
24300                            *BCAT ' ' *BCAT &QWSD) TOMSGQ(&QCON)
24700                CHGVAR      VAR(&ERRMSG) VALUE('System is performing +
24800                            dedicated functions - please try again +
24900                            later')
25000                CHGDTAARA   DTAARA(*LDA (501 70)) VALUE(&ERRMSG)
25100                RMVMSG      PGMQ(*EXT) CLEAR(*ALL)
25200                SNDPGMMSG   MSG(&ERRMSG) TOPGMQ(*EXT)
25300                GOTO        CMDLBL(ENDPGM)
25400                ENDDO
25500
25600 /* ************************************************************** */
25700 /* -----   T E S T   S S A D M N   D A T A   A R E A      ---- */
25800 /* -------------------------------------------------------------- */
25900
26000 /* Determine if Application System Data Area Exist:                */
26100 /*  1) Notify System Console if Data Area NOT Found:              */
26200 /*  2) Force Error Condition in LDA for Calling CL to Halt/Abort:  */
26300
26400                CHKOBJ      OBJ(&SSSECLIBR/&SSSEC) OBJTYPE(*DTAARA)
26500                MONMSG      MSGID(CPF9801) EXEC(DO)
26600                SNDBRKMSG   MSG('SSADMN Data Area NOT FOUND - CL PROGRAM +
26700                            ABORTED') TOMSGQ(&QCON)
26800                CHGDTAARA   DTAARA(*LDA (501 70)) VALUE('SSADMN Data +
26900                            Area NOT FOUND - Contact IS Department - +
27000                            Application Error')
27100                RTVDTAARA   DTAARA(*LDA (501 70)) RTNVAR(&ERRMSG)
27200                RMVMSG      PGMQ(*EXT) CLEAR(*ALL)
27300                SNDPGMMSG   MSG(&QCLP *CAT &ERRMSG) TOPGMQ(*EXT)
27400                GOTO        CMDLBL(ENDPGM)
27500                ENDDO
27600
27700 /* ************************************************************** */
27800 /* -----   & Q C L P   M U S T   H A V E   V A L U E     ---- */
27900 /* -------------------------------------------------------------- */
28000
28100 /* If Security is Active - A valid, i.e. none blk, parm should have */
28200 /*  been passed in &QCLP = Calling CL Program                      */
28300
28400                IF          COND(&QCLP *EQ '          ') THEN(DO)
28500                CHGDTAARA   DTAARA(*LDA (501 70)) VALUE('Calling CL +
28600                            Program did not provide SEC100CL with +
28700                            CL Program Name')
28800                RTVDTAARA   DTAARA(*LDA (501 70)) RTNVAR(&ERRMSG)
28900                RMVMSG      PGMQ(*EXT) CLEAR(*ALL)
29000                SNDPGMMSG   MSG(&QUSR *CAT &ERRMSG) TOPGMQ(*EXT)
29100                GOTO        CMDLBL(ENDPGM)
29200                ENDDO
29300
29400 /* ************************************************************** */
29500 /* -----   I N I T   &   B U I L D   V A R I A B L E S   ---- */
29600 /* -------------------------------------------------------------- */
29700
29800                CHGVAR      VAR(&USER)   VALUE(&QUSR)
29900
30000 /* Determine if user is executing a CL that does not require       */
30100 /*   Security Verification                                         */
30200
30300                IF          COND(&BYPASS *EQ 'P') THEN(DO)
30400                GOTO        CMDLBL(ENDPGM)
30500                ENDDO
30600
30700 /* Determine Holding Company ID from USERID */
30800
30900                CHGVAR      VAR(&HLDID)   VALUE(%SST(&QUSR 01 03))
31000                CHGVAR      VAR(&HLDLIBR) VALUE(&HLDID *CAT '00')
31100
31200 /* Determine Corporation ID from previous used LDA, if used before */
31300
31400                CHGVAR      VAR(&CORID) VALUE(%SST(&PCORLIBR 04 02))
31500
31600 /* Determine Store ID from previous used LDA, if used before */
31700
31800                CHGVAR      VAR(&STRID) VALUE(%SST(&PSTRLIBR 07 04))
31900
```

```
32000 /* Determine if user has a dtaara area 'USER ID' for special      */
32100 /*     administrative processing                                   */
32200
32300              CHGVAR     VAR(&OBJFND) VALUE('Y')
32400
32500              CHKOBJ     OBJ(&USERDTALIB/&QUSR) OBJTYPE(*DTAARA)
32600              MONMSG     MSGID(CPF9801) EXEC(CHGVAR VAR(&OBJFND) +
32700                           VALUE('N'))
32800
32900    /* Data Area Not Found */
33000
33100              IF         COND(&OBJFND *EQ 'N') THEN(DO)
33200              CHGVAR     VAR(&ADMINUSER) VALUE(' ')
33300              CHGVAR     VAR(&IN20)   VALUE('1')
33400              ENDDO
33500
33600    /* Data Area Found */
33700
33800              IF         COND(&OBJFND *EQ 'Y') THEN(DO)
33900              RTVDTAARA  DTAARA(&USERDTALIB/&USER (01 01)) +
34000                           RTNVAR(&ADMINUSER)
34100              ENDDO
34200
34300    /* Is user is an ADMINUSER */
34400
34500              IF         COND(&ADMINUSER *EQ 'Y') THEN(DO)
34600              CHGVAR     VAR(&MAINTAUTH) VALUE('Y')
34700              CHGVAR     VAR(&IN20)   VALUE('0')
34800              RTVDTAARA  DTAARA(&USERDTALIB/&USER (11 01)) +
34900                           RTNVAR(&ADMINLIBL)
35000              ENDDO
35100
35200 /* ****************************************************************** */
35300 /* -- L I B R A R Y   P R O M P T   I N P U T            -- */
35400 /* -----                                                  ---- */
35500
35600    /* User is NOT an ADMINUSER */
35700
35800
35900              IF         COND(&ADMINUSER *EQ ' ') THEN(DO)
36000
36100              CHGVAR     VAR(&KHLDID) VALUE(&HLDID)
36200
36300              IF         COND(&CORID *EQ ' ') THEN(DO)
36400              CHGVAR     VAR(&KCORID) VALUE('01')
36500              ENDDO
36600              ELSE CMD(DO)
36700              CHGVAR     VAR(&KCORID) VALUE(&CORID)
36800              ENDDO
36900
37000              IF         COND(&STRID *EQ ' ') THEN(DO)
37100              CHGVAR     VAR(&KSTRID) VALUE(%SST(&QCLB 07 04))
37200              ENDDO
37300              ELSE CMD(DO)
37400              CHGVAR     VAR(&KSTRID) VALUE(&STRID)
37500              ENDDO
37600
37700              ENDDO
37800
37900 /* ------------------------------------------------------------------ */
38000 /*        B Y P A S S   F O R   G E N E R A L   U S E R S      */
38100 /*              BACK OFFICE SYSTEM ONLY                         */
38200 /*       SELECT01CL - MODIFIED TO INSERT 'B' LDA 601            */
38300 /*       THIS WILL OMIT PROMPT SCREEN AFTER INITIAL MENU        */
38400 /* WWW 11.23.2000                                               */
38500 /* ------------------------------------------------------------------ */
38600
38700              IF         COND((&ADMINUSER *EQ ' ') *AND (&PBYPASS *EQ +
38800                           'B')) THEN(DO)
38900              GOTO       CMDLBL(NOPROMPT)
39000              ENDDO
39100
39200 /* -----                                                  ---- */
39300    /* ADMINUSER first pass setup after signon */
39400 /* -----                                                  ---- */
39500
39600              IF         COND((&ADMINUSER *EQ 'Y') *AND (&PFIRSTPASS +
39700                           *EQ ' ')) THEN(DO)
```

```
39800              CHGVAR    VAR(&KHLDID) VALUE('ZZZ')
39900              CHGVAR    VAR(&KCORID) VALUE('01')
40000              CHGVAR    VAR(&KSTRID) VALUE('0001')
40100              ENDDO
40200
40300     /* ADMINUSER first pass previously completed */
40400
40500              IF        COND((&ADMINUSER *EQ 'Y') *AND (&PFIRSTPASS +
40600                          *EQ 'F')) THEN(DO)
40700              CHGVAR    VAR(&KHLDID) VALUE(%SST(&PHLDLIBR 01 03))
40800              CHGVAR    VAR(&KCORID) VALUE(%SST(&PCORLIBR 04 02))
40900              CHGVAR    VAR(&KSTRID) VALUE(%SST(&PSTRLIBR 07 04))
41000              ENDDO
41100
41200 /* -----                                                    ---- */
41300              CHGVAR    VAR(&IN03)   VALUE('0')
41400              CHGVAR    VAR(&IN90)   VALUE('0')
41500 /* -----                                                    ---- */
41600
41700 SCRN01:      SNDRCVF   RCDFMT(SCRN01)
41800
41900              IF        COND(&IN03 *EQ '1') THEN(DO)
42000              CHGDTAARA DTAARA(*LDA (501 70)) VALUE('Normal Exit Of +
42100                          Program' *BCAT '-' *BCAT &QCLP)
42200              GOTO      CMDLBL(ENDPGM)
42300              ENDDO
42400
42500 NOPROMPT:
42600
42700 /* ************************************************************** */
42800 /* -- T E S T   S C R E E N   I N P U T   L I B R A R I E S    -- */
42900 /* -------------------------------------------------------------- */
43000
43100     /* Test For Holding Company Library */
43200
43300              CHGVAR    VAR(&HLDLIBR) VALUE(&KHLDID *CAT '00')
43400
43500              CHGVAR    VAR(&OBJFND) VALUE('Y')
43600
43700              CHKOBJ    OBJ(*LIBL/&HLDLIBR) OBJTYPE(*LIB)
43800              MONMSG    MSGID(CPF9801) EXEC(CHGVAR VAR(&OBJFND) +
43900                          VALUE('N'))
44000
44100              IF        COND(&OBJFND *EQ 'N') THEN(DO)
44200              CHGVAR    VAR(&ERRMSG) VALUE(' Selected Holding +
44300                          Company is not available on this system ')
44400              CHGVAR    VAR(&KERRMSG) VALUE(&ERRMSG)
44500              CHGVAR    VAR(&IN90) VALUE('1')
44600              GOTO      CMDLBL(SCRN01)
44700              ENDDO
44800
44900     /* Test For Corporation Library */
45000
45100              CHGVAR    VAR(&CORLIBR) VALUE(&KHLDID *CAT &KCORID +
45200                          *CAT '.0000')
45300
45400              CHGVAR    VAR(&OBJFND) VALUE('Y')
45500
45600              CHKOBJ    OBJ(*LIBL/&CORLIBR) OBJTYPE(*LIB)
45700              MONMSG    MSGID(CPF9801) EXEC(CHGVAR VAR(&OBJFND) +
45800                          VALUE('N'))
45900
46000              IF        COND(&OBJFND *EQ 'N') THEN(DO)
46100              CHGVAR    VAR(&ERRMSG) VALUE(' Selected Corporation is +
46200                          not available on this system ')
46300              CHGVAR    VAR(&KERRMSG) VALUE(&ERRMSG)
46400              CHGVAR    VAR(&IN90) VALUE('1')
46500              GOTO      CMDLBL(SCRN01)
46600              ENDDO
46700
46800     /* Test For Store */
46900
47000              CHGVAR    VAR(&STRLIBR) VALUE(&KHLDID *CAT &KCORID +
47100                          *CAT '.' *CAT &KSTRID)
47200
47300              CHGVAR    VAR(&OBJFND) VALUE('Y')
47400
47500              CHKOBJ    OBJ(*LIBL/&STRLIBR) OBJTYPE(*LIB)
```

```
47600              MONMSG     MSGID(CPF9801) EXEC(CHGVAR VAR(&OBJFND) +
47700                           VALUE('N'))
47800
47900              IF         COND(&OBJFND *EQ 'N') THEN(DO)
48000              CHGVAR     VAR(&ERRMSG) VALUE(' Selected Store is not +
48100                           available on this system ')
48200              CHGVAR     VAR(&KERRMSG) VALUE(&ERRMSG)
48300              CHGVAR     VAR(&IN90) VALUE('1')
48400              GOTO       CMDLBL(SCRN01)
48500              ENDDO
48600
48700 /* ************************************************************** */
48800 /* -- T E S T   F O R   S S L O C K                        -- */
48900 /* -------------------------------------------------------------- */
49000
49100     /* Test For Holding Company SSLOCK FLAG */
49200
49300 SSLOCKH:   RTVDTAARA  DTAARA(&HLDLIBR/SSLOCK (1 1)) RTNVAR(&SSLOCK)
49400
49500              IF         COND(&SSLOCK *EQ 'Y') THEN(DO)
49600              CHGVAR     VAR(&TEMP) VALUE(&KHLDID *CAT '-')
49700              CHGVAR     VAR(&ERRMSG) VALUE(&TEMP *BCAT 'is +
49800                           performing dedicated functions - try +
49900                           again later')
50000              CHGDTAARA  DTAARA(*LDA (501 70)) VALUE(&ERRMSG)
50100              RMVMSG     PGMQ(*EXT) CLEAR(*ALL)
50200              SNDPGMMSG  MSG(&ERRMSG) TOPGMQ(*EXT)
50300              GOTO       CMDLBL(ENDPGM)
50400              ENDDO
50500
50600     /* Test For Corporation SSLOCK FLAG */
50700
50800 SSLOCKT:   RTVDTAARA  DTAARA(&CORLIBR/SSLOCK (1 1)) RTNVAR(&SSLOCK)
50900
51000              IF         COND(&SSLOCK *EQ 'Y') THEN(DO)
51100              CHGVAR     VAR(&TEMP) VALUE(&KHLDID *CAT '-' *CAT &KCORID)
51200              CHGVAR     VAR(&ERRMSG) VALUE(&TEMP *BCAT 'is +
51300                           performing dedicated functions - try +
51400                           again later')
51500              CHGDTAARA  DTAARA(*LDA (501 70)) VALUE(&ERRMSG)
51600              RMVMSG     PGMQ(*EXT) CLEAR(*ALL)
51700              SNDPGMMSG  MSG(&ERRMSG) TOPGMQ(*EXT)
51800              GOTO       CMDLBL(ENDPGM)
51900              ENDDO
52000
52100     /* Test For Store SSLOCK FLAG */
52200
52300 SSLOCKS:   RTVDTAARA  DTAARA(&STRLIBR/SSLOCK (1 1)) RTNVAR(&SSLOCK)
52400
52500              IF         COND(&SSLOCK *EQ 'Y') THEN(DO)
52600              CHGVAR     VAR(&TEMP) VALUE(&KHLDID *CAT '-' *CAT +
52700                           &KCORID *CAT '-' *CAT &KSTRID)
52800              CHGVAR     VAR(&ERRMSG) VALUE(&TEMP *BCAT 'is +
52900                           performing dedicated functions - try +
53000                           again later')
53100              CHGDTAARA  DTAARA(*LDA (501 70)) VALUE(&ERRMSG)
53200              RMVMSG     PGMQ(*EXT) CLEAR(*ALL)
53300              SNDPGMMSG  MSG(&ERRMSG) TOPGMQ(*EXT)
53400              GOTO       CMDLBL(ENDPGM)
53500              ENDDO
53600
53700 /* ************************************************************** */
53800 /* -- T E S T   T O   S E E   I F   S E C U T I T Y   I S      -- */
53900 /* -- A C T I V A T E D   O N   S Y S T E M   -or-            -- */
54000 /* -- R E Q U I R E D   F O R   U S E R                       -- */
54100 /* -------------------------------------------------------------- */
54200
54300 /* Determine if security is active for this system */
54400
54500              RTVDTAARA  DTAARA(&SSSECLIBR/&SSSEC (1 1)) +
54600                           RTNVAR(&ASECURITY)
54700              IF         COND(&ASECURITY *NE 'Y') THEN(DO)
54800              GOTO       CMDLBL(NOSEC100R)
54900              ENDDO
55000
55100 /* If ADMINUSER - do not execute SEC100R */
55200
55300              IF         COND(&ADMINUSER *EQ 'Y') THEN(DO)
```

```
55400              CHGVAR  VAR(&FIRSTPASS) VALUE('F')
55500              GOTO       CMDLBL(NOSEC100R)
55600              ENDDO
55700
55800 /* **************************************************************** */
55900 /* -- M E N U   O P T I O N   T E S T I N G                 -- */
56000 /* -- T E S T   S C R E E N   I N P U T   L I B R A R I E S   -- */
56100 /* ---------------------------------------------------------------- */
56200
56300 /* SEC100R    verifies that the user has clearance to execute the   */
56400 /* procedure that calls this program                               */
56500
56600              CHGVAR     VAR(&PASSED) VALUE(' ')
56700
56800              OVRDBF     FILE(SSSECURE) TOFILE(&HLDLIBR/&SECFILE) +
56900                          SHARE(*YES)
57000
57100              CALL       PGM(SEC100R) PARM(&QCLP &QUSR &HLDID &KCORID +
57200                          &KSTRID &MAINTAUTH &ERRMSG &PASSED)
57300
57400              DLTOVR     FILE(*ALL)
57500
57600 /* ---------------------------------------------------------------- */
57700
57800     /* Did user pass or fail the security validation */
57900
58000              IF         COND(&PASSED *EQ 'N') THEN(DO)
58100              CHGDTAARA  DTAARA(*LDA (500 01)) VALUE(&PASSED)
58200              SNDBRKMSG  MSG('User ' *CAT &QUSR *TCAT ' at wstn ' +
58300                          *CAT &QWSD *TCAT ' attempted unauthorized +
58400                          execution of program ' *CAT &QCLP *TCAT +
58500                          '.') TOMSGQ(&QCON)
58600              RMVMSG     PGMQ(*EXT) CLEAR(*ALL)
58700              SNDPGMMSG  MSG(&QCLP *CAT ' ' *CAT &ERRMSG) TOPGMQ(*EXT)
58800              GOTO       CMDLBL(ENDPGM)
58900              ENDDO
59000
59100
59200     /* User Passed Security */
59300
59400              IF         COND(&PASSED *EQ 'Y') THEN(DO)
59500              CHGDTAARA  DTAARA(*LDA (500 01)) VALUE(&PASSED)
59600              ENDDO
59700
59800 /* **************************************************************** */
59900 /* -- A L L   S E C U R I T Y   P A S S E D                 -- */
60000 /* -- S E T U P   L D A   A N D   E X E C U T E   C L   P G M   -- */
60100 /* ---------------------------------------------------------------- */
60200
60300 NOSEC100R:     CHGDTAARA  DTAARA(*LDA (501 499)) VALUE(' ')
60400
60500              CHGDTAARA  DTAARA(*LDA (601 01)) VALUE(&SSMODL)
60600              CHGDTAARA  DTAARA(*LDA (611 01)) VALUE(&PBYPASS)
60700              CHGDTAARA  DTAARA(*LDA (621 01)) VALUE(&ADMINUSER)
60800              CHGDTAARA  DTAARA(*LDA (626 01)) VALUE(&FIRSTPASS)
60900              CHGDTAARA  DTAARA(*LDA (631 01)) VALUE(&MAINTAUTH)
61000              CHGDTAARA  DTAARA(*LDA (651 10)) VALUE(&HLDLIBR)
61100              CHGDTAARA  DTAARA(*LDA (661 10)) VALUE(&CORLIBR)
61200              CHGDTAARA  DTAARA(*LDA (671 10)) VALUE(&STRLIBR)
61300              CHGDTAARA  DTAARA(*LDA (681 10)) VALUE(&CURLIBR)
61400              CHGDTAARA  DTAARA(*LDA (691 10)) VALUE(&GLOLIBR)
61500              CHGDTAARA  DTAARA(*LDA (701 10)) VALUE(&USER)
61600              CHGDTAARA  DTAARA(*LDA (711 10)) VALUE(&USERDTA)
61700              CHGDTAARA  DTAARA(*LDA (721 10)) VALUE(&USERDTALIB)
61800              CHGDTAARA  DTAARA(*LDA (731 10)) VALUE(&SECFILE)
61900              CHGDTAARA  DTAARA(*LDA (741 10)) VALUE(&SECLIBR)
62000              CHGDTAARA  DTAARA(*LDA (751 10)) VALUE(&SECDDSLIBR)
62100              CHGDTAARA  DTAARA(*LDA (761 10)) VALUE(&SSSEC)
62200              CHGDTAARA  DTAARA(*LDA (771 10)) VALUE(&SSSECLIBR)
62300
62400              CHGDTAARA  DTAARA(*LDA (801 010)) VALUE(&QSYS)
62500              CHGDTAARA  DTAARA(*LDA (811 010)) VALUE(&QUSR)
62600              CHGDTAARA  DTAARA(*LDA (821 010)) VALUE(&QCON)
62700              CHGDTAARA  DTAARA(*LDA (831 010)) VALUE(&SYSP)
62800              CHGDTAARA  DTAARA(*LDA (841 010)) VALUE(&QWSD)
62900              CHGDTAARA  DTAARA(*LDA (851 010)) VALUE(&QCLP)
63000              CHGDTAARA  DTAARA(*LDA (861 010)) VALUE(&QMNU)
63100              CHGDTAARA  DTAARA(*LDA (871 006)) VALUE(&QNBR)
```

```
63200              CHGDTAARA  DTAARA(*LDA (881 006)) VALUE(&QDAT)
63300              CHGDTAARA  DTAARA(*LDA (891 006)) VALUE(&QTIM)
63400              CHGDTAARA  DTAARA(*LDA (901 001)) VALUE(&QTYP)
63500              CHGDTAARA  DTAARA(*LDA (911 008)) VALUE(&QSWS)
63600              CHGDTAARA  DTAARA(*LDA (921 010)) VALUE(&QPRT)
63700              CHGDTAARA  DTAARA(*LDA (931 010)) VALUE(&QOUQ)
63800              CHGDTAARA  DTAARA(*LDA (941 010)) VALUE(&QOUL)
63900
64000              IF         COND(&SSMODL *EQ '0') THEN(DO)
64100              CHGDTAARA  DTAARA(*LDA (951 70)) VALUE('ScotSystems, +
64200                            Inc. - Backoffice System')
64300              ENDDO
64400
64500              IF         COND(&SSMODL *EQ '1') THEN(DO)
64600              CHGDTAARA  DTAARA(*LDA (951 70)) VALUE('ScotSystems, +
64700                            Inc. - CStore System')
64800              ENDDO
64900
65000              CHGJOB     SWS('00000000')
65100
65200 /* ------------------------------------------------------------------ */
65300 /* Library List for ADMINUSERs  Addition/Modification WWW 10.24.2000 */
65400 /* ------------------------------------------------------------------ */
65500
65600              IF         COND(&ADMINLIBL *EQ 'B') THEN(DO)
65700              GOTO       CMDLBL(ENDPGM)
65800              ENDDO
65900
66000 /* ------------------------------------------------------------------ */
66100 /* Library List for Client Users                                     */
66200 /* ------------------------------------------------------------------ */
66300
66400              CHGLIBL    LIBL(*NONE) CURLIB(*CRTDFT) /* Clean it's +
66500                            clock */
66600
66700              ADDLIBLE   LIB(QTEMP) POSITION(*LAST)
66800              MONMSG     MSGID(CPF2103)
66900
67000              ADDLIBLE   LIB(QGPL) POSITION(*LAST)
67100              MONMSG     MSGID(CPF2103)
67200
67300              ADDLIBLE   LIB(&HLDLIBR) POSITION(*LAST)
67400              MONMSG     MSGID(CPF2103)
67500
67600              ADDLIBLE   LIB(&CORLIBR) POSITION(*LAST)
67700              MONMSG     MSGID(CPF2103)
67800
67900              IF         COND(&SSMODL *EQ '1') THEN(DO)
68000              ADDLIBLE   LIB(&STRLIBR) POSITION(*LAST)
68100              MONMSG     MSGID(CPF2103)
68200              ENDDO
68300
68400              ADDLIBLE   LIB(SSLIB) POSITION(*LAST)
68500              MONMSG     MSGID(CPF2103)
68600
68700              ADDLIBLE   LIB(SSCOMMANDS) POSITION(*LAST)
68800              MONMSG     MSGID(CPF2103)
68900
69000              IF         COND(&SSMODL *EQ '0') THEN(DO)
69100              CHGCURLIB  CURLIB(&CORLIBR)
69000              IF         COND(&SSMODL *EQ '0') THEN(DO)
69100              CHGCURLIB  CURLIB(&CORLIBR)
69200              MONMSG     MSGID(CPF2103)
69300              ENDDO
69400
69500              IF         COND(&SSMODL *EQ '1') THEN(DO)
69600              CHGCURLIB  CURLIB(&STRLIBR)
69700              MONMSG     MSGID(CPF2103)
69800              ENDDO
69900
70000 ENDPGM:      DLTOVR     FILE(*ALL)
70100
70200              ENDPGM
```

A.5.2 SEC100R RPG security program

This small RPG program is called by the CL security program SEC100CL (see A.5.1, "SEC100CL CL security program" on page 224). As the document header mentions, it validates the users' access to call other CL programs.

```
SEQNBR*...+... 1 ...+... 2 ...+... 3 ...+... 4 ...+... 5 ...+... 6 ...+... 7 ..
   100      *-------------------------------------------------------------------
   200      * SEC100R - ScotSystems  Date 03.07.2000
   300      *
   400      * Validate users access for usage of CL Program and update
   500      * LDA with maintenance authority
   600      *-------------------------------------------------------------------
   700   FSSSECUREIF  E         K        DISK
   800      *-------------------------------------------------------------------
   900      * External message - #LDAMS /  output to LDA
  1000      * Compile time tab - MSG    /  error message test
  1100      *-------------------------------------------------------------------
  1200   E                        #LDAMG     1 70              LDA Screem MsgS
  1300   E                        MSG      1 1 70              Msg Table
  1400      *-------------------------------------------------------------------
  1500      *   M A I N L I N E   P R O C E S S I N G
  1600      *-------------------------------------------------------------------
  1700      *
  1800   C           *ENTRY   PLIST
  1900   C                    PARM           CLPGM  10
  2000   C                    PARM           CLUSR  10
  2100   C                    PARM           CLHLD   3
  2200   C                    PARM           CLCOR   2
  2300   C                    PARM           CLSTR   4
  2400   C                    PARM           CLMNT   1
  2500   C                    PARM           CLMSG  70
  2600   C                    PARM           CLPAS   1
  2700      *
  2800   C           SOKEY    KLIST
  2900   C                    KFLD           CLPGM
  3000   C                    KFLD           CLUSR
  3100   C                    KFLD           CLHLD
  3200   C                    KFLD           CLCOR
  3300   C                    KFLD           CLSTR
  3400      *
  3500   C                    MOVE *OFF      *IN11
  3600      *
  3700   C           SOKEY    CHAINSOREC01              11
  3800      *----------
  3900   C           *IN11    IFEQ *ON
  4000   C                    MOVEAMSG,01    CLMSG
  4100   C                    MOVE *BLANK    CLMNT
  4200   C                    MOVE 'N'       CLPAS
  4300   C                    ELSE
  4400   C                    MOVE *BLANKS   CLMSG
  4500   C                    MOVE SOMNT     CLMNT
  4600   C                    MOVE 'Y'       CLPAS
  4700   C                    ENDIF
  4800      *----------
  4900   C                    SETON          LR
  5000 **
MSG-01 Not authorized for program -- Event has been logged
            * * * * E N D  O F  S O U R C E * * * *
```

A.5.3 SEC101PMT display file for the security prompt program

This is the display file used to prompt for the security information needed by programs SEC100CL and SEC100R.

```
SEQNBR*...+... 1 ...+... 2 ...+... 3 ...+... 4 ...+... 5 ...+... 6 ...+... 7 ...+..
   10   A*%%TS  SD  20000314  203515  WOODY       REL-V4R4M0  5769-PW1
   20   A*%%EC
   30   A                                         DSPSIZ(24 80 *DS3)
   40   A                                         PRINT
   50   A                                         MSGALARM
   60   A                                         CA03(03 'Exit')
   70   A          R SCRN01
   80   A*%%TS  SD  20000314  203515  WOODY       REL-V4R4M0  5769-PW1
   90   A  90                                     ALARM
```

```
100      A                               1  2DATE
110      A                                  EDTCDE(Y)
120      A                               1 71SYSNAME
130      A                               2  2TIME
140      A                               2 71USER
150      A                               3 32'ScotSystems, Inc.'
160      A                               6 22'Holding Company Identity Code .'
170      A            KHLDID      3A  B  6 56DSPATR(HI)
180      A                                  DSPATR(UL)
190      A  20                              DSPATR(PR)
200      A                                  CHECK(MF)
210      A                              13 22'Corporation Identity Code .....'
220      A            KCORID      2A  B 13 57DSPATR(HI)
230      A                                  DSPATR(UL)
240      A                                  RANGE('01' '99')
250      A                                  CHECK(RZ)
270      A                              15 22'Store Identification Code .....'
280      A            KSTRID      4A  B 15 55DSPATR(HI)
290      A                                  DSPATR(UL)
300      A                                  RANGE('0001' '9999')
310      A                                  CHECK(RZ)
311      A                                  DSPATR(PC)
320      A            KERRMSG     70A O 20  6
330      A  90                              DSPATR(HI)
340      A  90                              DSPATR(BL)
350      A N90                              DSPATR(ND)
360      A                              24 33'Cmd 3-End of job'
                            * * * * E N D  O F  S O U R C E  * * * *
```

Appendix B. WebSphere-specific security concerns

This appendix seeks to raise key issues related to WebSphere Application Server (WAS) security running under OS/400.

B.1 iSeries object security

This section discusses the various iSeries objects and IFS files that contain sensitive information and need to be protected. This section also describes the user profiles under which services run by default and what it means to change to other profiles.

B.1.1 WebSphere user profiles

When first installed, WAS takes advantage of two different user profiles on your system. The first, QEJB, provides the context in which the WebSphere administration server runs on your system. The second, QEJBSVR, provides the context in which your WebSphere application server runs by default. It may also be beneficial to create other user profiles under which various parts of WebSphere run. See B.1.5, "Running application servers under specific user profiles" on page 238.

B.1.2 Securing IFS files

In addition to enterprise beans and servlets, the administration server and application servers access IFS stream files and database files for configuration and persistence.

The following files may contain sensitive information and should be given close consideration to ensure no unauthorized access is granted:

- /QIBM/UserData/WebASAdv/default/properties/admin.properties
- /QIBM/UserData/WebASAdv/default/properties/sas.server.props
- /QIBM/UserData/WebASAdv/default/properties/sas.server.props.future
- /QIBM/UserData/WebASAdv/default/properties/sas.client.props

By default, each of these files is shipped with *PUBLIC authority set to *EXCLUDE. In addition, the QEJB profile is granted *CHANGE authority, and the QEJBSVR profile is granted *USE authority, to these files to allow them appropriate access.

B.1.3 Securing WebSphere database resources

There are two classes of database tables used by WAS. The first class is the *administration repository*, which holds all of the WAS server configuration and information about the application servers and beans. The second class is the tables that are used by user applications to persist data.

The administration repository, by default, is stored in the EJSADMIN library. The name of this library can be changed. See step 2 in "Implementing" on page 97 for more details about editing the admin.properties file. This library is created when the administrative server starts, if it doesn't already exist. Upon creation, the QEJB user profile owns the library, and *PUBLIC authority is set to *EXCLUDE.

Tables in this repository can contain user names and passwords and should, therefore, be treated with appropriate security considerations.

WAS uses tables to persist user data such as Enterprise JavaBeans persistence and servlet session data. There are several options to control which iSeries user profiles are allowed access to this user data. See B.2, "Database access security" on page 238, for more information.

B.1.4 Securing the WebSphere server

The process of enabling security places the server's user profile and password in a number of places that should be maintained in a secure way. The following files contain user identifiers and clear text passwords whenever WebSphere security has been enabled:

- /QIBM/UserData/WebASAdv/default/properties/sas.server.props
- /QIBM/UserData/WebASAdv/default/properties/sas.server.props.future

The user and password in the sas.server files are used for two reasons:

- The server authenticates itself when initializing. This authentication is required due to the second use of the user and password in this file.

- This user and password functions as the system identity for this server. Example cases may include when a bean's security has been deployed to use SYSTEM_IDENTITY for method delegation or whenever method calls are made from one server to another while using Local Operating System user registry.

Because there is always the chance of the security on these files being compromised, it makes sense to use a non-default user for the server identity and password. The default user is QEJBSVR. For example, if you are using the Local Operating System user registry on the iSeries server, you may choose to create and use an OS/400 user profile with no special authorities.

B.1.5 Running application servers under specific user profiles

It is possible to run your WebSphere Applications Servers under a user profile other than the default QEJBSVR user profile. In these cases, it is necessary for the new user profile to have access to several objects to which the QEJBSVR profile has access. This authority can be given to the new profile by adding QEJBSVR as the new profile's group profile. For example, if you want to run the application server under user profile JDOE, you need to use the Change User Profile (CHGUSRPRF) command and add QEJBSVR as JDOE's Group Profile.

For more information on configuring your application servers to run under a specified user profile, refer to the "Enabling user IDs to run application servers with Operations Navigator" section in *WebSphere Application Server 3 Advanced Edition for AS/400* found at:

http://www.as400.ibm.com/products/websphere/docs/doc.htm

B.2 Database access security

There are a number of database tables that are used to persist user data in the WebSphere environment. WAS provides a variety of different options for protecting access to these tables. In most cases, you have a choice between changing the user profile used by WebSphere to access the resource to one that already has authority to the tables, or adding authority for the profile that WebSphere is using to the iSeries tables. You can use these techniques in combination. You should consider changing the profile that WAS uses to access the data when accessing tables that existed prior to the installation of WAS or when using programs outside of WAS to access tables. The default profiles used will most likely be suitable for tables that are created by WAS and used only within WAS.

The database tables are accessed based on the authority in use for a specific database connection. Table 27 summarizes the security information for the different user database tables in WebSphere.

Table 27. Database access and user profile matrix

Type of data	Created by	iSeries library	User profile
Administrative repository	WebSphere	By default EJSADMIN. Can be changed in the administrative server admin.properties configuration file.	QEJB. All administrative servers run under the QEJB profile, so this is not configurable.
Servlet session data	WebSphere	By default, QEJBSESSON. Can be changed using the Session Manager Persistence Properties.	By default, the user profile that the application server runs under. Can be changed using the Session Manager Persistence Properties.
Servlet user profile data	WebSphere	By default, QEJBUSRPRF. Can be changed on the data source that is specified for the User Profile Manager.	By default, the user profile that the application server runs under. Can be changed using the User Profile Manager Datasource Properties.
Entity beans using container managed persistence	WebSphere or already existing	By default, EJB if created by WebSphere and not mapped. Can be changed using schema mapping in VisualAge for Java.	By default, the user profile that the application server runs under. Can be changed on the data source for an EJB container or an enterprise bean.
User-written database access in servlets, session beans, and bean managed persistent entity beans may use connection pools	WebSphere, by user code, or already existing	User defined	By default, the user profile that the application server runs under. Can be changed in the user code to explicitly use a user ID and password on the database connection.

Explanation of the database access and user profile matrix
Some of the terms from Table 27 are explained here:

- **Application server**: The application server runs under the user ID that is specified in the USER ID property on the application server. Any database tables that are accessed should allow access to the specified user ID. By default, the application server runs under the QEJBSVR user profile, so the database tables that are used need to allow access to the QEJBSVR user profile.

- **EJB container**: You can specify a data source on the EJB container. The User ID and Password properties on the EJB container data source control what user ID is used to access the tables defined by the data source. Specifying a user ID and password on the EJB container data source takes precedence over the user ID that the application server is running under. If no user ID or password is specified on the EJB container data source properties, the user ID that the application server is running under is used.

- **Enterprise bean**: You can specify a data source on the enterprise bean. The User ID and Password properties of the enterprise bean data source control what user ID is used to access the tables defined by the data source. Specifying a user ID and password on the enterprise bean data source takes precedence over the user ID that the application server is running under and a data source specified at the EJB container level. If a data source is specified at the enterprise bean level, but no user ID or password is specified on the enterprise bean data source properties, the user ID that the application server is running under is used independent of whether a data source was specified at the EJB container level.

B.2.1 Allowing WebSphere Application Server access to existing tables

Tables referenced through data sources can exist prior to their use by WebSphere Application Server, or they can be created from within WebSphere Application Server. If your table was created outside of the administrative server (perhaps created through interactive SQL or legacy data), the user ID that WAS uses must have *CHANGE authority to the table. To grant *CHANGE authority to a user ID, use either the Grant Object Authority (GRTOBJAUT) command or the GRANT SQL statement.

To manipulate the authorities for a user ID, use the Edit Object Authority (EDTOBJAUT), GRTOBJAUT, or Revoke Object Authority (RVKOBJAUT) commands. Or use the GRANT and REVOKE SQL statements.

Note: Using the GRTOBJAUT command and GRANT SQL statement, as shown in the following examples, will not yield results that are exactly equivalent. You can use the EDTOBJAUT command to view the exact authorities that are given after using each of these methods. Both methods will give a user enough authority to access and update database tables from WAS.

B.2.1.1 Using the GRTOBJAUT command
To use the GRTOBJAUT command, follow these steps:

1. You need to know the name of the iSeries file object that was used for the table that you want to access. To find the name of the iSeries file object, run the following query:

   ```
   Select SYSTEM_TABLE_NAME from lib/SYSTABLES where (TABLE_NAME = 'tablename')
   ```

   Here, your table is in the iSeries library *lib*, and *tablename* is the name of your table.

For example, if you are running your application server under QEJBSVR and need to access an existing table named ENTITYSIMPLE in the ADMNTEST collection, you need to run the following query:

```
Select SYSTEM_TABLE_NAME from ADMNTEST/SYSTABLES where (TABLE_NAME =
'ENTITYSIMPLE')
```

Note: The *TABLE_NAME* value is case-sensitive. In most cases, table names are all uppercase.

2. Once you know the name of the file object that was used for your table, you can grant a user ID *CHANGE authority to the file. To grant a user ID *CHANGE authority to a file, use the following command:

```
GRTOBJAUT OBJ(lib/filename) OBJTYPE(*FILE) USER(userid) AUT(*CHANGE)
```

Here the file is located in the iSeries library *lib*, the file name is *filename*, and the user ID is *userid*.

For example, if you are running your application server under QEJBSVR and the name of the file that was used for your table is named ENTIT00001 and is in library ADMNTEST, you need to use the following command:

```
GRTOBJAUT OBJ(ADMNTEST/ENTIT00001) OBJTYPE(*FILE) USER(QEJBSVR)
AUT(*CHANGE)
```

B.2.1.2 Using the GRANT SQL statement

To use the GRANT SQL statement, run the following query:

```
GRANT ALL ON lib/table TO userid
```

Your table is in *lib* (or the iSeries library), *table* is the name of your table, and *userid* is the user ID that the WebSphere Application Server is using.

For example, if you are running your application server under QEJBSVR and need to access an existing table named ENTSIMPLE in collection ADMNTEST from an interactive SQL session, use the command:

```
GRANT ALL ON ADMNTEST/ENTSIMPLE TO QEJBSVR
```

B.2.2 Hosting multiple instances of WAS on a single node: Security

It is not uncommon to host multiple instances of a WAS administrative server on a single node. If your application has container-managed persistence (CMP) entity beans, and you deploy these beans with WAS, then, by default, the beans' state will be written to the table named <bean name>BeanTbl in library EJB. For example, if you have a bean named Account, then the table name will be AccountBeanTbl. This is not a desirable behavior for an ASP environment. What can you do to run multiple instances of WAS on a single node and be able to separate data from the different customers?

There are two ways to perform this task:

- Use bean-managed persistence (BMP) entity beans
- Use EJB deployment tools in VisualAge for Java Enterprise Edition for CMP beans

BMP entity beans

The enterprise bean class stores the persistent information for the enterprise bean. Entity beans achieve bean-managed persistence by writing to a data source directly from their enterprise bean class. BMP can be advantageous when you are required to have more control over the persistence of your entity beans, for example:

- If your data source is not a database.
- If the container does not offer the support you need to persist the entity bean to the database.

Because an entity bean with BMP handles all of their own data source interaction, they can be more complex to write. You must use BMP if either of the following points is true about an entity bean:

- The persistent data for the bean is stored in more than one data source.
- The persistent data for the bean is stored in a data source that is not supported by the WebSphere Application Server.

Keep in mind that applications using BMP beans may have portability problems.

CMP entity beans

CMP entity beans delegate persistence to the EJB container. It makes them more attractive to use in a portable application. To use an existing or specific library or table name or to map a bean's persistent fields in a different manner than the WAS default, you have to use VisualAge for Java (VAJ) Enterprise Edition. It allows you to generate a database schema and schema mapping for an EJB group.

There are several ways you can do this (database collections are libraries on the iSeries):

- Hardcode the desired collection for the underlying EJB table:

  a. Create your CMP entity bean using VAJ.

  b. Generate the default DB schema.

  c. Modify the generated DB schema to specify the desired collection name in the qualifier field for the database table in the schema map.

  d. Generate the deployed code for the EJB, and then export the deployed EJB jar file.

  e. Configure a data source in WAS, and specify `*local` for the Database name property.

  f. Specify this data source on the **DataSource** tab for the EJB container.

  g. Deploy the EJB in WAS.

  The underlying EJB table will be created in the collection specified in the EJB's DB schema.

  This is an inflexible, yet simple approach because the DB collection is specified at development time. To change the collection name, the EJB's schema map has to be modified, and the EJB has to be redeployed.

- Specify the desired collection for the underlying EJB table at deployment time using the EJB's data source:

  a. Create your CMP entity bean using VAJ.

  b. Generate the default DB schema.

  c. Generate the deployed code for the EJB, and then export the deployed EJB jar file.

d. Configure a data source, and specify `*local/<myCollectionName>` for the Database name property where *<myCollectionName>* is the name of the DB collection where the EJB table is to be stored (for example: *local/BANKONE). Please note that this collection must exist on the iSeries (use the Start SQL (`STRSQL`) and `CREATE COLLECTION` commands to create the collection), and the QEJBSVR user profile must have *ALL authority to the collection.

e. Specify this data source on the **DataSource** tab for the EJB collection.

f. Deploy the EJB in WAS.

The underlying EJB table will be created in the collection specified on the data source (BANKONE in our example).

This approach is more flexible, since the collection used to store the EJB table can be configured at deployment/run time. Additionally, the EJB itself will not have to be modified to support multiple environments.

- Configure the collection for the underlying EJB table by using different user profiles:

a. Create your CMP entity bean using VAJ.

b. Generate the default DB schema.

c. Generate the deployed code for the EJB, and then export the deployed EJB jar file.

d. Create a new user profile with the same name as the desired collection that will be used to store the underlying EJB DB table.

For example, if you want your tables to be stored in a collection called BANKONE, you could create a new user profile called BANKONE. Please note that this user profile must have QEJBSVR specified for its group profile:

```
CRTUSRPRF USRPRF(BANKONE) TEXT('User profile for customer BANKONE')
GRPPRF(QEJBSVR)
```

e. Enable the user profile to run application servers with Operations Navigator. See the "Enabling user IDs to run application servers with Operations Navigator" section in *WebSphere Application Server 3 Advanced Edition for AS/400*, which you can find on the Web at: `http://www.as400.ibm.com/products/websphere/docs/doc.htm`

f. Specify this user profile for the application server (click the **Advanced** tab, and select the **User ID** property). This will allow WAS to run the application server under this user profile.

g. Configure a data source and specify `*local` for the Database name property.

h. Specify this data source on the **DataSource** tab for the EJB container.

i. Deploy the EJB in WAS.

The underlying EJB table will be created in a collection that has the same name as the user profile that the application server is running under (BANKONE in our example)

This approach is comparable to the second approach on the previous page in that they both solve the same problem dynamically, configuring the EJB DB collection at deployment or run time.

- Configure the collection for the underlying EJB table by using a library list. This approach is useful when EJBs are created to access existing DB tables on the iSeries and where multiple tables are involved. In this scenario, a library list can be used by the EJB container to locate such tables. These are the steps that you must follow for this option:

  a. Create a new job description on the iSeries, and specify the custom library list.

  b. Create a new user profile that specifies this job description. The application server can be configured to run under this user profile as in the third method.

  c. Create a data source for the EJB, and set the **Database name** property to `*local;naming=system`. The EJB will then search the library list for the user profile when it attempts to locate its underlying DB table.

For more information about using VisualAge for Java, see the "Developing enterprise beans in VisualAge for Java Enterprise Edition" section in *WebSphere Application Server 3 Advanced Edition for AS/400*, which you can find on the Web at: `http://www.as400.ibm.com/products/websphere/docs/doc.htm`

Appendix C. Special notices

This publication is intended to help the hardware and software distributors who want to sell or rent their products and for the independent software vendors (ISV) looking for alternative means of licensing their products. The information in this publication is not intended as the specification of any programming interfaces that are provided by V4R5 of OS/400 (5769-SS1) and other related products. See the PUBLICATIONS section of the IBM Programming Announcement for V4R5 of OS/400, Program Number 5769-SS1 for more information about what publications are considered to be product documentation.

References in this publication to IBM products, programs or services do not imply that IBM intends to make these available in all countries in which IBM operates. Any reference to an IBM product, program, or service is not intended to state or imply that only IBM's product, program, or service may be used. Any functionally equivalent program that does not infringe any of IBM's intellectual property rights may be used instead of the IBM product, program or service.

Information in this book was developed in conjunction with use of the equipment specified, and is limited in application to those specific hardware and software products and levels.

IBM may have patents or pending patent applications covering subject matter in this document. The furnishing of this document does not give you any license to these patents. You can send license inquiries, in writing, to the IBM Director of Licensing, IBM Corporation, North Castle Drive, Armonk, NY 10504-1785.

Licensees of this program who wish to have information about it for the purpose of enabling: (i) the exchange of information between independently created programs and other programs (including this one) and (ii) the mutual use of the information which has been exchanged, should contact IBM Corporation, Dept. 600A, Mail Drop 1329, Somers, NY 10589 USA.

Such information may be available, subject to appropriate terms and conditions, including in some cases, payment of a fee.

The information contained in this document has not been submitted to any formal IBM test and is distributed AS IS. The information about non-IBM ("vendor") products in this manual has been supplied by the vendor and IBM assumes no responsibility for its accuracy or completeness. The use of this information or the implementation of any of these techniques is a customer responsibility and depends on the customer's ability to evaluate and integrate them into the customer's operational environment. While each item may have been reviewed by IBM for accuracy in a specific situation, there is no guarantee that the same or similar results will be obtained elsewhere. Customers attempting to adapt these techniques to their own environments do so at their own risk.

Any pointers in this publication to external Web sites are provided for convenience only and do not in any manner serve as an endorsement of these Web sites.

Any performance data contained in this document was determined in a controlled environment, and therefore, the results that may be obtained in other operating environments may vary significantly. Users of this document should verify the applicable data for their specific environment.

This document contains examples of data and reports used in daily business operations. To illustrate them as completely as possible, the examples contain the names of individuals, companies, brands, and products. All of these names are fictitious and any similarity to the names and addresses used by an actual business enterprise is entirely coincidental.

Reference to PTF numbers that have not been released through the normal distribution process does not imply general availability. The purpose of including these reference numbers is to alert IBM customers to specific information relative to the implementation of the PTF when it becomes available to each customer according to the normal IBM PTF distribution process.

The following terms are trademarks of the International Business Machines Corporation in the United States and/or other countries:

e (logo)®	Redbooks
IBM ®	Redbooks Logo
Advanced Function Printing	AFP
AIX	AnyNet
AS/400	AS/400e
CICS	CICS/400
COBOL/400	CT
DB2	DB2 Universal Database
DRDA	Infoprint
Integrated Language Environment	Intelligent Printer Data Stream
IPDS	LANClient Control Manager
Language Environment	MQSeries
Net.Data	Netfinity
Network Station	OfficeVision
OfficeVision/400	OS/2
OS/390	OS/400
PartnerWorld	Print Services Facility
RPG/400	RS/6000
S/390	SecureWay
SP	System/38
System/390	VisualAge
WebSphere	XT
3090	3890
400	Lotus
LearningSpace	Lotus Notes
Domino	Lotus QuickPlace
Notes	QuickPlace
Sametime	Tivoli
Cross-Site	

The following terms are trademarks of other companies:

Tivoli, Manage. Anything. Anywhere.,The Power To Manage., Anything. Anywhere.,TME, NetView, Cross-Site, Tivoli Ready, Tivoli Certified, Planet Tivoli, and Tivoli Enterprise are trademarks or registered trademarks of Tivoli Systems Inc., an IBM company, in the United States, other countries, or both. In Denmark, Tivoli is a trademark licensed from Kjøbenhavns Sommer - Tivoli A/S.

C-bus is a trademark of Corollary, Inc. in the United States and/or other countries.

Java and all Java-based trademarks and logos are trademarks or registered

Appendix D. Related publications

The publications listed in this section are considered particularly suitable for a more detailed discussion of the topics covered in this redbook.

D.1 IBM Redbooks publications

For information on ordering these publications, see "How to get IBM Redbooks" on page 253.

- *Building a Portal with Lotus Domino R5*, REDP0019
- *IBM AS/400 Printing V*, SG24-2160
- *Complementing AS/400 Storage Management Using Hierarchical Storage Management APIs*, SG24-4450
- *Cool Title About the AS/400 and Internet*, SG24-4815
- *Understanding LDAP*, SG24-4986
- *LDAP Implementation Cookbook*, SG24-5110
- *Lotus Domino for AS/400: Performance, Tuning, and Capacity Planning*, SG24-5162
- *V4 TCP/IP for AS/400: More Cool Things Than Ever*, SG24-5190
- *The AS/400 NetServer Advantage*, SG24-5196
- *AS/400 Internet Security: Implementing AS/400 Virtual Private Networks*, SG24-5404
- *Lotus Domino for AS/400: Implementation*, SG24-5592
- *IBM Network Station Manager V2R1*, SG24-5844
- *Patterns for e-business: User-to-Business Patterns for Topology 1 and 2 using WebSphere Advanced Edition*, SG24-5864
- *Domino and WebSphere Together*, SG24-5955
- *Porting UNIX Applications Using AS/400 PASE*, SG24-5970

D.2 IBM Redbooks collections

Redbooks are also available on the following CD-ROMs. Click the CD-ROMs button at http://www.redbooks.ibm.com/ for information about all the CD-ROMs offered, updates and formats.

CD-ROM Title	Collection Kit Number
System/390 Redbooks Collection	SK2T-2177
Networking and Systems Management Redbooks Collection	SK2T-6022
Transaction Processing and Data Management Redbooks Collection	SK2T-8038
Lotus Redbooks Collection	SK2T-8039
Tivoli Redbooks Collection	SK2T-8044
AS/400 Redbooks Collection	SK2T-2849
Netfinity Hardware and Software Redbooks Collection	SK2T-8046
RS/6000 Redbooks Collection (BkMgr Format)	SK2T-8040
RS/6000 Redbooks Collection (PDF Format)	SK2T-8043
Application Development Redbooks Collection	SK2T-8037
IBM Enterprise Storage and Systems Management Solutions	SK3T-3694

D.3 Other resources

These publications are also relevant as further information sources:

- *AS/400 Physical Planning Reference*, SA41-5109
- *AS/400 Client Access for Windows 95/NT - Setup*, SC41-3512
- *OS/400 Backup and Recovery V4R5*, SC41-5304
- *OS/400 Work Management V4R4*, SC41-5306
- *Backup Recovery and Media Services for AS/400*, SC41-5345
- *Printer Device Programming Version 4*, SC41-5713
- *Installing and Managing Domino for AS/400* is located at http://notes.net
- *WebSphere Application Server 3 Advanced Edition for AS/400* is found at http://www.as400.ibm.com/products/websphere/docs/doc.htm. Click **Version 3.0.2** under the Advanced Addition bullet, and then click the **HTML** link for the *WebSphere for AS/400 Documentation Center* document.

The following publications are available in softcopy only from the AS/400 Online Library: http://publib.boulder.ibm.com/pubs/html/as400/onlinelib.htm

- *Internet Connection Server and Internet Connection Secure Server for AS/400 Web Master's Guide*, GC41-5434
- *AS/400e Security - Reference*, SC41-5302
- *TCP/IP Configuration and Reference Guide*, SC41-5430

The following publications are available in softcopy only from the iSeries 400 Information Center at:
http://publib.boulder.ibm.com/pubs/html/as400/infocenter.html

- *Up and Running with Domino for AS/400*, SC41-5334
- *Client Access Express for Windows - Setup*, SC41-5507

D.4 Referenced Web sites

These Web sites are also relevant as further information sources:

- *WebSphere Application Server 3 Advanced Edition for AS/400*:
  http://www.as400.ibm.com/products/websphere/docs/doc.htm
- IBM Redbooks and redpapers: http://www.redbooks.ibm.com
- WebSphere Application for iSeries site:
  http://www.as400.ibm.com/products/websphere/docs/doc.htm
- Notes.net home page: http://notes.net
- iSeries 400 Information Center:
  http://publib.boulder.ibm.com/pubs/html/as400/infocenter.html
- WebSphere Commerce Suite site:
  http://www-4.ibm.com/software/webservers/commerce
- Tivoli Security Management Solution site:
  http://www-4.ibm.com/software/secureway

- WebSphere Host On-Demand site:
  http://www.ibm.com/software/network/hostondemand
- Novera's jBusiness: http://www.novera.com
- LANSA home page: http://www.lansa.com
- ASP Prime Solution Center:
  http://as400.rochester.ibm.com/developer/asp/index.html
- IBM Application Development site: http://www-4.ibm.com/software/ad
- iSeries and AS/400 Technical Support Web site:
  http://www.as400service.ibm.com
- PartnerWorld for Developers: http://www.ibm.com/as400/developer
- WebSphere Studio: http://www-4.ibm.com/software/webservers/studio
- IBM @server Introduction Capacity Advantage site:
  http://www-1.ibm.com/servers/eserver/introducing/capacity.html
- BEA/WebXpress and their WebLogic server: http://www.bea.com
- Bluestone's Sapphire/Web server: http://www.bluestone.com
- Baltimore Technologies MIMEsweeper site: http://www.us.mimesweeper.com
- WebSphere Development Tools for AS/400:
  http://www-4.ibm.com/software/ad/wdt400/news.html
- ICSA Labs, a division of TruSecure Corporation:
  http://www.icsalabs.com/index.shtml
- Datalogics home page: http://www.datalogics.com
- Help/Systems home page: http://www.helpsystems.com
- ACS: http://www.acs-inc.com
- AmQUEST, Inc.: http://www.amquest.com
- Berbee Information Networks: http://www.berbee.com
- Digica: http://www.digica.com
- DPS, Inc.: http://www.dpslink.com
- Eviciti: http://www.eviciti.com
- J.J.Croney & Associates: http://www.j2ca.com
- Prominic.NET: http://www.prominic.net
- SunGard Computer Services: http://www.sungard.com
- Triangle Hosting Services: http://www.bcafreedom.com
- WebSphere Web site address with a list of PTFs:
  http://www.as400.ibm.com/products/websphere/services/service.htm
- Sun Microsystems Enterprise JavaBeans Technology:
  http://java.sun.com/products/ejb/index.html
- IBM HTTP Server (Powered by Apache):
  http://www.iseries.ibm.com/products/websphere/docs/
  apacheWebServerSupport35.html
- Information about WebSphere Application Server:
  http://www.iseries.ibm.com/products/websphere

- Good site to search for Domino and iSeries information:
  - http://search400.com
  - http://www.lotus411.com
  - http://www.searchdomino.com
- Latest Domino PTFs: http://www.iseries.ibm.com/domino/support
- IBM Workload Estimator for iSeries 400 Web site
  http://as400service.ibm.com/estimator
- BlueNotes Office Portal (sample Domino portal): http://www.bluenotes.com
- AS/400 Technical Studio:
  - http://www.as400.ibm.com/techstudio
  - http://www.as400.ibm.com/tstudio
- *Installing and Managing Domino for AS/400:* http://www.notes.net/doc
- Lotus Developer Network: http://www.lotus.com/developer
- Webinar/Webcast Schedule: http://www.lotus.com/developertraining
- Masters Broadcast information: http://www.lotus.com/masters
- Lotus Dev-Net site: http://www.lotus-dev.net/
- Iris Sandbox: http://www.notes.net/sandbox
- IBM DeveloperWorks: http://www.ibm.com/developer
- To register for the Developers e-Newsletter: http://www.lotus.com/lwm
- DevCon 2000 Information: http://www.lotus.com/devcon
- StoreReport.com home page: http://www.storereport.com
- ScotSystems home page: http://www.scotsystems.com
- SecureWay Host On-Demand:
  http://www-4.ibm.com/software/webservers/hostondemand

How to get IBM Redbooks

This section explains how both customers and IBM employees can find out about IBM Redbooks, redpieces, and CD-ROMs. A form for ordering books and CD-ROMs by fax or e-mail is also provided.

- **Redbooks Web Site** http://www.redbooks.ibm.com/

  Search for, view, download, or order hardcopy/CD-ROM Redbooks from the Redbooks Web site. Also read redpieces and download additional materials (code samples or diskette/CD-ROM images) from this Redbooks site.

  Redpieces are Redbooks in progress; not all Redbooks become redpieces and sometimes just a few chapters will be published this way. The intent is to get the information out much quicker than the formal publishing process allows.

- **E-mail Orders**

  Send orders by e-mail including information from the IBM Redbooks fax order form to:

	e-mail address
In United States	usib6fpl@ibmmail.com
Outside North America	Contact information is in the "How to Order" section at this site: http://www.elink.ibmlink.ibm.com/pbl/pbl

- **Telephone Orders**

United States (toll free)	1-800-879-2755
Canada (toll free)	1-800-IBM-4YOU
Outside North America	Country coordinator phone number is in the "How to Order" section at this site: http://www.elink.ibmlink.ibm.com/pbl/pbl

- **Fax Orders**

United States (toll free)	1-800-445-9269
Canada	1-403-267-4455
Outside North America	Fax phone number is in the "How to Order" section at this site: http://www.elink.ibmlink.ibm.com/pbl/pbl

This information was current at the time of publication, but is continually subject to change. The latest information may be found at the Redbooks Web site.

IBM Intranet for Employees

IBM employees may register for information on workshops, residencies, and Redbooks by accessing the IBM Intranet Web site at http://w3.itso.ibm.com/ and clicking the ITSO Mailing List button. Look in the Materials repository for workshops, presentations, papers, and Web pages developed and written by the ITSO technical professionals; click the Additional Materials button. Employees may access MyNews at http://w3.ibm.com/ for redbook, residency, and workshop announcements.

IBM Redbooks fax order form

Please send me the following:

Title	Order Number	Quantity

First name _____ Last name _____

Company _____

Address _____

City _____ Postal code _____ Country _____

Telephone number _____ Telefax number _____ VAT number _____

☐ Invoice to customer number _____

☐ Credit card number _____

Credit card expiration date _____ Card issued to _____ Signature _____

We accept American Express, Diners, Eurocard, Master Card, and Visa. Payment by credit card not available in all countries. Signature mandatory for credit card payment.

Index

Symbols

Application Service Provider Business Model: Implementation on the iSeries Server